▼ COMMUNICATION STUDIES

'Students and teachers alike will warmly welcome this book. It addresses the needs of AS students in a lively, pragmatic, intelligent, and above all, accessible way, and is written by authors who understand fully the needs of their audience. A must for any AS student!'

Patrick Russell, George Abbot School

This fully comprehensive and easy-to-use textbook covers all aspects of Communication Studies for students following the AS and A Level syllabus.

The authors, who are experienced Communication Studies teachers and examiners, introduce students step-by-step to the main forms of communication – verbal, non-verbal, intrapersonal and group; they provide guidance on developing effective communication skills and advise on how these skills can be used to prepare for and pass examinations. Individual parts address:

* Studying Communicaction * Effective Communication * Texts and Meanings in Communication * Communication Practice * Themes in Personal Communication * Using Communication Skills to Pass Examinations

Communication Studies: The Essential Introduction will give students the confidence to tackle every part of an introductory course in Communication Studies. Its key features include:

* Activities * Worked examination questions * Suggestions for further reading * Glossary of key terms * Worksheets and assignments * Case studies showing how theoretical concepts can be applied in everyday situations

Andrew Beck was Chief Examiner for A Level Communication Studies until 2001 and is Head of Communication, Culture and Media at Coventry University. **Peter Bennett** is Chief Examiner for A Level Communication Studies and Head of Communications at Rowley Regis College. **Peter Wall** is Chair of Examiners for AQA's Communication and Media Studies specifications.

COMMUNICATION STUDIES

THE ESSENTIAL INTRODUCTION

Andrew Beck, Peter Bennett and Peter Wall

London and New York

First published 2002
by Routledge
11 New Fetter Lane, London EC4P 4EE

Simultaneously published in the USA and Canada
by Routledge
29 West 35th Street, New York, NY 10001

Routledge is an imprint of the Taylor & Francis Group

© 2002 Andrew Beck, Peter Bennett and Peter Wall

Typeset in Bell Gothic by Keystroke, Jacaranda Lodge, Wolverhampton
Printed and bound in Great Britain by TJ International Ltd, Padstow, Cornwall

British Library Cataloguing in Publication Data
A catalogue record for this book is available from the British Library

Library of Congress Cataloging in Publication Data
A catalog record for this book has been applied for

ISBN 0–415–24751–9 (hbk)
ISBN 0–415–24752–7 (pbk)

▼ CONTENTS

List of figures   vii
List of diagrams   ix

Introduction   1

PART 1: STUDYING COMMUNICATION   5

1 Studying   5
2 Communication   21

PART 2: EFFECTIVE COMMUNICATION   27

UNIT 2

PART 3: TEXTS AND MEANINGS IN COMMUNICATION   53

1   Communication as text   53
2   Texts and meanings   60
3   Decoding and de-coding   70
4   Words and pictures: signs and signatures   79
5   Taking the process further   93
6   Putting it back together   103
7   Some print texts and sample tasks   112

UNIT 1 — 40%

PART 4: COMMUNICATION PRACTICE *→ COURSEWORK*   123

UNIT 3

PART 5: THEMES IN PERSONAL COMMUNICATION   139

1   Verbal communication   139
2   Non-verbal communication   150
3   Intrapersonal communication: self and self-concept   165
4   Intrapersonal communication: ideas about the development of the self
         and personality   175
5   Intrapersonal communication: self and self-presentation   186

6   Group communication: what groups are and what they do   196

7   Group communication: inside groups   201
8   Group communication: how groups work and when they don't:
     leadership and lethargy   211

**PART 6: USING YOUR COMMUNICATION SKILLS TO PASS
EXAMINATIONS**   **221**

Glossary   239
Resources   247
Bibliography   249
Index   254

▼ FIGURES

1.1	Computer screen with search results for key word enquiry	18
1.2	Hump-back bridge hazard sign	22
2.1	Job advertisements	28
2.2	E-mail set-up	49
3.1	Crowds leaving Old Trafford. Courtesy of Dale Smith	54
3.2	Still from *Once Were Warriors* (New Zealand Film Commission, 1994). Courtesy of the Kobal Collection	58
3.3	*PC Format* postcard. Courtesy of *PC Format*	61
3.4	Cover of *PC Format*, July 1998. Courtesy of *PC Format*	64
3.5	*PC Format*, no. 84, July 1998, p. 200. Courtesy of *PC Format*	66
3.6	Edvard Munch, *The Scream*, 1893. Photo: J. Lathion © Nasjonalgalleriet, Oslo, 1999	68
3.7	Still from *The Truman Show* (Paramount 1998). Courtesy of the Kobal Collection	71
3.8	*The Italian Job* (Paramount 1969)	73
3.9	Still from *Trainspotting* (Figment/Noel Gay/Channel 4 1996). Courtesy of the Kobal Collection	74
3.10 & 3.11	S CLUB 7, *Bring It All Back* CD. © Polydor Ltd. Courtesy of Polydor Ltd	76–7
3.12	Cambridge Youth Project 'Ordinary' flyer. Courtesy of Selina Dean of Cambridge	80
3.13	Cambridge Youth Project 'Quiet' flyer. Courtesy of Selina Dean of Cambridge	81
3.14	Dog/Cat/Horse?	82
3.15	Mexican frying an egg	82

3.16	'Killer Queen' poster. Courtesy of FilmFour	84
3.17	Norman Parkinson, *New York, New York* (1955). Courtesy of Hamiltons Photographers Ltd	86
3.18	Cartoon	86
3.19a	Baby drawing (Paul Mendez)	89
3.19b	Norman Rockwell, detail from 'The Tantrum', cover of the *Saturday Evening Post*, 24 October 1936	89
3.19c	Baby photograph. Courtesy of www.digitalvisiondownload.com	89
3.20	*The Toy Box.* Courtesy of Rowley Regis College	91
3.21	*Art Alive!* flyer. Courtesy of the Barber Institute of Fine Arts, University of Birmingham	92
3.22	The death of Harold. Detail from the Bayeux Tapestry	95
3.23	'Right behind You' postcard. Courtesy of the National Union of Students	98
3.24	Blair Witch website. www.blairwitch.com	99
3.25	*Eve* advertisement	102
3.26	'Who Needs Ted Hughes?', *Q* magazine, no. 151, April 1999, p. 28. Courtesy of *Q* magazine	105
3.27	*The Sims.* Courtesy of Electronic Arts	109
3.28	Egg Card advertisement, www.egg.com	113
3.29	Illustration from Alan Moore and Dave Gibbons, *The Watchmen* (Titan Books Ltd, 1987)	115
3.30	'The Four Stages of Royal Life' by Scrank from *The Independent on Sunday*, 6 August 2000	116
3.31	Lancaster University flyer. Courtesy of Lancaster University	117
3.32	Planet Happy card	118
3.33	Routledge Media Arena website	120
5.1	Truth Machine advertisement	163

▼ DIAGRAMS

1.1 Obtaining and retaining information 6

1.2 The SQ3R model 11

1.3 Simple process model of communication 24

1.4 General model of semiotics 25

3.1 Shannon and Weaver's Mathematical Theory of Communication 87

3.2 Gerbner's model of communication 94

3.3a Jakobson's elements of communication 101

3.3b Jakobson's functions of communication 101

5.1 White's Gatekeeping model 165

5.2 Roger's Concentric Circle model 169

5.3 The Johari Window 172

5.4 Jung's psyche (after Stevens) 181

5.5 Psychometric model (after Cattell) 182

5.6 Political attitudes axis 186

5.7 Burton and Dimbleby's group communication model 203

5.8 Bales's IPA model 206

5.9 Teacher–group model 208

5.10 Network of group interactions I 209

5.11 Network of group interactions II 209

▼ INTRODUCTION

Communication is at the heart of our everyday lives. From the moment we wake in the morning, thinking about the challenges of the day ahead, to the moment we drift off to sleep last thing at night, we are constantly in the process of communicating. We do so either as senders of messages or receivers of messages. In some cases, such as our early morning thoughts, the communication is within and to our self.

Just think how important the process of communication is in so many everyday situations:

- We speak to, listen to, and interact with other people. We do this face-to-face or on the telephone. We communicate in formal situations (such as sitting in class listening to a teacher) as well as in informal situations (chatting with friends or family).

- We use written language to communicate. We read and write letters, notes, reports, essays, instructions and shopping lists. Many of us use electronic technology to send and receive e-mails or to surf the Net.

- Wherever we go we are the receivers of messages. Newspaper headlines, billboards, street signs, shop windows, public announcements and traffic lights all send us messages. In a media-saturated society they compete for and demand our attention to the point where it is impossible to ignore them.

- We use the mass media as a source of messages that offer us both information and entertainment. We listen to the radio, to CDs or minidiscs; we watch television and DVDs and read newspapers and magazines.

- We communicate with ourselves when we think, consider, plan, or have a sudden moment of anxiety.

- Even when we think we are not communicating, we usually are. Facial expressions, bodily posture, even the way in which we occupy the space about us, are all methods of communicating our attitudes, ideas and feelings to the world at large. Indeed, it has been argued that it is impossible *not* to communicate.

As communication is such an important part of our everyday lives, it is hardly surprising that people have chosen to study it. By doing so, it is possible to understand more fully how communication works. Some people believe that such study can help make us more efficient and effective communicators.

Some commentators have tried to represent Communication Studies as a new arrival on the scene. This is easy to disprove. Key theorists such as Saussure and Peirce, whose work forms a foundation for Communication Studies, were born and worked in the nineteenth century. Fundamental models of the communication process (such as Shannon and Weaver's) were devised and published in the late 1940s. Since the 1970s Communication Studies has been an established discipline in British secondary, further and higher education. What sometimes confuses people about Communication Studies is that it draws on, and its work is informed by, work in other related disciplines. Thus, as a student of Communication Studies, you will encounter elements of Psychology, Sociology, Philosophy, Linguistics as well as Cultural Studies. But you'll still be studying communication, and you'll be studying the world from the perspective of Communication Studies.

Since Communication Studies was first mapped out as an area of study, there have been many advances in Communication and Information Technology. Mobile phones, personal computers, digital and interactive technology have all had a profound impact on how, what, where and why we communicate. If anything, the pace of technological change is increasing, and these advances in Communication and Information Technology may well be set to have an even greater influence on our lives in the future. It is against this background that this book has been written.

HOW THIS BOOK IS ORGANISED

This book aims to give you a start in your study of communication. It opens up a path into an often complex discipline. It looks at the principal theories that have been developed about, while at the same time exploring the character of, communication in a modern technological age. It is designed to help you explore and understand communication from both theoretical and practical perspectives. We offer you advice on how to enhance your own communication skills. We look at key perspectives in communication by considering approaches to textual analysis. We explore key aspects of the communication process between individuals and within groups.

You might be working with the book by yourself or with a group of fellow students led by a teacher. Whichever way you're using the book, here are a few hints on how to make best use of it.

You can work with the book in any order you wish. If you start at the beginning and proceed right the way through to the end, then you should appreciate that there's a structure here. Parts 1 and 2 set the scene for your studying Communication. Part 1 introduces you to effective study skills and to what often strikes students when first approaching the study of communication – there is more than one way of looking at it. Part 2 looks at ways and means by which you can become more effective communicators and examines the forms and functions of communication in a number of contexts. Parts 3, 4 and 5 are of special interest to students preparing for AQA's AS Communication Studies. Part 3 introduces you to the tools you can use to analyse communication texts; it also introduces you to a wide range of (sometimes complementary, sometimes conflicting) theories about communication. Part 4 focuses on preparing, undertaking and writing up communication practice, practical project work for Communication Studies examinations. Part 5 looks at themes in personal communication; it introduces you to key concepts relating to verbal and non-verbal communication, intrapersonal communication and group communication. Finally, Part 6 offers advice and assistance to preparing for and sitting public examinations in Communication Studies.

On the other hand, you might want simply to dip into the book without working through it in sequence. If you want to do this, then look to the titles of each part, to the titles of the sections into which Parts 1, 3 and 5 are divided. And in all parts look to the headings that break up the text and which tell you what's coming.

Whenever a key term is introduced you will find that we offer a definition of that term. Whenever we want you to explore a concept, theory or perspective we offer activities (in shaded boxes). It's often the case that we want you to engage in that activity before you go any further – because what you'll discover doing that activity will inform how you read the next part of the text. It's sometimes the case that we will explain something to you and then ask you to undertake an activity to reinforce your learning or to test the truth or reliability of what we've said. Shorter definitions of key terms in the text are offered in the Glossary at the end of the book.

We hope this book offers you a readable introduction to Communication Studies. We hope it helps you in your explorations of Communication Studies and that it stimulates you to take your studies further. If that's what you want, then the Further Reading sections and Bibliography will help you find out more about the world of Communication Studies.

Andrew Beck, Peter Bennett and Pete Wall
Leamington Spa, Stourbridge, Wakefield
February 2001

PART 1: STUDYING COMMUNICATION

In this first part of the book we will look at the two parts of 'studying' and 'communication'.

■ We will offer guidance to help you prepare yourself for effective study.

■ We will describe techniques and strategies you can use to study effectively and efficiently.

■ We will introduce you to two contrasting approaches to the study of communication: the process and the semiotic.

▼ 1 STUDYING

In this section we will consider the skills necessary to make an effective student of Communication Studies. We will look at ways of preparing yourself for effective study, including:

■ How to motivate yourself

■ How to acquire and practise study techniques

■ How to gather and use information

■ How best to use study resources

The most important skill you need to develop is how to be an active student. Many students are passive. They believe that if they arrive on time for classes, read the right books and take notes, then all they will have to do is turn up at the examination and regurgitate what they have 'learned'. Such students might be likened to empty containers passing along a conveyor belt, believing that knowledge and information can simply be poured into them. At the end of the conveyor belt all they have to do is spit out this knowledge and information, before joining the next conveyor belt that will take them on to the next stage of their study.

Such a model may once have had some use. However, modern assessment methods, especially in a discipline such as Communication Studies, are concerned with something other than testing your skills to absorb and regurgitate facts. Nowadays, students are expected to apply what they have learned. It is this competence in applying what you have learned that is tested in both coursework and examinations.

Research has shown that active learning is a far more effective method than passive learning. In the 1970s researchers at the California Institute of Technology investigated different methods of obtaining and retaining information. We can summarise what they found in the form of this diagram:

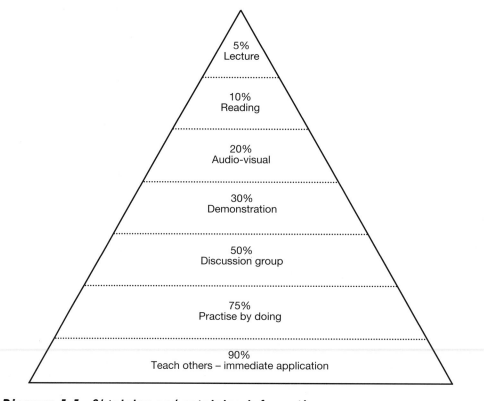

Diagram 1.1 *Obtaining and retaining information*

The diagram shows the percentage of information retained by participants 48 hours after obtaining it by the methods shown. As you can see, the active processes at the bottom of the pyramid are far more effective than the passive ones at the top. It's also worth noting that those methods that seem to be most time-effective (one hour lecture or one hour textbook-reading session) are least effective in terms of the information retained. On the other hand, those methods that are less time-effective, such as a discussion group, where you will have to take turns, listen to other opinions as well as stating your own position, are more effective in terms of retaining information. Clearly, those learning methods that will be most time-consuming will also be the most effective in the acquisition of knowledge and the development of skills.

If you are to engage actively in the learning process, you will need to be prepared to set time aside to do this. For example, you will find it useful to get together with other groups of Communication Studies students to discuss some of the key issues you are trying to get to grips with. Similarly, the shared viewing (and subsequent discussion) of a live television programme or video tape or a DVD may well prove helpful in formulating ideas around an important topic. Whatever device is employed, it is clear that it is far better to do than to be done to. Active participation in the learning process will always achieve much more than passive consumption of other people's work.

Making your learning active rather than passive clearly goes far beyond the immediate demands of succeeding in your Communication Studies course. Ultimately, it is a life skill that not only will have applications in study at a higher level, but will also influence your effectiveness in your chosen career. But let us get back to some of the basics of studying communication.

Here are some key questions that can help you focus your studies. Each of these questions relates to a key aspect of study.

Question	Aspect
Why am I studying?	Motivation
How do I keep myself studying?	Gratification
How do I maintain my attention when studying?	Climate
Where should I study?	Location
What techniques or strategies should I use when studying?	Study techniques

Let us consider each of these aspects in turn.

MOTIVATION

A good question to ask yourself is 'Why am I studying?' Sadly, many students drift into a course of study without considering what they hope to get from it. So it is a good idea to ask yourself why you are studying communication. The answer may well be a negative one, such as 'Because I could not get on to the biology course'.

It might be that you have identified the course as a means to an end – 'If I pass the examination, I will get the job I want or a place on the degree course.'

Fortunately, most students have much more positive reasons for joining the course. Whatever the case, it is essential that you recognise the value that the course and subsequent examination have for you. If you cannot see these, then ask someone, perhaps your teacher, for help. What you must avoid doing is coming up with the answer: 'I don't know'. If you can't see why you're studying, you could experience difficulty staying with that course of study.

Assuming that you can find positive answers to your goals in taking the course, it is probably a good idea to put these down in writing. You might also consider putting this 'statement' in a prominent position. In this way, if your attention starts to wander or you feel aimless and demotivated or unsure about what you should be doing, you will be reminded of these goals and should get yourself back on the right track of engaging in productive activity to realise these goals.

You may also like to consider telling close friends, family and colleagues about your goals. These people may be a valuable source of support through their concern to ensure you achieve the goals you have set yourself.

GRATIFICATION

Gratification is about the often difficult job of how to keep yourself going with your studies. Here are three strategies that can help you keep up your levels of motivation:

State your goals

You should see immediately that this relates closely to the point made above. However, let's consider two sorts of goal. Long-term goals are generally a fair distance in the future. They are likely to include such issues as completing a piece of assessed coursework or passing a particular unit in the examination. Short-term goals are much closer: 'by the end of the week' is a short-term goal. Setting yourself these short-term goals is an important method of keeping yourself on the right track. So, for example, you may have decided that by the end of the week you will be able to apply the process model of communication. You will probably find it helpful to use a diary or the calendar on your PC to note down these short-term objectives. Alternatively, prepare a list at the beginning of each week setting out what you want to achieve. Crossing them off one at a time can be very therapeutic, and you will feel suitably gratified by your achievement.

Give yourself rewards

What should immediately follow the achievement of a short-term goal is rewarding yourself. Although achieving the goal is a gratification in itself, you can add to this feeling by indulging in an activity that you enjoy in order to reinforce your achievement. Earning leisure time by achieving short-term goals can be a most effective motivating factor throughout your course of study, if not your life. If you have put in an appropriate amount of hard work, then the reward of leisure time can gratify you, refresh you, and provide you with the energy and impetus to maintain yourself in your studies.

Surface your satisfaction

Surfacing your satisfaction can help keep you studying. Don't be afraid to share your successes and achievements with your family and friends. Their pats on the back can be a source of great encouragement. Keep an eye out for television and radio programmes that have relevance to your study. Demonstrate your knowledge and skills to yourself and others by critically discussing these programmes. Similarly, keep a look-out for magazines and books that may be relevant to Communication Studies. Be prepared to talk about what you have learned whenever the conversation permits. In other words, do not make your newfound knowledge a secret – surface it. In this way you will derive satisfaction from being able to talk about topics in a constructive, detailed and animated fashion. Not only should your achievement not be a secret, but your satisfaction in your achievement should also be shared.

CLIMATE

Effective time management is another important aspect of making yourself effective in your studies. Preparing yourself a weekly timetable is the first step to ensure this effective personal time management. For study purposes build every aspect of your life in any given week into this timetable. You need to include such items as work, travel, eating, sleeping as well as the recreational time you have earned.

Of course, all the time management in the world cannot take account of unforeseen and pressing matters. The secret of dealing with these is to timetable them away. This does not mean ignoring them. What it means is that you should find an appropriate time and place to deal with them rather than letting them intrude on your studies. At first sight this may seem harsh, but it is far better to deal with them in this way than to commit time and energy to a problem that may even resolve itself without any action on your part.

Finally, remove any people who might intrude on your study time. Inform people in your family and social circle that you have studies to complete and tell them politely but firmly that you do not wish to be disturbed.

If you organise your time in the above fashion, you should create an effective climate in which to devote your complete attention to your studies.

LOCATION

As human beings, we tend to associate specific locations with specific activities. Therefore it is a good idea to find a specific location that you can associate with study. If you are fortunate enough to be able to designate a space in your home exclusively for study, so much the better. If not, you may have to consider opting for a space at your school or college or, if that is inconvenient, perhaps a local library. Alternatively, you may have to compromise around such a deal as using the kitchen for a study space when it is not being used for other purposes. What is important is that other people recognise and acknowledge your space and respect your right to peace and tranquillity when you occupy it.

Once you have established your space, it is a good idea to customise it to your needs. A clear space in which to work that is well lit and comfortable is a good starting point. Increasingly important is access to a computer. If you are sharing the use of a computer, you should check the advice in Part 2 about saving information on a disk.

Ideally your workspace needs to have all the materials that you are likely to need close at hand. This means not only obvious things like paper and pens but also textbooks, dictionaries and other appropriate reference works. There will be occasions when you will also need audio-visual equipment for playing video and audio-tapes. The fewer excuses you have for leaving your workstation to search for resources, the more likely you are to stay focused on your studies.

Getting your workstation right for your needs will inevitably be a matter of trial and error. Be prepared to make changes if there are aspects that do not suit your style of working. On the other hand, be prepared to hang on to those aspects that you feel make you more effective in your studies.

STUDY TECHNIQUES

If you are going to be an active student, there are a number of techniques that you need to learn. Let us look at three key skills that you will need before considering how these might fit into formulas that will help you remember how to be an active student.

Reviewing

Before you begin any study session, such as reading a textbook, locate where the topic falls into your study programme. You can do this by making a review, either mentally or on paper, of all you have studied so far. In this way what you are about to study can be seen as a key jigsaw piece in the larger picture of your study. The reason why you are studying it should also emerge. If you do not engage in this review, it is likely that the study you are undertaking will be aimless and you will simply be going through the motions without perceiving how it fits into the pattern as a whole.

Previewing

Make sure you know what you are about and that it is appropriate for your needs. Later in this section, when we look at using textbooks, we consider some of the key points you need to check before proceeding to use a book. Carefully previewing a source of information (whether it's a book, programme or lecture) should ensure that you do not waste time considering material that is inappropriate to your needs. It also makes sense to preview the shape of the study session. Knowing when a session will start and when it will end should indicate to you just how long your active study session is going to take.

Questioning

The activity of questioning both yourself and others can make your study more active. Raise your awareness levels at the start of a study session by asking yourself questions about what you need to know and what the writer or speaker is going to say. If you have asked yourself these questions before the session begins, you will find yourself more alert and able to maintain this questioning frame of mind throughout the session.

Make a note of those points you find questionable or mysterious. When the session is over follow up these issues, either by asking people who may know or by seeking clarification from other sources. When you start engaging in this questioning activity it is a good idea to write down your questions. As you become more experienced you are likely to find that it will become something you can do without consciously thinking about it.

A USEFUL FORMULA

Here is a useful formula that should help you become skilled in active study when you are using a textbook or other written source of information. It should help you to apply some of the techniques described above. The formula is SQ3R. This stands for:

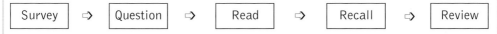

Diagram 1.2 The SQ3R model

1   **Survey** is the activity of reviewing and previewing what you know, what you need to know, and how this fits into the larger plan of your study.

2   **Question** is about using this technique to ensure purposeful engagement with the study materials.

3   **Reading** should be active. It is recommended that you read through any material twice: the first time to give you the main ideas; the second to make notes.

4   **Recall** is about digesting what you have read. Once you have read through the material, stop and tell yourself the main points. This will help you to test how effective your reading has been. If you have taken notes, ideally these will be an accurate account of the original material.

5   **Review** is the final stage of the process. This involves looking back at the four previous stages and checking the effectiveness of the process of study. You need to carry out the following:

   ■ Check that the questions you wanted answered have been answered. You should also see if any new questions have emerged and think about how you might answer them.
   ■ Re-read the material to ensure you have grasped all the important points.
   ■ Check to see if there are any gaps in your notes. If so, you should fill them in. This is also a good point at which to check for connections between the material you have just studied and those topics you have previously studied.

LISTENING

It is useful to make a distinction between hearing and listening. Most people can hear, in that they can receive and distinguish sounds within a specific frequency range. Hearing, however, is a passive activity. It is something that happens *to* us, rather than something that we do. On the other hand, listening is active. You may have come across the common notion that people 'hear but do not listen'. In a class or lecture it is very likely you will hear the words being spoken. You may not necessarily listen to them. There may be a number of reasons why you do not listen:

- You are not interested in what is being said
- You are preoccupied with a personal problem
- Something is taking place nearby that you find more interesting

In *Interpersonal Communication* (1999) Peter Hartley identifies another problem that can occur when we listen. He suggests that there are people who appear to be listening but who are not doing so. He categorises them into three groups:

1 **Pretend listeners**: These are people who seem to be listening and responding to what is being said but whose minds are in fact elsewhere
2 **Limiting listeners**: They listen in a limited way by tending to focus on specific comments or topics and distorting or misinterpreting other things that are said to them
3 **Self-centred listeners**: Such people are concerned only with their own views and are looking only for your agreement

ACTIVITY . . .

Consider occasions when you have been talking to someone and they have exhibited one of the above listening patterns. What do you think was their reason for doing so? Do you think you could ever be accused of listening in any of these ways?

Most people are born with the capacity to hear; listening is a skill they have to develop. The best sort of listener is one who is active. Active listening implies helping the transmitter to get their message over as effectively as possible. An effective listener demonstrates a willingness to participate in the communication process. This can be achieved in a number of different ways. These include:

- Paying attention to and showing interest in the message
- Indicating if we are understanding the message or not
- Showing how we are reacting to the message

A good listener will also be aware that some signals will indicate that they are bored or growing impatient. Clearly, it is best to avoid these and identify positive strategies to support a speaker in getting the message across.

As you will see in Part 5, Section 2, where we look at non-verbal communication (NVC), eye contact is one important method for signalling your response to what someone is saying. Similarly, head nods can be used to encourage a speaker to expand, develop or simply continue with a particular train of thought. Smiling or laughing at a humorous comment can demonstrate that you have picked up the subtle implications of what they are saying. Equally, laughing in the wrong place can be quite discouraging to a speaker, so make sure that a witty comment was intended as such.

You should listen in order to comprehend and make sense of another person's utterances. To achieve this you must not only listen carefully and avoid getting distracted but you should also avoid being selective in what you hear. For example, you are likely to fail to grasp a message if you insist on jumping in before a person has finished speaking. This way you will only understand a half-formulated communication. In order to make sure you have understood a message, you need to finish listening to it and to evaluate it. As Hartley (1999) points out, 'Delay evaluation of what you have heard until you fully understand it.' This means you need to check at various points in the communication process that you are understanding what is being communicated. For example, you might use a quizzical look or even a direct verbal intervention to encourage a speaker to reformulate a message to overcome some barrier to your understanding. This may simply be an unfamiliar word that needs defining.

Evaluation is an important process. We need to grasp all of the message and not just part of it. This can be difficult if a message is complex or technical or if it uses terminology unfamiliar to you. In order to become effective at listening we need to practise it.

ACTIVITY . . .

We can think faster than we can speak. When you are listening to someone else speaking, what are your thought processes? How do you exploit the difference in speed between what you think and what they say?

NOTE-TAKING

The skill of making notes from a range of sources (such as lectures, class discussion or reference books) is vital for every student. Similarly, making sense of your notes from these sources over a period of time can mean the difference between success and failure.

The key to effective note-taking is to be conscientious and to stick to an organisational method that works. For many students this will mean not only taking an initial set of notes but also revisiting these notes while they are fresh and expanding or developing them in such a way that they will make sense later. Many students find the most efficient method of doing this is to transfer hand-written notes on to a computer at the earliest opportunity. If no computer is available, then writing them up in long hand into a logical and clear format is the next-best thing.

Choose a topic you have covered recently, either in Communication Studies or another subject. Now look through your notes and see how easy it is to retrieve information on the topic. What has the result told you about your level of organisation?

ORGANISATION

Organisation is a skill closely linked to note-taking. The most accurate and detailed set of notes imaginable will be quite worthless if you cannot retrieve them for use when you want them.

Whatever system of storage you have, be it a computer or simple A4 binder, you need to develop a method of filing and organising your notes in such a way that you can confidently gain access to them whenever you need to refer to them. If you are able to store information on a computer hard disk, don't forget to make a back-up copy on a floppy disk – especially if you are not the only person using the computer.

However, the need for organisation goes far beyond simply filing your notes for easy retrieval. Probably the single most effective way to improve your skill in studying lies in organising your time. This is frequently termed 'time management'. The simple act of drawing up a timetable or action plan of how you can utilise the hours in your day can help you to optimise the use of your time. This can be especially important to a Communication Studies student; time spent on recreational activities and time spent on study can sometimes become blurred. A visit to the cinema, for example, might well be considered a pleasurable social activity as well as an aspect of your study of communication. It is up to you to try to make sure you get the best of both worlds.

INFORMATION RETRIEVAL

We live in an information-rich society. Indeed, many people see a new division within society between those who have access to information and those who don't. In general students belong to the former category, especially where they have access to the Internet and the skills and knowledge necessary to retrieve information from it. However, the privilege of such access has its downside. So much information is now available through the average student's PC that it is very easy to suffer from an overload. It is important to learn how to be selective in gaining access to and retrieving information. Equally important is how to make the most effective use of what you have obtained.

Despite some potential drawbacks, the Internet has become a real boon to students, allowing instant access to information 24 hours a day. For the student who has taken the trouble to learn how to use it effectively, it is a valuable shortcut to rich sources of information which just a few years ago might well have involved waiting several weeks for a library to obtain a book from elsewhere in the country.

SOURCES OF INFORMATION

Even though we live in an age of electronic information, books are still an important source for the Communication Studies student. Indeed, many publishers believe that books are set to grow in both importance and popularity as society is keen to have access to more and more information encouraged by such innovations as the Internet.

Using a textbook is an important skill that needs to be developed. The first challenge is to find the right book. You will need to consider both the content of the book and the level at which it is pitched.

A lot of Communication Studies books are aimed at students who are well ahead of A Level and are used to a much more sophisticated level of language and concepts than people at your stage of study. Unless you are prepared to spend hours wrestling with complex language and concepts (and spending lots of time looking up unfamiliar words), these books will not be very helpful. Equally there is a wide range of Communication Studies books covering a variety of different topics. Finding the best one for your needs is bound to be tricky. Here are some tips to help you select the right book at the right level.

- **Check cover copy**. If you are browsing in a library or bookshop, read the copy (the words) that appear on the book's cover to see if the book covers the topics you are looking for.
- **Check the contents page** to assess further if it covers the right ground. You may also find information about the level at which the book is aimed. Ideally you want a book that is geared to the needs of a reader looking for an introduction to the topic. You can check this further by reading half a page of the text inside the book to see how easy or difficult you find it to grasp.
- **Check the name of the writer(s)**. It may also be a good pointer to the usefulness of the book. Is this a writer whose name you have heard mentioned in other books or in class perhaps? You will find in the Resources section at the end of this book some suggestions for further reading. (You'll need to decide which authors you find talk to you at a level and in a way that you can understand and feel happy with.)

Once you have found the right book, the next step is to learn how to get the best from it. It is always a good idea to read the introduction to any textbook. This should tell you about the approach the writer is going to take and what they intend to cover.

It is unlikely that you will have the time to read a whole book, so you need to learn how to select the sections that are especially relevant for what you are doing. One device that may help here is the index. This will outline for you all the references to a particular topic. Where these are fairly detailed you will find they run across several pages (e.g. 68–73), so that is always a good place to start looking. Note also that most textbooks give a chapter summary at the beginning of every chapter. This gives an outline of what is covered in the chapter. It is a good idea, therefore, to check each chapter in turn to see if it is likely to contain any relevant material. To help you with this, look at the section headings within each chapter as a way of navigating your way to the information you are looking for.

The next stage is to make some notes. Some students like to photocopy useful sections of books. If you do this, you need to check with your school or college that you are not breaking copyright laws. Whilst photocopying can be a useful tool, it is often much better to make some notes from the book you are using. There are a couple of reasons why this is so. First, the process of transferring information in this way helps to reinforce your learning. Not least because you have to read and understand the original before you can write down your own version. Second, it is important to acquire and practise the skill of summarising other people's ideas in your own words. Taking notes will help you to perfect this skill. On a very few occasions you will want to lift direct quotations from a book. When you do so, don't forget to remind yourself they are direct quotations by putting them in inverted commas. This way you will not forget to attribute the ideas to their original source when you come to write up your essay or report.

EFFECTIVE READING

Most people can read. However, many people have just one method of reading; this is to look at every word. This means that they are slow readers. Reading for the efficient taking in of information is a skill that has to be learned. If you only read at one speed, it is likely that you are reading inefficiently and spending a lot more time than is necessary. The faster you read something, the less time it takes. This means you are less likely to get bored by the process. In the same way that a car has different gears for different situations, so too should you have different speeds for different types of material. Here are some of the different speeds at which you should be able to read, together with suggestions for the uses to which these reading speeds should be put.

1   **Scanning**: It is possible to scan information at between 1,000 and 2,000 words per minute (wpm). Scanning is useful when you are seeking a specific item of information such as a name, a statistic or a key phrase from a document. It takes practice to be able to look at printed information at this speed, but it will save you a lot of time and trouble.

2   **Skimming**: Skimming at 800 to 1,000 wpm is about moving your eyes left to right and from top to bottom of a page in order to locate information you are looking for. You will not read every word or phrase. However, skimming should enable you to grasp the gist of a document. It is particularly useful when you are standing in a library or bookshop trying to decide whether a book is going to be worth taking home with you.

3   **Rapid reading**: For most general reading you want to aim at a speed within this range. If your reading speed is below 300 wpm, it is likely you are wasting your time. If you think that by reading slowly you are taking in everything, bear in mind that you do not need to exceed a level of between 70 and 80 per cent comprehension and retention of information. This is due in part to the fact that up to 30 per cent of what you're reading will be redundant. (Redundancy is defined and explored in more detail in Part 3, Section 4, but basically if a communication is low on new information and highly predictable, then it is said to be redundant – it's easy to understand and you don't have to examine every single word closely in a written communication.)

4 **Slow Reading**: A speed of 150–300 wpm is the sort of speed at which you might need to read if you are dealing with difficult material containing ideas or language that you are unfamiliar with. If you need to have complete understanding of a document, you will need to read at this speed if you are to comprehend the material.

5 **Studying**: 10 to 200 wpm. At this speed you will be doing some very close reading of a text. You may well find yourself going back over material to consider its meaning. You may also be taking notes as you read. You are not reading slowly because you can't help it, rather you are doing it to ensure you completely grasp the material you are tackling.

Don't forget to write down all the details of a book you use. Later in this section we look at the important practice of referencing and describe a procedure for referencing books. Every time you use a book make a note of:

Author
Title
Publisher
Date of publication
ISBN (International Standard Book Number)

It is also a good idea to make a note of the page numbers from which your notes have been taken. If you are using a reader or collection of essays by different people, don't forget that you also need a note of the name of the individual contributor whose work you are using.

An important reason that you need to make a note of the source of your information is that when you come to use it in an essay or a piece of coursework you have to attribute it. That means that you should not try to claim that it is an original idea of your own but should acknowledge the source from which it comes. Otherwise you can be accused of plagiarism, which means taking and using other people's ideas without properly acknowledging them.

ACTIVITY . . .

At what speed are you reading this part of the book? Is the speed you are reading appropriate to:

- the content of the book

- your purpose in reading it?

THE INTERNET

The Internet is a great boon to all students but for the Communication Studies student it also offers some unique advantages as well as disadvantages. The chief advantage is the way it provides swift access to contemporary information. A problem with much of the information in a textbook is that it may become out of date.

If you are using a computer that doesn't belong to you, make sure you have a plentiful supply of disks on which to store things you find. It is a good idea to reserve one disk for keeping a list of bookmarked sites that you have found especially useful. If you download something to a disk for future reference, keep a detailed note of the contents of that disk on the label so you can find it again without having to search through each of your disks in turn.

Most of the sites relevant to Communication Studies are pitched at a sophisticated level of understanding. This is because a lot of research into the discipline takes place in higher education, especially in the United Sates. Just as you will have found it necessary to dip into a textbook to see if it is useful or not, so it is with a website.

However, before you do this, it is a good idea to learn how to use a search engine to the best effect. Search engines such as Yahoo, Lycos or Google are the means by which you can enter keywords to identify what you are looking for. They will list all of the sites on the Internet that seem relevant to your search. This often amounts to several thousand, so it will pay you to do some initial research into how to get the best from the search engine you have chosen to use. Click on the help icon on the home page of the search engine and it will tell you how you can use such devices as inverted commas and plus and minus signs to limit your search. It is really worthwhile familiarising yourself with these devices if you are going to make searches that produce a manageable amount of information for you to follow up.

Figure 1.1 *Computer screen with search results for key word enquiry*

BIBLIOGRAPHY AND REFERENCES

It is important that you acknowledge other people's ideas when you produce work for Communication Studies. To lift material from published sources without acknowledging where it came from is called plagiarism. Widespread access to the Internet has made plagiarism more prevalent in some academic disciplines. Of course, in a complex area such as Communication Studies there is a huge amount of published material that you may wish to refer to across a range of different disciplines. The fact that material is available from such diverse sources makes it more important that you properly acknowledge what you have used. Referencing and acknowledging source material is important whatever level of academic study you are engaged in. Proper referencing enables the reader to check the source you have quoted. By doing so they are able to ensure that you have accurately represented what that person has said. It may be that you have interpreted material in a specific way. A reader checking back may feel that the material you have quoted is open to other interpretations and that you have chosen one that particularly suits your own argument.

A bibliography is a list of sources, usually books, that you have cited (or used) in an essay. Whenever you produce a written piece of work, it is essential that you give such a list at the end. You will find a bibliography at the end of most textbooks. Communication Studies students will need to make references to a wide range of publications: books by a single author; contributions made by an author to a collection or anthology; a journal article; a publication from an organisation or corporation; a newspaper article; a television programme; a film; a website; or a song or a piece of music.

The Harvard System of referencing is the most frequently used in Communication Studies. Below you'll find examples of how you should refer to the various sources listed above using the Harvard System.

When you make your own bibliographies or references, make sure that you stick to the punctuation and type style given. Right down to the use of the comma, the colon and the full stop.

Book:
Strinati, D. (2000) *An Introduction to Studying Popular Culture*, London: Routledge.

Contribution made by an author to a collection or an anthology:
de Saussure, F. (1996) 'The object of linguistics', in P. Cobley (ed.) *The Communication Theory Reader*, London: Routledge.

Journal article:
Brophy, P. (1986) 'Horrality – the textuality of contemporary Horror films', *Screen*, 27 (1): 2–13.

Publication by an organisation or corporation:
Independent Television Commission (1991) *The ITC Code of Advertising Standards and Practice*, London: ITC.

continued . . .

A newspaper article:
Brown, M. (2001) 'Bubbling Over', *The Guardian*, February 12.

Television programme:
Coronation Street (2001) ITV, December 16.

Film:
Soderbergh, S. (1999) *The Limey*, Artisan Pictures Inc.

Website:
Taylor & Francis,
    http://www.mediastudiesarena.com/mediastudiesarena/books/textbooks.html
    (2001, February 12)

Song or piece of popular music:
Scanner vs. D.J. Spooky (1999) 'Synchronism', *The Quick and the Dead*. Sulphur
    Records, MELCDDDI.

WRITING AN EVALUATION

It is common in much academic study to ask students to produce their own evaluation of
work they have done. In the Assessment and Qualifications Alliance (AQA) GCE
Communication Studies coursework units students are required to produce an evaluation
or review of the work they have done. This takes the form of a self-assessment in which
you are asked to identify and consider what you have achieved. You will sometimes hear
the process described as self-reflexivity. This means that you are being asked to look in
on yourself and reflect on what you have achieved. Implicit in this process is the notion
of how you might improve on what you have done, if you were given the chance to do
it again. In both AQA coursework units, marks that count towards your final grade are
awarded for this process.

The process of evaluation does not invite you to seize the opportunity to praise the work
you have produced in the hope that an examiner will agree with you about its value.
Evaluation should be more concerned with the process of learning than of fishing for
marks. In Communication Studies the evaluation presents you with the opportunity to link
the theory that you have learned to the process of communication that has been part of
your practical work. For example, if you have given an oral presentation, your evaluation
of it should to some extent focus on theories of interpersonal communication. You might
like to address such issues as your use of register and language more generally. You may
also like to consider how you dealt with feedback from your audience but linking in some
of the theoretical work you have done on the role of feedback.

CRITICAL THINKING

Critical thinking is a key term in the evaluation process. 'Critical' does not carry with
it the negative connotation of finding things that are wrong. 'Critical' in this sense means
the skill to stand back from the work you have produced and to make an assessment of

it. This assessment should be objective, avoiding any sense of bias because it is your own work. Indeed, the best type of evaluation looks at what has been produced as though it were done by someone else.

'Critical' carries with it the sense of analysing in order to understand how something functions. This should be an important signal that you are expected to do more than simply describe the process of preparing a presentation or making a project. Critical thinking requires you to go deeper and show you understand why you worked in the way that you did.

Similarly, your evaluation needs to concern itself with the issue of how effective was your communication in terms of its purpose and the audience at which it was aimed. You may wish to consider how it might be improved. Equally important is to think about what you have learned from the process not only in terms of communication theory but also in terms of your own skills as a communicator (including what you need to do to develop and improve these skills).

Now that we have looked at ways of studying effectively, we will move on to see how those skills can be used to study communication itself.

▼ 2 COMMUNICATION

In this section we will briefly outline two contrasting approaches to the study of communication.

- We will look at the *process* approaches to studying communication.
- We will look at the *semiotic* approaches to the study of communication.

It is probably this capacity to communicate with ourselves and with others which, more than any other single factor, distinguishes the human animal from other animals. More than the capacity to communicate in many different forms, the capacity to think and to organise those thoughts into systems distinguishes the human animal from other animal societies. We can act, we can reflect upon our actions, and we can draw conclusions about the actions of others. As Colin Cherry (1978) has observed, 'Self-awareness and the sense of social responsibility have arisen as a result of organised thoughts. Systems of ethics and law have been built up. Man has become self-conscious, responsible, a changeable creature.'

CODES

One of the first things we discover when studying communication is that all communication is coded. Although we all use codes in our communication behaviour right from our earliest days, we are not always aware of this. Awareness of the existence of codes often first arises when we encounter groups of people using what we term 'jargon'. Indeed, our awareness often first reveals itself as frustration. 'If that's what they meant, why didn't they say so?' It's a common complaint of students and people in the working world that other people 'wrap up' what they're trying to say in fancy words, in jargon, in long words that sound impressive but which don't seem to mean very much when closely analysed. Of course, these complaints are all too often justified. People do tend to wrap up or dress up what they're saying in a way they think will impress other people. Developing the ability to see through people who do this is what Neil Postman has termed 'acquiring a crap detector'.

On the other hand, we must be careful not to reject completely those expressions that puzzle us. Certain groups of people express themselves in certain ways because that is the agreed and commonly used method. In other words, they use codes. Codes are sets of signs and symbols which have meaning for people who are members of specific social or working groups (even families often have their own coded ways of speaking which prevents outsiders gaining access to those families and engaging in constructive communication with them). You can often tell what a person's job is by paying close attention to the words they use and the ways in which they express themselves. All signs and symbols work as a shorthand method of communication.

For example, if you were driving a car or riding a bike and came across this road sign, you'd know what it meant.

Figure 1.2 Hump-back bridge hazard sign

It would be silly – and dangerous – if you were presented with a sign that said:

> If you continue driving or riding on the road that you are now driving or riding on, you will encounter a hump bridge. Take care to reduce speed to ensure you don't damage your vehicle, and use your eyes and ears because vehicles approaching from the other side of the bridge may be obscured by the hump of the bridge and may not be as careful as you are.

It would be silly because we know what the road sign means, and when we come across it we consciously or subconsciously remind ourselves of the advice that was presented in the second written sign. Thus we can see that there exist codes to which we already have the key. We know how to unlock the door of specific coded communications and extract their meanings. It's for this reason that we don't have mayhem on our roads. If we all stick to the conventions and guidance in the coded system of road signs, then all road users get along with one another.

Although we will look at theories that have been devised to explain and to study the communication process in greater detail in Part 3, it is appropriate to take a brief look at them here. It's also appropriate to state quite clearly that there is more than one approach to the study of communication. In one way it is quite easy to explain why this should be so – different types of communication require different types of study, analysis, explanation and evaluation. In other ways it is less easy – different theories seem to compete to explain the same or similar kinds of communication.

You would imagine that a book about communication would easily be able to define the word. But it's not that easy. As John Fiske admits in the first sentence of his *Introduction to Communication Studies* (1990), 'Communication is one of those human activities that everyone recognises but few can define satisfactorily'. Colin Cherry, an early commentator on communication working in the 1950s, offered this definition which is a good starting point: 'Broadly: the establishment of a social unit from individuals, by the shared use of language or signs. The sharing of common sets of rules, for various goal-seeking activities. (There are many shades of opinion)' (Cherry 1978). A number of conclusions can be drawn from this: (*a*) Cherry conceives of communication as a social act; and (*b*) he conceives of communication as sharing (this isn't surprising given that we derive the word 'communication' from the Latin verb *communicare*, which means 'to share').

In the study of communication two main schools of thought exist.

SCHOOL OF THOUGHT   Where groups of academics come together because they feel the same way about particular issues.

The first school of thought, usually known as the process school, characterises communication as the transmission and reception of messages. The second school of thought, usually known as the semiotic school, conceives of communication as the generation and sharing of meanings.

THE PROCESS SCHOOL OF COMMUNICATION

This approach to the study of communication originated in the study of telecommunications. Claude E. Shannon was employed by the Bell telephone corporation in America in the 1940s. To begin to solve problems occurring in telecommunications, he devised what he called a mathematical model of communication. He was concerned to eliminate or lessen the effect of disruptions to the communication process. He called this 'noise'. He believed that if you could place a mathematical value on 'noise', then you could work out by how much the signal being transmitted would have to be boosted to overcome the 'noise'. As this model originated in telecommunications, it is concerned with the transmission of signal and the effectiveness of transmission. So the process school of thought came into being, a school of thought which interpreted communication as being about the process of transmission and reception of signals.

A simple model of the process approach to communication can be represented by this diagram:

| Source | ⇨ | Transmitter | ⇨ | Channel | ⇨ | Receiver | ⇨ | Destination |

Diagram 1.3 Simple process model of communication

The source is the idea in someone's mind. The transmitter is the physical device used to communicate with. The channel is the medium used to communicate through. The receiver is the physical means of receiving a transmitted signal. And the destination is the original idea now in the mind of the person communicated with.

ACTIVITY . . .

Take the road sign for a hump-back bridge and explain how it functions in terms of the process approach to communication.

THE SEMIOTIC SCHOOL OF COMMUNICATION

This approach to the study of communication takes its name from the Greek word for sign: *semeion*. Independently of each other, the Swiss linguist Ferdinand de Saussure and the American philosopher Charles Peirce (pronounced 'purse') took *semeion* and devised the words 'semiology' and 'semiotics' (de Saussure 1983; Peirce 1966). In many ways semiotics is more concerned with how communication works than about why communication exists or what communication is. It assumes that all codes are arbitrary, that there isn't any logical reason why we use one particular sign. It assumes that the meaning we get from signs comes in part from the creator of the sign, in part from our experience of the sign, and in part from the sign itself. In other words, communication is an active dynamic process.

SIGN The basic unit of communication, the building block from which all communication is constructed.

Our thinking about semiotics can be helped by this diagram (where 'produce' is the origin of the message, 'consumer' is the destination of the message, and 'text' is the message itself). What we call 'meaning' is what is generated as a result of an interaction between all three elements.

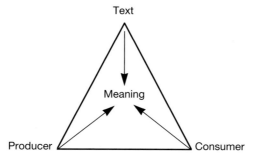

Diagram 1.4 *General model of semiotics*

ACTIVITY . . .

State the basic differences between the process and semiotic schools of thought.

FURTHER READING

Barrass, R. (1984) *Study! A Guide to Effective Study, Revision and Examination Techniques*, London: Chapman & Hall.

Chambers, E. and Northedge, A. (1997) *The Arts Good Study Guide*, Milton Keynes: Open University Press.

Cherry, C. (1978) *On Human Communication: A Review, a Survey and a Criticism*, 3rd edn, Cambridge, Mass/London: MIT Press.

Drew, S. and Binham, R. (1997) *The Student Skills Guide*, Aldershot: Gower.

Fiske, J. (1990) *Introduction to Communication Studies*, 2nd edn, London: Routledge.

Fry, R. (1997) *How to Study*, London: Kogan Page.

PART 2: EFFECTIVE COMMUNICATION

In this part we look at how you can develop the skill of effective communication. We consider the development of this skill in the contexts of written communication, verbal communication, and the use of new technology.

■ We look at written communication and verbal communication.

■ We explore forms of written and verbal communication.

■ We look at verbal communication in formal contexts.

■ We map out some contemporary applications of Communication and Information Technology.

We are all born with the capacity to communicate. We are all capable of making utterances and gestures that enable us to send messages to other people. Being able to communicate well is, however, a skill. It is a skill that we need to learn if we are to do it effectively.

So what makes a person an effective communicator? Unfortunately, contrary to the claims of countless self-help guides, there is no simple answer to this question. Effective communication is a result of a combination of factors. It relies on the capacity of the communicator to utilise a range of different skills, some of which we are probably born with, some of which we have to learn.

To help you to become a more effective communicator you should bear in mind that you will need to communicate in a range of different situations. Some of these will require you to use skills in communicating formally. Making a speech and writing a report are examples of formal communication. Others will require you to communicate informally, for example sending a note to a friend, or chatting to a stranger on the bus. Whatever the situation, there are some useful guidelines that you should bear in mind when you start to compose your message.

The first point relates to the concept of empathy. Empathy is the act of putting yourself in someone else's shoes in order to see issues and ideas from their perspective rather than

Sales Office Administrator

wanted for busy electronic component distributor based in glorious countryside near Balsall Common. Excellent computer, **communication and interpersonal skills are a pre-requisite**. Excellent career prospects for someone wanting to move into a fast-moving sales environment. Salary £12,000 p.a. plus bonus plus benefits.

A.P.B. GROUP LIMITED
CONSTRUCTION OR ENGINEERING GRADUATE

An opportunity exists to join our management team in a busy civil engineering environment.
Practical experience of sites and a good knowledge of Health & Safety Law an advantage.
Must have good communication skills, be computer literate & have a full clean driving licence.
Applications in writing to:
Mr A Graham, Managing Director
A.P.B. Group Limited

Grade G Community Nurse (RNMH)

£20,830 – £24,090 per annum

Full-Time, 37½ hours per week

We are constantly seeking to expand and improve our Learning Disability Service, and we have your future very much in mind too, with a clear career structure and a whole range of personal development opportunities, including individual performance reviews, clinical supervision, good in-house training opportunities and excellent support and mentoring.

This role offers considerable autonomy in decision making and scope to see your own progressive ideas implemented. You will manage a caseload and a team of community staff, assessing client need, implementing and evaluating care programmes and setting standards of care, as well as being involved in teaching staff and students.

A good communicator and teamworker, with the ability to lead and develop people, you must be innovative, highly motivated and able to work on your own initiative. RNMH, diploma/degree in Community Health Studies and ENB 807 or equivalent are essential.

Car driver essential, lease car scheme in operation.

This post offers the chance to live and work in one of England's most attractive areas, close to the Cotswolds, yet within easy reach of the UK motorway network and the major cities of Coventry and Birmingham.

Please quote job reference number: 41/1934

Lecturer/Senior Lecturer in Management Sciences
(Temporary for one year)
£14,902 – £30,636 pa

You will contribute to the teaching of Management Science and/or Applied Statistics at both undergraduate and postgraduate levels, as well as play an important role in research and course-related activities.

With a good first or higher degree in the Management Sciences area, you will have at least two years' lecturing or professional experience. Evidence of research/professional collaboration and an interest in one or more of the following: multivariate analysis, survey analysis, data warehousing and data mining would be an advantage.

You will be a team-player with **good communication and presentation skills** and the ability to work under pressure to meet deadlines.

Suitably experienced candidates may be appointed at senior lecturer level.

Please quote reference 535/00 Interview data 13 December 2000

Figure 2.1 *Job advertisements – the importance of communication skills* your own. Another way of saying this is that you should be sensitive to the needs of your audience. One way to do this is to consider how you would respond to the message if you were one of them. We have all sat through a long boring class in which the teacher has paid little heed to the feelings and needs of the audience. Similarly, each of us has been trapped in a conversation with a boring and uninteresting person who seems completely insensitive to the response, or perhaps more accurately the lack of response, he or she is getting from his victim. In both cases the communicator is showing a lack of sensitivity to the audience. The more sensitive you are to the needs of your audience, the more likely you are to communicate effectively with them.

The second point you should consider is how best to organise the information you want to communicate to make it comprehensible to the receiver. This is especially true of a formal communication situation, such as making a speech or writing a report. The need to plan and organise information into a logical and user-friendly structure is vital. Taking time to plan and organise your message is also a useful tool in less formal contexts. Take, for example, a situation where you need to telephone someone in order to obtain information. Planning what you are going to say in advance will almost certainly produce a more positive result than dialling the number and finding yourself tongue-tied when the caller answers. Often a simple checklist will remind you of the points you want to make.

The third point to remember is not to underestimate the importance of feedback. Feedback is a key aspect of the communication process. Feedback is the way people let us know how they are responding to the information we are giving them. A room full of people all with puzzled looks on their faces should indicate to a presenter that there is a lack of clarity about the information that is being transmitted. Similarly, people falling asleep while you are talking to them does not always mean that they need a good night's rest. Learning to recognise feedback and responding to it is an important factor in communicating effectively.

ACTIVITY . . .

Observe other people communicating in a range of different situations: your teacher in class, your family at meal times, or your friends or classmates during breaks.

- How effective are they at communicating?

- Is there any evidence that they have planned what they are going to say?

- How sensitive are they to the needs of their audience?

- What do you think makes some people better at communicating than others?

WRITTEN COMMUNICATION

Let us start by looking at written communication. Writing has been a highly prized skill throughout history. With a largely illiterate population until the middle of the Victorian era, being able to write conferred great powers on those who possessed it. Today, although most of the population has at least a functional level of literacy, people who are able to write effectively and confidently are often seen as an intellectual and cultural elite, a privileged minority. Our education system, and more specifically the examination system, privileges skills in written communication above most of the skills taught in school.

When it comes to writing, very few people get it right first time. Writing is invariably a process of drafting, editing and redrafting to arrive at an acceptable finished product. This calls on the writer to be prepared on occasion not only to revise many times over, but also to listen to and, where necessary, act on the advice and criticisms of other people. A book like this one, written by three people, has undergone not only a heavy editing process, but also substantial redrafting and revision before it was considered fit for students.

Effective writing is about clarity, precision and concision. Good writing is also appropriate to the purpose, context and audience for which it is intended. An effective writer is one who creates a message with these points in mind.

So how are clarity, precision and concision achieved in written communication? As you will see from the resources section at the end of the book, there are a number of books that offer advice on how to write effectively. Some of these, such *The New Fowler's Modern English Usage* (1998), are most useful for checking grammatical accuracy. Perhaps the best way to improve your own style of writing is to consider the work of people who have perfected the art of writing with purpose and efficiency. George Orwell is a good example of a writer whose work bears these hallmarks of clarity and precision. In fact Orwell wrote a particularly helpful essay entitled 'Politics and the English Language' (Orwell 2001) in which he outlines the principles of good writing. The essay is well worth reading, but the following summary of Orwell's key points should help you start thinking about how you can improve your own style of writing.

1   Never use a metaphor, simile or other figure of speech which you are used to seeing in print. The first person to write the phrase 'raining cats and dogs' used a witty figure of speech to describe stormy weather. To use the phrase now is simply to repeat a cliché or worn-out method of saying something. It is best therefore to avoid using a cliché. Instead try to find a fresh way of expressing yourself that will have an impact on your reader.

2   Never use a long word when a short one will do. In other words, try to keep it simple. There may be occasions when you need to use a long word because it is technically correct and there is not a simple word you can use instead. Look out, though, for occasions when you lapse into long 'formal' words which can sound pompous. 'Endeavours to engage her in caresses' is a line from a poem by T. S. Eliot in which he pokes fun at young clerk. 'Tries to kiss her' would be a more simple and direct way of expressing the idea.

3   If it is possible to cut out a word, cut it out. A helpful exercise when you are revising what you have written is to read through and delete any words that are unnecessary.

4   Never use the passive where you can use the active. This refers to sentence construction. A simple active construction has a subject doing something to an object, for example: 'The child [subject] kicked [verb] the ball [object]'. A passive

construction puts this object at the beginning of the sentence. For example, 'The ball was kicked by the child'. You can see that, if you use the active, your sentence will be more direct and more dynamic. Often people will use a passive construction when they wish to evade responsibility. In this way we have people saying things like 'The train was delayed by my actions' rather than 'I delayed the train'.

5   Never use a word or phrase from another language, a scientific word or a jargon word if you can think of an everyday English equivalent.

6   Break any of these rules rather than say anything plain silly. In the end common sense should always prevail over rules. Provided you are writing with clarity and precision, you shouldn't become obsessed by rules. The acid test must always be to consider how the receiver will react to your words.

You may wish to consider an additional point to Orwell's advice. That is the importance of writing short sentences. Never strain a sentence by trying to include more information than it is capable of holding. Too many ideas in one sentence can make it indigestible. If you find yourself writing a long sentence, try to break it down into two or more shorter sentences. In this way your meaning should become clearer.

A useful source of information and ideas on writing clearly is the website of the Plain English Campaign (www.plainenglish.co.uk).

As we have suggested, it is important to bear in mind your purpose and the context in which you are writing. Just as you need the right tools to change a wheel on a car, so you need the right tools for the job of writing. A note for the milkman, an academic essay and a love letter are examples of different types of message. However, the context and purpose of each are so different that each requires an individual approach if it is to be effective. Each of these messages demands the use of a different set of conventions. If you ignore these conventions, you will produce a message that loses its impact because of its inappropriateness. Most written communication is intended to inform. It is a method of passing information from one person to another, or to a group of people. However, there are often additional reasons for writing beyond the simple act of informing. For example, you may wish to persuade someone to do something. On the other hand you may wish to entertain. You may wish to do both at the same time.

ACTIVITY . . .

What do you think are the main differences between a note for the milkman, an academic essay and a love letter? Try writing the opening of an essay in the style of a love letter and vice versa.

The message that you compose and the intention you have in composing it may not necessarily be the same as the message and intention that the recipient receives. What you thought to be an entertaining and persuasive message may be read as tedious and threatening.

The risk of misunderstanding can be reduced if you remember to place yourself in the position of the recipient. You need to take into account a number of factors when you consider your audience. The most important of these is the level of knowledge or expertise that they have of the topic about which you are communicating. This should determine the register you will adopt. For example, if you are explaining some aspect of an academic subject to another student, you can assume that s/he will have a basic vocabulary to describe key aspects of the subject. In Communication Studies, for example, that student would probably have some understanding of terms used in semiotics, such as 'denotation' and 'connotation'. If, on the other hand, you were writing for a person with no knowledge of semiotics, it would be inappropriate to use subject-specific jargon.

JARGON means the specialised vocabulary which people who have knowledge and understanding of a particular subject use when communicating with one another. The legal profession and the computing industry are places where you can expect to find professional jargon. Similarly, someone who repairs your car will use jargon to describe a fault or problems with the engine. Some people hide behind jargon. They use a vocabulary that is baffling to people who do not share their expertise in the subject.

Despite the fact that many people feel uncomfortable around jargon, its use is frequently essential to make yourself understood in a precise way. For example, when you are analysing a text for Communication Studies, you will need to employ some of the terms you have learned for semiotic analysis. If it is a print text, you would also need to use the vocabulary for describing the presentation of information through typographical devices, such as italics or 72 point type. Taking account of the level of expertise that your audience possesses is an important matter if you are to make yourself understood.

Similarly, it is important to estimate the level of linguistic sophistication your reader possesses. It is easy to get this wrong. If you employ too high a register, you are likely to confuse your reader. On the other hand, too low a register may appear patronising and insensitive and, although the reader may understand what you have written, s/he may be so antagonised that communication isn't achieved.

REGISTER describes the level of language being used. The appropriateness of a register is determined by the audience being addressed, the context in which they are being addressed, and the subject matter being communicated.

STRUCTURE

Structure is an essential ingredient in creating an effective written message. Structure means planning and arranging your ideas in such a way that they have a logical organisation. This will enable the person receiving the message to decode it. Structure is a means of organising the flow of your ideas into a form that can be readily assimilated by your audience.

If you are to achieve a logical structure to your written communication, you must be prepared to think ahead about what you want to say. This means working out a plan of what you intend to say before you put pen to paper. One way of doing this is simply to take a piece of paper and write down everything that comes into your head about the message you are going to create. Once you have done this, try to number the points in a sequence that will take you from the start of what you want to say to the end. This numbered sequence will then form your plan. You may well find that each numbered idea represents an individual paragraph for what you want to say.

The paragraph is an important tool in writing. Paragraphs are used to put together connected ideas. A paragraph is a group of sentences each covering the same theme. A new paragraph should represent for the reader the next stage in the development of an idea or argument.

ACTIVITY . . .

Look at how a news story is constructed in a newspaper. It does not matter whether it is tabloid or broadsheet. You will notice newspaper paragraphs are generally much shorter than, say, in an academic essay. This strategy helps the reader digest the information in manageable portions.

Now look at the structure of a newspaper story. Consider the sequence in which the information is given. What do you notice about the ordering of the paragraphs? Why do you think typographical devices are used so the first paragraph is made to stand out from the others?

TYPOGRAPHY   The use of different types and styles of lettering in printed texts.

WRITING A LETTER

In an age of fast-developing electronic communications technology, the importance of the letter has begun to diminish. It still remains, however, an important method of communicating information. Choosing the most appropriate channel of communication is an important element in the success of a message. Often you will be called upon to decide whether a letter or a telephone call is the more appropriate channel. You may consider a fax or an e-mail or a mobile phone text message as an alternative.

A letter does offer certain advantages to both the sender and the receiver of a message. It is a good idea to take these into account when deciding how to send your message. Unlike a telephone call, a letter is a permanent form of communication. It also carries with it some degree of formality. In business, a letter often signifies the transmission of a formal message between two people or organisations, as opposed to the relative informality of a telephone call. Perhaps most importantly, a letter gives the receiver time to consider a response. A telephone call can often put the receiver 'on the spot' with the demand for an immediate answer. A letter allows time for the receiver to think about the contents and respond in a more assured and comfortable way. Of course, the danger is that no response at all will be forthcoming.

ACTIVITY . . .

Imagine you need to get some information for a project from a large organisation, such as a television company or a national charity. Why do you think a letter would be an effective way of doing this? What points would you need to bear in mind when writing your letter?

Your response to this activity should have included the importance of addressing your letter to an appropriate recipient. Ideally this should be a named person in the organisation. You can usually find the names of people with specific roles, such as public or customer relations, by doing some research on the Internet or in a library. Failing that, you can either phone and ask reception for the name of such a person, or you can write to the person using either a job title or the departmental name. (The formal term for someone's job title is their designation.) For example, you might direct your letter to the Head of Customer Relations.

You should also have considered the content of your letter. Every week large organisations receive letters from students asking for help and information. Many respond by sending out an all-purpose information pack which they hope will cover the needs of most students. This is due in part to the fact that most commercial organisations are too busy to answer individual queries. It is also due to the fact that many students don't state precisely what they want in their letters. An effective letter will make clear exactly what it is you require. It must also meet those important guidelines of clarity, precision and concision. Indeed, it can be argued that a good letter will not exceed one side of A4 paper.

VERBAL COMMUNICATION

Verbal communication is generally much less formal than written communication. Many of the verbal messages that we produce are quite casual exchanges with other people. As a consequence many people tend to speak without thinking.

In Part 3 we will look at verbal communication in the wider context of themes in human communication in general and the more specific context of language. What follows here has a more practical orientation and is intended to help you become a more effective communicator.

Clearly, it would be ridiculous to suggest that every utterance should be carefully prepared in advance. Spontaneity is an important characteristic of verbal exchanges. However, you will find there are a number of occasions when planning in advance what you are going to say is important. These situations include:

- Asking for and giving information
- Making a telephone call
- Making a presentation
- Contributing to a meeting

Our general principles of effective communication are important here. Remember to:

- Think about the needs of your audience
- Organise what you have to say into a logical structure
- Respond to feedback

Similarly, the importance of speaking with clarity, precision and concision cannot be over-emphasised.

SEEKING INFORMATION

ACTIVITY . . .

Imagine you are walking through a town or city that you know well. Someone asks you the way to the town hall. What factors would you bear in mind about your audience before composing your reply?

Your response to the above activity should tell you a lot about the principles of effective verbal communication. First, you would need to make some assessment of the person asking for the information. You may need to consider such points as:

1 How do they intend to get to the town hall – on foot, by car? If it is not immediately apparent, you may need to ask.
2 An elderly person or a person with a disability may not be able to follow the route you were going to describe. If, for example, that route involved climbing steps, then you might need to think of an alternative route.

This is a good example of empathy – where you are looking at the message from the viewpoint of the recipient, imagining yourself in their position.

Second, before you compose your reply, it is important that you plan what you are going to say. It may be that there is a map of the town nearby and you can show the person the route using that. Otherwise you need to construct the journey mentally and organise it in such a way that it is clear to recipient. You need also to cut out unnecessary detail that might confuse.

Think of those occasions when you have asked for directions and received a bewildering response. What aspect of the message you received was it that made it difficult for you to understand? When you are looking for directions in a crowded street, what criteria do you use in choosing someone to ask?

If you are to compose an effective message offering directions, you will need to:

1   Assess the needs of the recipient, identifying any possible barriers to effective communication.
2   Think through the most efficient way of explaining the route to be taken.
3   Organise your directions into a simple, easy-to-follow form. This probably means giving the information in sequence, reinforced by offering such handholds as key landmarks.
4   Look for feedback signals from the receiver. Head nods or confused facial expressions should help you assess the effectiveness of your communication.
5   Be prepared to repeat or reinforce all or some of your message in the light of this feedback.

KEY TERM

FEEDBACK   The response received by the sender to a message.

MAKING A TELEPHONE CALL

Making a telephone call to give or obtain information requires a very similar approach. However, because the telephone is a channel of communication that relies exclusively on sound, it requires other factors to be taken into account.

Just as we suggest the need to plan your message for face-to-face communication, so it is important to do so with a telephone call. A checklist of points that you wish to make can be a useful guideline for handling the call. Indeed, it is always a good idea to have pen and paper nearby, not only to note down what you want to say, but also to note down points from the person at the other end. Breaking off a conversation to find a pen will make you seem amateur and disorganised, as well as disrupting the communication process.

When you initiate a telephone call start by making it clear who you are. It is always a good idea to give your name, even if you are not known to the person you are calling. Next explain clearly and concisely what it is you want. If it is a large organisation, this is a good point to ensure you are speaking to the person best able to help you.

Suppose when you make a call you are greeted by an answering system. Many people at this point hang up and try to call later. This can be frustrating for the person you are calling, especially as Caller ID and Ringback systems allow the source of the call to be traced. It is a good idea to ensure that you have a message ready to leave on the answering system. This should include your name, telephone number and brief details of what you want. Some people also leave the time and date of the call, although increasingly this information is stored automatically by answering machines.

Responding to feedback remains an important part of telephone communication, even though visual signals such as facial expression are not available to us. On the telephone, as well as listening to the words that people say in response, you need to be aware of paralanguage. (Paralanguage is discussed in detail later.) Be prepared to pick up on and respond to such non-verbal clues in the voice as intonation, volume and hesitation. Silence can often say more than speech at the other end of the telephone.

PARALANGUAGE Communication which is in the form of utterances other than the words themselves, e.g. the volume of one's voice.

KEY TERM

MAKING A PRESENTATION

One communication context that you are almost certainly going to have to deal with is making a presentation. A presentation is a formal talk made to a group of people and usually requires the support of visual aids, such as overhead transparencies (OHTs). For the AS Communication Studies Unit 1, you are expected to give a talk lasting approximately 10 minutes, with a question-and-answer (Q&A) phase of up to 5 minutes. Your presentation will be based on an investigation you have made into some aspect of personal communication skills. Before preparing your presentation, you should have already produced a 500-word essay based on your investigation. Your essay, therefore, will used as the basis for your presentation. This means that most of the information you need to communicate as part of your presentation should have been collected and organised into a written form. In making your presentation, you will need to assimilate this material into a form appropriate to a verbal presentation.

You should have realised by now that one key to achieving this is organisation. In preparing your presentation it will help if you start by deciding on how you intend to structure it. Begin by making an outline plan of how your presentation will evolve. You are not necessarily bound by this plan – you can go back and change it if you need to. By having such a plan, you will at least have a framework that should enable you to structure your talk so that you can communicate the important information within the 10-minute time limit. The advice on written communication about jotting down the points you want to make and numbering holds good here. Remember too the importance of creating logical links between your points. You should consider carefully how you might control the flow of information to your audience in such a way as to hold their attention throughout.

PREPARING YOUR NOTES

Notes should be notes. Do not be tempted to write the content of your presentation as continuous prose, like an essay. If you do, it is very likely you will deliver it in a dull monotone with your head looking down on to a piece of paper. Reading a prepared speech is guaranteed to disaffect your audience. It is much better to write notes on small individual cards. Ideally these will be little more than key words to remind you of the individual points you need to make. By doing this, then you will have to exercise some degree of creativity.

The beginning and end of your presentation are especially important. You should aim for an opening that will make an impact on your audience and put them in a frame of mind where they want to listen to what will follow. Although you may feel nervous at the start of your talk, you should aim for a confident opening. A brief anecdote to relax your audience and get them on your side is one way of breaking the ice. It is also important that you make clear to your audience precisely what it is you are going to tell them about. It may also help if you run through an outline programme so that they are aware of the structure of your talk and can identify the points of specific interest and importance.

This is also a good point to let your audience know what you expect of them. Some speakers welcome interruptions; many speakers do not. If you do not want to be interrupted, then tell your audience that you prefer that they wait until the end to ask questions.

Organising the room in readiness for your presentation can have an important impact on how it is received. There are a number of different styles for arranging a room for an audience and each can affect the way in which audiences respond. Rows of desk set out like a classroom are probably best avoided. Desks in rows can remind an audience of the authority and discipline of the classroom. Many speakers like a U-shape (or horseshoe shape) arrangement, usually without desks, that makes for a comfortable, barrier-free space between speaker and audience.

An alternative is a 'cabaret'-style arrangement. Here three or four people are grouped at individual tables. This allows them to network in groups while still focusing on the presentation. This approach is especially useful if you want your audience to work together for any part of the presentation.

Whatever layout you decide on, it is important that each individual in your audience is able to see and hear all that is going on. When organising your room before the audience arrive, check to make sure that all visual aids, such as overhead projectors (OHPs) and televisions are clearly visible from every seat.

The opening of your presentation is important. You want to make a good impression on your audience. The problem is that all but the most experienced and accomplished of public speakers is bound to feel nervous. Dealing with nerves is something you must learn to do. The wrong way to confront it is to put your head down and try to get through the presentation as quickly as possible. We all have a tendency to speak too quickly when we are nervous or excited. Take deep breaths, speak slowly and look directly at your audience. If you spot a friendly face smiling back, focus for a while on that person to help gain confidence.

Indeed, eye contact is one of the many non-verbal aspects of your communication repertoire that you can harness to ensure you have maximum impact on your audience. Being prepared to look directly at your audience, rather than averting your eyes, is an important way of keeping their attention and showing your sincerity. Your whole posture will communicate to the audience how you feel about what you are doing. If you stand up straight, not only will you feel more confident, but you will also transmit a sense of your authority to the audience. Similarly, your tone of voice should communicate to the audience a sense of confidence and authority. By speaking clearly and directly to your audience, you will show them that you are confident about what you are telling them and in doing so you should hold their attention.

ACTIVITY . . .

Spend some time watching professionals speaking, politicians for example. What do you learn from them about how to address an audience? Pay particular attention to their:

- body language and gestures

- facial expressions

- vocal pitch and emphasis

- speed of diction and pausing

- use of humour/anecdotes.

Maintaining eye contact with your audience will also ensure that you are alert to any feedback signals. It is to be hoped that the sorts of signals you will be receiving will be those that suggest people are paying attention, understanding and enjoying your presentation. If you become aware of any negative feedback signals, such as people not paying attention or looking bewildered, then it may be necessary for you to assess the situation quickly and take any necessary remedial action. This may call for quick thinking, but one useful strategy is simply to stop your presentation at the next convenient point and ask for feedback. For example, you may ask if everyone is clear about the points you are making. Even if none of the audience is brave or forthright enough to speak up, you will at least have demonstrated your awareness of their needs. Indeed, the simple act of breaking off from the presentation momentarily may help regain the focus of the audience.

USING VISUAL AIDS

Many speakers nowadays like to support their presentations with visual aids. A programme such as PowerPoint will allow you to generate high-quality, professional-looking overhead transparencies with quite minimal design skills. Alternatively, it is possible to use a fairly basic word processing package to produce less ambitious OHTs that will still be far more clear than those produced by hand. The danger is that as transparencies become easier to produce, speakers will use them without thinking of what advantage they offer. Another danger is that audiences think that the more effort presenters put into their visual aids, the less effort they will put into the content of their presentation.

In deciding what aids you intend to use, a good starting point is to ask what work you expect the visual aid to do. The content of the presentation must precede the visual aids. Visual aids must aid, they must help, they must assist. At worst visual aids can be a distraction from what you are saying. A good visual aid should be seen as a reinforcement of what you are saying. It is always a good idea to ask yourself 'What work is this visual aid doing?' You should be able to come up with a clear answer to this. If you cannot, then it is probably best not to use the aid at all.

There are a number of pitfalls in using visual aids that are obviously to be avoided. A common mistake that people make is to use visual aids that are too small to be read by the whole audience. If you are using an OHT or a poster, for example, make sure that the smallest point size is at least large enough to be read from all parts of the room. A common reason for using type that is too small is the attempt to get too much information on to a visual aid. This should be avoided at all costs.

Always think carefully about why you are using the aid. Too many presenters seem to think that all they have to do is to read what an OHT says. This is not only pointless, it is insulting to your audience as it may suggest that they cannot read. A good OHT should be a method of reinforcing a point in such a way that it gets the attention of the audience and also helps it stick in their mind.

One particularly effective way of using an OHT is to divide it into sections and mask each of these. As a speaker, you can then reveal the OHT section by section simply by lifting the masking from each. This strategy helps keep the attention of the audience both by avoiding giving them too much information in one go and also by providing some element of suspense as they wait for the next section to be revealed.

Using a programme such as PowerPoint to develop your OHTs also allows you to develop hand-out materials that you can use to support the visual aids. For example, the audience can have a print copy of the transparency to save them the trouble of copying it. At the same time it is possible to provide a space at the side of this for additional notes. Any such attempt to make the work of the audience easier is likely to be well received. If you are going to provide a hand-out at some point in your presentation, you should tell your audience in advance; this will save them wasting time taking notes.

Another type of visual aid that you may wish to use is a short video sequence. For example, a short extract from a television soap opera may provide a useful illustration of a particular point you are making. A well-chosen clip used appropriately can have a telling impact on your audience. Again, however, don't allow the visual aid to become a distraction. Leaving the television set switched on when nothing is playing is almost guaranteed to distract an audience. Some people are so conditioned to television that they will watch white noise on the screen rather than listen to a live speaker. So be prepared to switch on the television only at the point when you intend to introduce the clip into your presentation and switch it off again immediately afterwards. Obviously it is a good idea to make sure in advance that the video you intend to use is cued up and that the equipment will function at the push of the appropriate button. Better still, get someone who is familiar with the equipment to help you.

It is always a good idea to practise your presentation before you actually deliver it. You can do this in front of a friend or family member if they are willing to help and you feel confident. Otherwise you can simply use a mirror as your 'audience'. This practice session will help you to identify any problems that you may encounter and allow you to address them before your actual performance. A common difficulty is mistiming your presentation. Make sure that your practice run-through is at the same pace as you intend to deliver your presentation and use a stop-watch to time it. If necessary you can then adjust your timing accordingly. Make sure that you are fluent in your presentation. If there are any sections where you find yourself faltering, try to find out what is causing this. It may be that simply changing some of the words on a cue card will cure the problem. Finally ensure that your delivery is going to be clear and confident while remaining sensitive to the needs of your audience.

You will often hear it said that a good presentation has a beginning, a middle and an end. Similarly, advice on public speaking is often given in the form of 'stand up, speak up and shut up'. Often too little attention is paid to the way in which you should 'shut up'. It is important that you signal the end of your presentation. Otherwise the audience may be left in doubt as to what is happening if you simply allow it to drift to a close. One way in which to close is to announce that you have finished and are now happy to answer any questions. This approach also has the benefit of making it clear to the audience that they now have a role to perform.

The Q&A phase of a presentation is a chance for you to impress with your knowledge and grasp of your chosen topic. It is important, however, that you see this phase as an extension of your presentation; that means that you must stay in control of this phase of the presentation at all times. You must learn to control any discussion through yourself, rather than allowing members of the audience to discuss issues between themselves.

You can help make sure that you remain in control by using your position at the front of the group to control the proceedings. Make sure that it is *you* who decides who will ask the question by making it clear who you want to speak next. Ask people to raise their hand if they wish to ask a question. If several people do so at the same time, indicate the order in which you want them to speak.

When someone asks a question, give yourself time to respond properly. Don't just say the first thing that comes into your head. Try to frame a considered response that will answer the question fully. At the same time look for the opportunity to develop the point further by steering it towards an issue that you feel confident about or would have liked to have developed in your presentation.

There are several strategies you can use to give yourself time to think when you have been asked a question. A stock phrase such as 'Well, that is an interesting question' is a useful tactic to employ. Another method of playing for time is to repeat the question back with some slight rephrasing. You can say: 'So the question you are asking is . . .' Summarising the question is also an effective way of checking you've understood the question asked of you.

Usually there is a time limit on the Q&A phase of a presentation. One test of your skill in maintaining control is how well you bring the phase to its conclusion. Keep an eye on the clock. In the heat and excitement of debate, it is easy to lose track of time. In good time indicate that questions will have to come to an end. For example, you may indicate that there is time for just two more questions. At the same time you can identify who the questioners will be. In this way you can bring your presentation to an orderly conclusion.

Finally at the end of your presentation, make sure you put all your notes and visual aids back together in a logical and organised fashion. This way you will have them ready for the next time you give the presentation as well as being available for assessment, if this is required as part of your course.

CONTRIBUTING TO A MEETING

Another situation in which good verbal communication skills are required is taking part in meetings. As you will see from the sections on group communication, meetings are formalised situations in which a group gets together for a specific purpose. There are many different types of meeting. Some, such as annual general meetings (AGMs), form part of an ongoing procedure that plays a key role in the functioning of a group or organisation. Other meetings, such as a group of students getting together to plan a coursework project, may be less formal or only take place to achieve one immediate purpose. Whatever type of meeting you are involved in, you will need your communication skills if you are to play an effective role in the meeting.

Most meetings have someone who takes charge. This person is usually called the chair. The chair's functions are many and will vary from meeting to meeting. However, it is his/her responsibility to ensure that correct procedures are followed in the meeting. The chair also determines the order in which issues are discussed. This is set down in the form of an agenda, usually written, published and circulated prior to the start of the meeting.

AGENDA FOR A MEETING

The next Communication meeting will take place at 1500 hours on Friday, 7 September 2001 in room 203.

Agenda

1   Apologies for absence
2   Minutes of previous meeting
3   Matters arising
4   Financial matters
5   Main restaurant
6   Any other business
7   Date of next meeting

As we have suggested, meetings vary in their degree of formality. As you can see from the example, a typical meeting will start with a welcome from the chair and introductions if new people are present.

It is common in meetings for people to introduce themselves by saying a few words about what they do or what their interests are. Suppose you are attending a meeting for the first time and jot down some notes with which to introduce yourself. Remember that the type of meeting and the sort of people attending are likely to determine how you do this.

Other typical formalities at a meeting are opportunities for people who are absent to have their apologies read out and also a check on the accuracy of the minutes of the previous meeting.

MINUTES OF A MEETING

Minutes of Communication Meeting held at 1500 hours on Friday, 7 September 2001 in Room 203 for Front Office Cashiers, Restaurant Cashiers and Night Auditors

Present: J. Ellroy
D. Hammett
E. Leonard (Chair)
S. Paretsky
R. B. Parker (Secretary)
I. Rankin

1   *Apologies for absence*:   R. MacDonald.
2   *Minutes* of 3 August 2001 meeting were confirmed.
3   *Matters arising* from 3 August 2001 meeting minutes:
   — Incorrectly completed registration cards are to be passed back to Reception;
   — Present difficulties for charging for room service will be removed when revised charges are introduced at the end of this month.
4   *Financial matters*
   — Mr Leonard thanked front office cashiers for helping restaurant cashiers during the busy holiday period.
   — Ms Parker informed the meeting that from October all assistant front office cashiers will be given additional training to work with new financial procedures.
5   *Main restaurant*
   — Ms Parker reported that prices for the carvery have now been clarified.
   — The question of breakfast price for children was raised. It was felt that half adult price was insufficient discount for children.
6   *Any other business*
   — Mr Rankin, who will be leaving next month, was thanked and wished well for the future.
   — Mr Ellroy was congratulated on his promotion to front office cashier.
7   *Date of next meeting* was set for Friday, 5 October 2001.
8   *The meeting closed* at 1540 hours.

These minutes are likely to be important to the current meeting because the first agenda item usually requires the group to work through them, discussing matters that have arisen out of the previous meeting.

If you have a contribution you wish to make to the discussion of any item, you should always do this through the chair. It is important that you do not address your remarks to individual members of the group, but rather you should make your point to the group as a whole by addressing your comments through the chair. Of course, getting the attention of the chair in order to be able to contribute is in itself a skill. An effective chair, however, will be conscious of the need to encourage everyone to contribute, so quietly waiting your turn rather than butting in is probably the better strategy.

Once you have the opportunity to make your contribution, there are a number of points to bear in mind. First make sure that what you are saying is relevant to the point being discussed. Don't, for example, raise an issue that is better covered under another agenda item. Second, remember our advice about clarity, concision and precision. Try to plan what you want to say and say it clearly and succinctly. If you can link in your ideas to build on the contribution of a previous speaker, then do so. Finally, do not take issues personally. Remember that meetings are about debates and issues, not personalities, even though it may seem like it at times. Your contribution will be much more highly valued if you stick to the issues under consideration, rather than making personal attacks on other members of the group.

COMMUNICATION AND INFORMATION TECHNOLOGY

We have just spent time looking at types of written and verbal communication that can be described as traditional. This is because in many respects they have changed little over a long period of time. Although we have mentioned the use of computers and software programmes such as PowerPoint, the impact of technology has not been central to our discussion of the principles of effective communication. The world of communication is constantly changing. Some people feel that it is doing so at an alarming rate. Chief among these changes is the way in which communication technology is becoming central to our lives. Indeed, some people argue that one of the chief social divisions is between those who have access to communications technology and those who do not. These groups have become known as the information rich and the information poor.

The communications revolution is having a profound impact on the way each of us lives our life. The number of people who work from home using communication technology to connect to the office has increased rapidly in recent years. E-mail, mobile phones and tele-conferencing have all affected people's working patterns to the point where the workplace itself is a far less significant feature of their lives. Traditional information sources such as newspapers and books are confronted by competition from electronic media such as the Internet. In our homes, technology is beginning to converge to the point where mass communications technology such as the television and personal communication technology, such as the telephone, are joining forces. Not only does our television set offer a vast choice of digital programming, but it also allows us to receive personal text messages sent from someone's mobile phone, to edit our own programmes, to choose the news we want to see and take a virtual tour of our favourite supermarket. We now have portable communications technology that will allow us to do many of these things on the move.

USING A PC

It is difficult for anyone who has grown up using a personal computer to appreciate how the Information and Communication Technology revolution has influenced the way in which we communicate. Writing and creating documents is now much easier thanks to the features that a personal computer offers. We will now look at how to get the best from your PC when you are writing and creating documents.

Perhaps the singular most telling advantage that a PC brings to writing is the capacity to store what you have written. A computer's hard disk together with CDs and floppy disks enables us to store documents we have created and to retrieve them whenever necessary. These facilities are all available to writers even on the most basic of word processing packages.

What this means for most users of the technology is that it is now much easier to get down ideas, shape them, save them, revise them and edit them. In addition the computer allows a final version to be produced and printed with layout and design to a high degree of sophistication.

So how can you get the best from using a PC? Well, every user of a computer will have developed a method for getting the best from it, but it is useful to consider here some of the ways in which you can use this tool to help you become more effective in your own communication. Assuming that you have the basic skill to open a word processing package and to use the keyboard, however slowly, then you are on the road to getting the best from your PC as a communication tool. Listed below are some ideas to help you become a more effective communicator using a PC.

Use the PC to get your ideas down quickly. Once you have opened a document do not worry about simply getting your ideas down in note form. Sometimes just a set of headings is enough to act as a reminder of your ideas. The flexibility of a word processing programme will then allow you to move from section to section filling in the detail as appropriate. The drag and drop facility will later allow you to shift round blocks of text or even single words to re-order the material as you require. You may find it useful to use some method of formatting your document, such as using headings in bold or uppercase letters as a way of getting down main headings and then filling in the text below them.

The typeface that you use to create a document does not have to be the same typeface you will use for the final version. It makes sense, therefore, to experiment with different typefaces when you are inputting words. Some typefaces on the screen are more friendly on the eye than others.

Another advantage of using PC as a writing tool is that it can help you to organise your ideas as you go along. In addition to organising your material under headings, PCs allow you to create bullet points and to number paragraphs. It is certainly worth spending some time familiarising yourself with these features to see how you can get them to work for you. Intelligent use of bullet points or numbering can help bring clarity to your writing by separating out and structuring your ideas into a logical order.

Do not forget to save your work at regular intervals. This is especially important if you are using a PC that is accessible by other people. Do not wander off and leave a document open. Other people may not respect your privacy or may even shut down your work to get on with their own. Even if you have exclusive use of a computer, back up your work at intervals using a floppy disk or CD. Unexpected crashes or power cuts should not then wreck your hard work.

It is a good idea to devise a system of file names for your documents. This is especially true when you have different versions of the same material. Numbering different versions should help. If you do get mixed up between versions of a document, look at the 'properties' menu. This will tell you when the document was first created and when it was last revised.

PCs have allowed people a lot more flexibility about the way in which they write. The fact that it is easy to save a document and then revise it at a later date has given people a lot more freedom to try out ideas and then go back and develop and revise them at a later date. Many people use a PC to get down their ideas quickly without too much concern at this stage for style or the observation of grammatical conventions. Once the ideas are in place, these can be attended to later. Most word processing packages have grammar and spell checks to help you with these aspects of writing.

Spend some time familiarising yourself with the grammar and spellcheck functions of your software. It is possible to have them running as you write so that errors are indicated as you input material. Some people find this irritating and prefer to disable the function and run the checks at the end of a session or even when they have completed the whole document. One function you may like to keep running is auto-correct which automatically corrects common errors such as transposed letters or literals. Look in the auto-correct menu at some of the options for setting this up.

Remember, too, that software packages are designed to work in many different countries. Do make sure that you have yours set to the appropriate version of English (English [United Kingdom] will avoid American Spellings).

The cut-and-paste facility on your PC saves you a lot of time. This allows you to copy material from another document and to paste it into the one you are working on. It means that if you have previously worked on an idea, it is a simple matter to lift any appropriate material into what you are currently working on.

Be aware, though, that if the material is not your own you must attribute it to its source. Lifting other people's ideas without giving them credit is called plagiarism and is heavily frowned upon, especially in academic circles.

Once you have finished putting all the material you feel is appropriate into a document then it is time to do a final edit. You may find it useful to go back to the beginning of this chapter and look at the section on writing style. One job you can very easily do on a PC is to run through a document and look for all the redundant words that can be deleted. If you have been set a word limit, then use the word-count menu to check you are inside this.

Many word processing packages have a useful readability index included. This tool calculates how accessible your document is to the reader by checking on sentence and paragraph lengths. A number of indices may be used. For example, the Flesch Reading Ease Score uses word length and sentence length to calculate readability on a 100 point scale. You should aim to score between 60 and 70 to make your writing accessible. Another handy statistic that is usually available tells you the number of passive sentences you have written. Remember Orwell's advice on style and try to keep the number of such sentences to a minimum.

Many people find editing a document on screen difficult. Reading through a long document on screen can cause eyestrain. You may find it useful to print out your document and make any amendments or corrections on this hard copy. This also has the advantage that you can work anywhere and at anytime. Of course, the downside is that you will have to spend time making the changes on the computer later.

Editing may also involve some reorganising of your material. Assuming you have created appropriate headings and, where necessary, subheadings, you should have a logical structure in place. Make sure that the material itself is organised logically under these appropriate headings.

Do not forget to choose the most appropriate typeface or font for your document. It is an easy matter to change the font to see which looks best. Many people feel that Times New Roman, for example, gives your document a sense of authority. A typeface such as Courier, on the other hand, has more of a typewritten quality that may suggest that the document is an initial draft or suggestion, rather than a definitive statement.

Remember that a properly edited document will be friendly to the reader. From the title at the head through to the last paragraph, there should be a consistency of style and format that make it easy for a reader to find their way through the document.

CREATING DOCUMENTS IN SPECIFIC FORMATS

There are likely to be a number of occasions when the document you need to produce will fit into an existing format. These formats include letters, reports and memoranda. Similarly, you may wish to create a document such a curriculum vitae (CV) that you can update at later intervals. Templates and Wizards are particularly helpful tools if this is what you want to do.

A template is a pre-existing format that you can select which will wrap up your own document. Often a package will offer several alternative styles of template, each appropriate to a particular context. For example, if you are preparing a letter, you will be offered a choice of template according to the type of letter you want to produce, from a formal business letter to an informal letter to a friend or relative. If none of the templates is appropriate for your needs, you may wish to create your own, for example a letterhead. Indeed, it is possible to create and file a range of stationery templates in a corporate style for yourself.

GETTING TO GRIPS WITH E-MAIL

Electronic mail or e-mail has become one of the most popular methods of communication, especially in the business world. It has fundamentally changed the way in which many people and organisations communicate. At the same time it has created a raft of issues relating to confidentiality and security.

E-mail is a system that uses the Internet to send messages between people and organisations. Perhaps its most important feature is that it enables almost instantaneous communication anywhere in the world. In this way it has many of the qualities of the telephone or fax as a method of getting information quickly from one source to another. However, unlike a telephone call, e-mail is in the form of a permanent written communication. Maybe more importantly, unlike the telephone call it does not demand an instant response, despite the speed at which it travels. Experienced and practised e-mailers, however, often expect almost instantaneous replies to their e-mails.

GETTING CONNECTED

In order to send or receive e-mail you will need access to a PC with a modem connected to a telephone line. You will also need to have an account with an Internet Service Provider (ISP), many of which provide free access and connection. You will most likely have to pay for a local telephone call to this provider. Once connected, you may be asked to register with the ISP's e-mail service. However, many people prefer to register with an e-mail service that is not tied to a specific ISP. This means that if you change providers at a later date you can keep the same e-mail address.

Your e-mail address is very like your postal address or telephone number. Changing it means you have to tell everyone the new one. So it is a good idea to get yourself an address and hang on to it. This is especially true if you have obtained a distinctive and memorable address. As the Internet gets busier, the demand for e-mail addresses gets greater and people with common family names will find it more difficult simply to use their name as the first part of their address.

It is also worth bearing in mind that when you set up your e-mail account it is possible to have several different accounts. This could be for different members of a family. Some people choose to have more than one identity for different groups of contacts.

Before you choose an e-mail service it is worth checking to see if you will be able to access your e-mail from any computer with an Internet facility. Usually you will be given a password that allows you to pick up and send messages from anywhere in the world. This is a very useful facility if you move around a lot.

If you are going to send a lot of e-mails, it is a good idea to get a programme that will allow you to compose your messages offline. This means writing them when you are not connected to your ISP and running up a telephone bill for yourself or someone else. A package such as Outlook Express will enable you to write your messages and store them until you are ready to send several in one batch. At the same time as you connect to send out these messages, you will also receive any incoming messages. This method will allow you to send and receive your mail once or twice a day using fairly short connection times.

Figure 2.2 E-mail set-up

Whatever package you use for sending e-mails, you will be provided with an onscreen form to use.

The spaces, or 'fields', at the top obviously require you to fill in details, in much the same way as a memorandum. Getting the address completely accurate, down to the last dot, is vital, otherwise your message will not be delivered. As you use e-mail more and more you will build up an address book of contacts. Simply clicking on the address book icon will enable you to call up your list and select the person you wish to write to.

The abbreviation c.c. stands for carbon copy. This allows you to send a copy of your e-mail to other people. Generally this is done when you need to keep someone else informed of your message to someone else. It can also be used as a lever to get the receiver to take action because another person, perhaps their boss, has been made aware of the contents of the message.

The abbreviation b.c.c. stands for blind carbon copy. In essence this means that the receiver of the e-mail will not be aware that you have sent a copy to someone else. Obviously this could be seen as a little underhand. However, there may be situations when you may need to use this function.

With regard to the subject of your e-mail, ideally every e-mail you send should be about just one topic. If you need to discuss more topics, then it is recommended that you use a separate e-mail for each. The reason for this is that it will help the receiver to retrieve the information in your e-mail more easily at a later date, if this proves necessary. Always try to indicate the content accurately in the subject field. It is tempting to be witty in choosing a subject but this can be frustrating for the receiver if he or she is later searching for one of your messages on a particular topic.

Keeping your message to a single topic also makes it easier for the receiver to reply. An important facility in e-mail software is the reply button. This enable you to send a reply to the message by automatically reproducing the appropriate details on the e-mail form but also printing the original message to which you are composing your reply. This has the advantage that the receiver does not have to search out the original message in order to make sense of the reply.

E-mail is a relative newcomer as a method of communication. As such it does not carry with it a lot of the heritage of the letter, for example. Doubtless one day famous people will have their collected e-mails published, probably on a website. For the moment there is not a great deal of case history that determines the rules of composing e-mails.

The codes that do exist are determined by efficiency and courtesy. Writing each individual e-mail on one topic is an example of both. Such an e-mail, as we have suggested, is easier for the receiver to deal with and therefore more efficient. Equally, it is courteous not to overburden the receiver with information by sending e-mails that run to several 'pages' and cover a whole range of topics. Such courtesies are an example of 'netiquette'.

KEY TERM

NETIQUETTE   Describes the conventions for using e-mail as this channel of communication is used more widely. This new word is derived from a contraction of the two words 'network' and 'etiquette'. There are a number of sites, such as those of university computer service departments, which spell out their own rules for using e-mail. You may find it helpful to visit one of these to see what advice they offer.

One especially useful rule to bear in mind is to think about the receiver of your communication at all times. Earlier (see page 35) we spoke about the importance of empathy with the receiver of a message. This is especially true of e-mail. Many people are new to the medium. They may not be skilled in using the keyboard. Extending to them courtesy and tolerance is essential. Similarly, when you are sending messages you should bear these points in mind:

- Be as brief as possible. Do not fill the screen with unnecessary words. It is hard on the eyes.
- If you pass on other people's messages, do not change or edit them. Do not forget to acknowledge the original sender.
- Do not impersonate other people. Do not use the potential anonymity of e-mail to harass or intimidate other people.
- Reply promptly to messages you receive. If you are away for a period of time set up the auto reply function in your programme to let people know.

COMMUNICATION STUDIES: THE ESSENTIAL INTRODUCTION

- Remember that the legal constraints that apply to print documents are equally applicable to e-mail. Be careful, for example, not to make defamatory comments about people and publish these to a third party. You risk a libel action if you do.

You should also remember the importance of organisation when dealing with messages. Most of you will deal with your snail mail (i.e. ordinary postal mail) by filtering incoming messages, saving important ones, and throwing away junk mail. Similarly with e-mail, file the important messages and delete those you do not need to keep. With outgoing e-mail keep a copy of everything. You may wish to save hard disk space by saving only those messages you need to.

Finally, remember that, unless you go to the trouble of encrypting a message, e-mail is potentially an insecure medium. Examination boards, for example, do not allow examiners to send draft examination papers by e-mail. If you have confidential material you wish to send, snail mail may be the better option.

ATTACHMENTS

If you have a long and complex document or even an illustration to send, then you can use a file attachment to your e-mail message. All you have do is to click on the attachment icon, usually a paperclip, and either type in the name of the file you wish to send or click on browse and select it from the list. Remember that to open the file the receiver must have compatible software. They may not be able to open a word-processed document if they are using e-mail through their television set.

This attachment function allows a large amount of material to be transmitted to and from and between computers. It is an invaluable resource for example for writers who work collaboratively or where documents need to be previewed, edited and revised by a group of people who are geographically remote. It allows amendments and suggestions to be communicated quickly between people without postal delays and the need for extensive re-typing.

FURTHER READING

Allen, R. E. (1990) *Oxford Writers' Dictionary*, Oxford: Oxford University Press.

Carey, G. V. (1971) *Mind the Stop*, Harmondsworth: Penguin.

Fowler, H. W. (1998) *The New Fowler's Modern English Usage*. Oxford: Oxford University Press.

Gowers, E. (1987) *The Complete Plain Words*, 3rd edn, Harmondsworth: Penguin.

Orwell, G. (2001) 'Politics and the English Language', in *Inside the Whale and Other Essays*, Harmondsworth: Penguin.

Partridge, E. (1999) *Usage and Abusage*, Harmondsworth: Penguin.

Roget, P. (2000) *Roget's Thesaurus of English Words and Phrases*, ed. B. Kirkpatrick, Harmondsworth: Penguin.

PART 3: TEXTS AND MEANINGS IN COMMUNICATION

In this part of the book we will be dealing with the ways in which communication texts generate meanings.

■ We will define, identify and undertake practical work on communication texts.

■ We will introduce two useful approaches to the study of text – the semiotic approach and the process approach.

■ We will explore these approaches practically and in some detail to provide you with an analytical toolkit.

■ We will address both the limitations and the strengths of both the semiotic and the process approaches.

▼ 1 COMMUNICATION AS TEXT

In this section we will be looking to define and identify communication texts.

■ We will be asking 'What is a text?' and looking at a wide range of answers.

■ We will be starting to offer critical tools with which textual analysis can be performed.

When Raymond Williams made his formal definition of Communication as an area of study in 1962, he began with the question 'What do we mean by communication?' This part addresses this question but it will do it practically rather than theoretically, examining where communication is to be found rather than redefining what it is. Williams provided some significant clues in his initial survey arguing for a new 'emphasis': 'that society is a form of communication, through which experience is described, shared, modified and preserved' (Williams 1962: 10).

Williams' book *Communications* makes powerful appeals for a new set of ways of looking at reality which are still relevant today. Here is his invitation to students of communication:

> We need to say what many of us know in experience: that the struggle to learn, to describe, to understand, to educate is a central and necessary part of our humanity. This struggle is not begun, at second hand, after reality has occurred. It is in itself a major way in which reality is formed and changed . . . Communication begins in the struggle to learn and describe.
>
> (Williams 1962: 11)

THE WHOLE WORLD AS OUR TEXT

Figure 3.1 *Crowds leaving Old Trafford. Courtesy of Dale Smith*

ACTIVITY . . .

Look at the image of Old Trafford. Try to identify those elements that communicate to you. Where are we? What is the event likely to be? Who are these people (age, gender, class)? How do we know all of this?

Stepping into the above photograph is an act of engagement with the world of communication and of communication texts. What is principally represented in the photograph is a piece of the built environment in the south of Manchester entitled 'Old Trafford'. What this structure represents, that is what is communicated by it, is a matter for debate, possibly heated debate. If, as a reader of this communication you are a member of what Desmond Morris called 'the football tribe', you are likely to have a strongly positive or negative attitude towards it. On the other hand, if you are ignorant of or uninterested in 'ball-based Saturday afternoon rituals', your response is likely to be neutral or even aggressive. In fact it might be said that instead of communicating, the image is in fact operating as a barrier to communication, causing communication to deteriorate.

KEY TERM

COMMUNICATION TEXT   Discrete unit of communication, that is anything that can be identified as communicating in its own right; a signifying structure composed of signs.

KEY TERM

COMMUNICATION BARRIER   Anything that impedes the communication process or causes it to deteriorate. There are four types of identifiable barrier to communication:

1   **Mechanical**: physical impediments
2   **Psychological**: internal pressures on sender/receiver
3   **Semantic**: lack of or partial understanding
4   **Organisational**: structural dysfunctions in groups

For merchandising purposes, 'Old Trafford' has been labelled 'the theatre of dreams'; in other words this meaning has been assigned to it. You can buy miniature representations of the football ground with this legend engraved on the base, where the significance of the word 'theatre' can easily be seen as a reference to the concentrated atmosphere of 'the cauldron'. This is an interesting representation in the sense that when you stand outside Old Trafford, or in fact inside it, you are struck by the awesome size of it and are tempted by its resemblance to a Gothic cathedral rather than to a theatre. We use the word 'tempted' because clearly making connections between places like a football stadium and a cathedral is making links between the activities that take place in them. This is to confuse form (that is shape and structure) with function (that is use and purpose).

ACTIVITY

Look at some specific buildings in your area where you either live or study. Look for buildings under the following categories:

- cathedral, church, mosque, temple

- civic building (e.g. town hall)

- house

- hospital

- library

Then consider the degree to which your description of them, or your thoughts about them, or the vocabulary you use about them derives from either their form (that is, what you see) and/or their function (that is, what you know about them).

What you are doing in the above activity is clarifying your perception of the world around you and recognising the extent to which even that perception is shaped by your experiences of language, culture and society. You are being asked to consider the extent to which even seeing is an 'interested' activity, that is, it isn't 'objective'. When we see 'Old Trafford', we are looking at a coded message which we must and will decode according to our experiences and experience. The essence of Communication Studies is in the recognition that our experience of the world as human beings is essentially the experience of communication texts – which must be understood.

ENCODE/DECODE In process explanations these twin verbs describe the process through which thought is converted from its abstract state and is given a concrete form by the sender (encoding) and then returned to its abstract state by the receiver (decoding).

COMMUNICATION AND MASS MEDIA TEXTS

Clearly, no understanding of our perception of 'Old Trafford' would be complete without a consideration of the role of the mass media in our perception and interpretation of human activities. It was Bill Shankley who claimed, for example, that 'Football's not a matter of life and death; it's more important than that', but it was newspapers and television that broadcast his words and repeated them until they stuck.

ACTIVITY . . .

A recent Communication Studies A Level question (AEB, 1999) asked candidates to 'consider the media coverage of a sport of your choice'. Looking at a sport other than football, consider what meanings the press and television give to sport, that is:

- What words do they use?

- How do they treat the participants?

- What values do they attach to the sport concerned? Compare these to the reasons why you play sport or why you believe sport should be played.

Whatever your findings, it is very difficult not to conclude that much of sport's social meaning is constructed by mass media for a range of purposes: from ensuring that there are eight pages or three minutes of sport on any day to reopening old wounds and restating matters of national identity. When, in advance of a new European championship semi-final between England and Germany, The *Daily Star* used the headline 'HERR WE GO: Bring On The Krauts' there was widespread criticism. The Star described Germany as 'the old enemy' and ended its front page with the slogan 'LET BATTLE COMMENCE'. Interestingly the coverage was very like that reserved for explicit campaigns of war such as the Falklands and the Gulf conflicts, with a call to fans to support 'the England boys' and including a pastiche of the Kitchener 'Your Country Needs You' First World War propaganda poster.

It is not our job here to analyse this text in depth but rather to reflect the degree to which our society is represented by and in such texts. If we as individuals are sometimes betrayed or revealed by what we consciously and unconsciously say, this may be equally true of the deliberate and accidental pronouncements of our society in its forms of mass communication.

ACTIVITY . . .

Take a single copy of a national newspaper.

- Analyse its values solely from its headlines.

- Try to describe the newspaper's 'personality'.

- List its preoccupations (themes), its 'heroes' and its 'villains'.

THE ILLUSTRATED MAN: THE HUMAN FIGURE AS TEXT

In the stadium illustration that appears at the beginning of this part, some people are represented moving in front of the camera. These people would probably have opinions as to the meanings of 'Old Trafford' and sport. They themselves are communicating at a number of levels. In other words, they constitute 'text' in a number of ways: as a crowd/group held together by a common context and purpose; as a group sharing certain demographic variables like gender, ethnicity and age, uniformed to some extent; as a series of individuals expressing their own identities through subtle modifications of clothing, of hairstyle, of attitude. This photograph is merely a still frame from a real movie which is their lives and in which the theme is communication.

How specifically do you express your own individual personality? List the most significant TEN ways (e.g. 1. My hairstyle, plus comment – 'it's been this long since . . .') PROMPT: your clothes, appearance, props, locations, roles.

In exploring what makes up your expressed identity, you are in fact rehearsing the content of much of your communication course. This will include a consideration of such matters as domestic architecture, interior design, industrial and commercial design, clothing, hairstyle, body adornment and modification as well as the various sorts of language we use. Communication Studies begins with reading the self and then extends to other people.

Figure 3.2 *Still from Once Were Warriors (New Zealand Film Commission, 1994). Courtesy of the Kobal Collection*

ACTIVITY . . .

Consider the significant elements of the appearance of the man in the illustration and the ways in which he can be read; that is, what are the factors that will likely affect the way he is read? Make two lists: features of the man as text which might affect reading; and features/characteristics of reader which might affect reading.

This is an extreme version of the confrontations that we have every day with 'other people' and we all have our own ways of dealing with this world of 'otherness', i.e. with those people who are not us. It is relatively easy to classify those people whom we encounter on a day-to-day basis in terms of the relative depth of our relationship with each of them: from family and intimates through workmates and fellow students to relatively infrequent 'total strangers'. As we meet (to us) new people, we like to think that we judge them according to their behaviour and react to them accordingly. On reflection, however, it is probably truer to say that we judge them according to our behaviour, our experience, our norms and our prejudices.

ACTIVITY . . .

Who are your friends? How long have you known them? Where did you meet? To what extent are they 'similar' to you in looks, interests, gender, ethnicity, or class? To what extent is this 'sameness' extended the closer you get to 'home' (i.e. how far are your best friends especially like you)?

Friendship is a loaded activity, it depends heavily on social experience and therefore is bound to be value-laden. What we communicate to others subconsciously may in fact operate as an informal and unconscious 'invitation to treat', a beacon for potential relationships. In other words, who we are, superficially, might be a significant factor in the relationships we form. After all, what are relationships but exchanges of communication, structures within which codes are employed and messages are delivered? What are relationships, after all, but communication texts?

When Umberto Eco proclaimed in 1973, 'I speak through my clothes,' he was just identifying one element of a considerable paradigm, a set in which every gesture and intonation, every affectation and attitude is potentially significant. This set constitutes the human figure as communicator, the variety of codes through which this significant text has significance. The tension remains between those elements that are intentional and those that are not: those that are given to be read and those that simply 'leak'.

PARADIGM   A sign set from which one might be chosen to contribute to a syntagm. Paradigms define their individual members with reference to all others in the set. To select from a paradigm is at that moment to reject all other signs in that set, just as by selecting something (or nothing) to cover your feet today you have rejected all other possibilities. This choice from a paradigm of 'foot coverings' has contributed to the syntagm which constitutes the things you are wearing today. When Peugeot's 'lion' went 'from strength to strength', it got its strength partly from the paradigm of 'elite animals' from which it was chosen and partly because that paradigm does not include 'weasel', 'frog' and 'sloth'.

NON-VERBAL LEAKAGE The tendency of non-verbal codes wholly or partly to contradict or to undermine intentional and verbal communication, e.g. lack of eye contact may betray the telling of an untruth.

ACTIVITY . . .

Take one example of a youth subculture (e.g. punk, headbanger) and classify its intentional non-verbal communication or iconography, i.e. its visual sign-system. Compare this with a similar list for an adult 'genre', e.g. teachers, business people, lawyers, doctors.

As in almost all cases in Communication Studies, context is a primary determinant. Teachers and doctors, for example, in a social context may display their identity in less obvious ways or not at all. Context will affect the reading but will rarely invalidate texts altogether. Mepham (1974) has claimed: 'social life is structured like a language'. As such it is of primary interest to us as students of its particular vocabulary, grammar and syntax.

▼ 2   TEXTS AND MEANINGS

In this section we will begin to look at how communication texts work.

- We will introduce key concepts such as representation, genre and convention.

- We will consider the potential of certain texts to have multiple meanings, whilst other texts are deliberately more focused.

- We will be exploring the different kinds of reading which texts might encourage or allow.

'WHERE DO I BEGIN AND WHAT SHOULD I PRESUME?'

Having established what a communication text is, it seems appropriate to address what they do, how they are constructed and, most importantly, how we respond to them. We might usefully start simply by looking carefully at what is in front of us, or in certain contexts, by listening carefully or by paying particular attention to the material used. This is what this section will help you with. It will, within a limited technical vocabulary, offer you ways of approaching texts for the first time.

Let's have a look at this advertisement:

Figure 3.3 *PC Format* postcard. *Courtesy of PC Format*

Our primary concerns are to describe what is there, what is represented in, on and by this particular text. What the text clearly does is to give physical form to a message, a meaning, a set of ideas. These ideas have been conceived in the form of this text: having presented themselves to the author(s), they are being re-presented to us (i.e. presented again, for a second time).

REPRESENTATION is usefully defined by O'Sullivan *et al*. in their important book *Key Concepts in Communication and Cultural Studies* (1994) as 'the process of putting into concrete forms . . . an abstract ideological concept'. Thus communication texts must be addressed in terms of their representations and the degree to which these leave room for the reader to explore meanings.

In this case what is represented are four women and four 'props': some spectacles, a video camera, a brain in a bubbling jar, and a mini-computer, complete with mouse. The women are all looking out, in different ways, towards the reader/receiver/camera – in this case, us. They are surrounded by a sort of white light which crudely highlights them and binds them together against a polished black background which carries a logo 'PC FORMAT' and some indication of what it is we are looking at – a promotional card for a computer magazine. The women seem superficially to be different but there are obvious ways in which these representations of women, because that's what they are, are alike.

ACTIVITY . . .

List the similarities and differences between these representations of women. These may be to do with their physical appearance, the way in which they are photographed, their costumes, or simply their presentation on this page.

You may find that these representations of women fit into a broader social 'model' of how women are usually represented and thus perceived. You may decide that with their consciously styled appearance, their careful make-up and their almost seductive glances, they conform to a stereotype of women often used in the media.

STEREOTYPE A stereotype is a mould into which reality is poured, whatever its individual shape. A stereotype is a simplified and generalised image of a group of people, which is created out of the values, judgements and assumptions of its creators, in most cases society itself. A stereotype of women might suggest their motherliness or, in this case, their function as decorative aesthetic objects to be appreciated for their beauty and allure.

More importantly you may begin to ask yourself what are the connections between four attractive young women and a personal computing magazine. This can be addressed in at least two ways – logically (by systematically identifying in detail what is there) and imaginatively (by imagining what kind of story the text is telling).

In 1970 the American Communication theorist George Gerbner suggested that in order to establish the potential meaning of any piece of media content or output it is useful to consider the following aspects:

- ■ **Existence**: what is there
- ■ **Priorities**: what is important
- ■ **Values**: what is valued
- ■ **Relationships**: what is related to what else

Subjecting PC FORMAT's postcard to this formula quickly produces results, which could be represented in this way:

- **Existence**: four 'girls', four props, a black background, words
- **Priorities**: their glamour, their beauty, the aesthetic dimensions
- **Values**: the glamour of the girls is an index of the magazine's values
- **Relationships**: the advertisement is designed to appeal to our sense of ourselves in terms of our status, our intelligence, our sex appeal

CONTENT ANALYSIS Gerbner's formula arose out of work he was doing on the content of American television. For example, Gerbner looked at violent acts and suggested that an average week produced 400 victims of violence. This is a statistical approach to analysis, which is useful for establishing trends within media output (e.g. the roles women have in television advertising compared to those of men).

In this case, the logical approach is a little longwinded because the message, though potentially patronising not to say sexist, is easy to understand. We know where this text is coming from and to whom it is speaking. The imaginative approach to textual analysis would suggest that we engage with the form, style and content in an unaffected and open way, but even this gives little significant extra information. What we know about this text is heavily dependent on the way it functions within the conventions of a genre.

GENRE This term describes the subdivisions of the output of a given medium (e.g. television, film, in this case magazine publishing). A genre is a type, a particular version of a communication medium. For example, soap opera is a television genre, for it represents a particular approach to theme, style and form.

ACTIVITY...

Consider the different genres of magazine available in your local newsagent. Identify three significant genres of currently available magazines and list their apparent characteristics. Select one genre, which might usefully be 'computer games magazines', and devise an A4 cover mock-up for a new addition to this genre.

Selecting examples from the genre of 'computer games magazines' makes the story of our original much clearer. What we are seeing from looking more widely at the genre of the text is the degree to which the production of any text is guided by particular ways of presenting and representing reality. The example that follows confirms that our original text contains a compilation of images which almost certainly featured on the magazine's cover at some point. In essence the text is delivering exactly what its readers expect, a predictable collection of reviews, previews and advice presented in an exciting and visually glamorous fashion.

Figure 3.4 Cover of *PC Format*, July 1998. Courtesy of *PC Format*

CONVENTION Where people agree to follow guidelines in the practice of communication. These guidelines may be stated or unstated, explicit or implied. To represent 'real life', a communication medium is necessary. For the communication medium to make sense, it must be ordered by conventions. In the case of a magazine cover, conventions of illustration, typography, colour and content are used.

Concluding that our original text is highly conventional is not to deny other interpretations but rather to identify the most likely intention of the piece. In terms of the possible things the text could say, one stands out as most likely, as most desired by the text itself. The conversation a text offers is called a discourse. This is conventionally referred to as the 'dominant discourse'. MacDougall (2000) explains it like this: 'What the text tries to do is offer a winner – a discourse that is privileged over others.'

The dominant discourse of the PC FORMAT text privileges a context in which the audience is assumed to be young, heterosexual men who will easily make connections between slick, fast women and slick, fast machines. It is not necessary to be a feminist to find this depressingly immature but it is important to understand that any such response goes against the grain of the semantics of this text.

SEMANTICS The study of the relationship between signs and meanings.

The conventions of a particular format are often most apparent when that format is subjected to criticism and especially via parody or pastiche. When a young female reader of PC FORMAT wrote in to complain about 'scantily clad females canoodling about new PCs' and suggested that perhaps one of the male reviewers should appear instead, the magazine mocked up a version of a cover which featured a young Scottish reviewer (Figure 3.5 overleaf). This self-parody successfully apes the conventions of the format but only goes some way to understanding the issues of representation.

ACTIVITY . . .

Compare and contrast the two covers (Figures 3.4 and 3.5) with those featured earlier in this section. List the similarities and differences, and consider the reasons why the role-reversal did not produce exactly the same results.

Clearly, all readings of these texts are being made in relation to the dominant discourse; even if we reject it out of hand, we can't ignore it. These are classic examples of what Eco

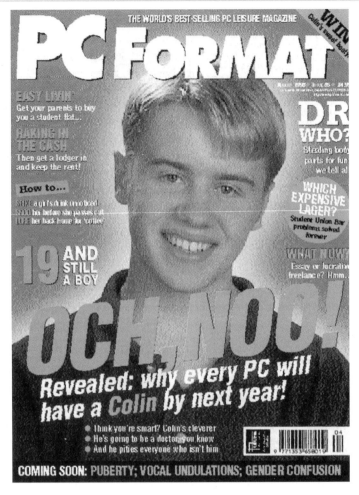

Figure 3.5 *PC Format, no. 84, July 1998, p. 200.*
Courtesy of *PC Format*

(1979) has called *closed texts*, texts in which one reading is significantly privileged. Other readings can be offered but they do not enhance the experience of the text, rather they are likely to frustrate readers and/or lead them to reject the text. *Open texts*, by comparison, are those in which individual readings are not significantly 'preferred' and in which the potential polysemy of the text is emphasised, even celebrated.

The image on page 68 was originally a painting by Edvard Munch. It, like many of the texts in this part, represents a woman but, unlike most of what we've observed, it is very much open to interpretation. Here the imposed discipline of Gerbner's formula (Gerbner 1970) might produce useful results, by asking key questions about what it is we are seeing. Some degree of emotional and imaginative engagement might also add to our understanding and response. Here is a text that demands a reading. This is not a criticism of those rather transparent mass media texts we looked at earlier; it is simply a reminder of the range of communication texts. This text has a very different function and context. Munch's painting, which he called *The Scream*, is clearly a communication text, albeit a sophisticated one, which employs artistic conventions to represent a particular kind of reality.

ACTIVITY . . .

Use Gerbner's formula to respond logically/systematically to Munch's text. Briefly add your own personal response to this text: what do you feel and think about it?

It is difficult to talk in this context about 'dominant discourse' because beyond the interpretative title, which sort of tells you what is going on, there are few clear clues. This text is open in the way that most mass media texts are not; it has no clear editorial position. This text has alternative readings but it would be difficult to categorise or even explain them in the way that Stuart Hall, among others, has done for media texts.

In their 1980 book *Culture, Media, Language*, Stuart Hall and his co-authors present three main types of reading of media texts, each of which has to do with the reader's social context (i.e. where the reader is in social terms). These are:

■ **The dominant-hegemonic**: the reading that the text prefers; the dominant discourse; the reading that relates the text to society's ideological norms.

■ **The negotiated**: the reading that broadly accepts the dominant discourse but which modifies it according to personal circumstances.

■ **The oppositional**: the reading that contests the dominant discourse and takes some alternative and opposed meaning from the text.

Hall is interested in the ways in which communication media reflect particular social and cultural views, which he argues are those of dominant groups and classes in society. The adjective hegemonic is chosen to reflect this perspective, since hegemony, a term used by Gramsci, represents the way the ruling classes maintain their power by manipulating the way we think about ourselves and our world. In simple terms Hall would argue, for example, that our 'harmless' magazine promotion is implicitly promoting all manner of social and political propaganda – about the desirability of consumerism, about social and intellectual elitism, about the position and value of women. This is not just about what the text intends to say but about the ways in which all texts fit into a pattern of social communication, which on the largest scale is about society talking to itself.

Figure 3.6 Edvard Munch, *The Scream*, 1893. Photo: J. Lathion
© Nasjonalgalleriet, Oslo, 1999

COMMUNICATION STUDIES: THE ESSENTIAL INTRODUCTION

HEGEMONY   The Italian writer Antonio Gramsci explained why the majority of people in a culture do not adopt the values and beliefs of their own class. He argued that the dominant minority within cultures present the values and beliefs of their own class as somehow 'natural' and thus universal. In this way people end up promoting the values and beliefs of the dominant or ruling class rather than of their own class.

It is possible to see *The Scream* in these terms, with the dominant-hegemonic as the need to see the text as a work of art (and thus in some unspecified sense valuable) and an oppositional reading as one that rejects these notions of cultural value. Most practical readings of text are negotiated, a compound of the two previous positions mixed with significant personal response. With this sophisticated example still in mind, let us turn to a common case of media-manipulated response, of moral panic in action.

MORAL PANIC   Cohen has described moral panic as what occurs when 'a condition, episode, person or group of persons emerges to become defined as a threat to societal values and interests' (Cohen 1980: 9). Classic cases would include media coverage of issues such as AIDS, punk rockers, or the 2000 campaign by the *News of the World* to 'name and shame' paedophiles.

Recently statistics for teenage pregnancies were published for Western Europe and Britain was once again top of this league. A quality Sunday newspaper ran a full-page article entitled 'Too Much Too Young'; this was accompanied by a still from a Channel Four documentary on the same subject. The image was of two young people in school uniforms, the boy with a loosened tie and a depressed or uninterested gaze, the girl with a short skirt and a heavily pregnant stomach. The fact that we could not get permission to show you this image does much to support the brief reading that follows. Channel Four, who own the image, simply said that it had been especially commissioned by them to advertise a forthcoming documentary. The 'stories' told by the photograph and the article become more interesting to us as students of communication from the moment that permission is denied.

In the case of the newspaper article, the dominant-hegemonic reading is fairly clear: we are being encouraged to share the newspaper's shock, horror and outrage at ever more precocious and promiscuous children, and the inevitable outcomes of under-age sex. The preferred reading thus runs something like this: here are two *children*, not yet out of school uniform, who have experimented with sex and who are now in considerable trouble – which is nobody's fault but their own.

PREFERRED READING   The reading a text's producer would like receivers to make. The producer will compose the text in a way which ensures this occurs.

For many of us this is not an entirely convincing reading, though the gist seems plausible enough. There is plenty of room in their unspecified non-verbal communication (their postures, facial expressions and gaze focus are all relatively open to a range of interpretations) for negotiated readings. Partly these will be informed by our 'relationship' to Britain's 'child sex' statistics; we possibly all know, know of or are people who have had under-age sex or even teenage pregnancy. All of these experiences elaborate the dominant-hegemonic reading, which offers the issue of child sexuality as a fuel for a moral panic.

Oppositional readings might start in an examination of the physical evidence provided, where the slightly-too-well-composed image, with bulging belly in a central position, might prompt an accusation of contrivance. This is validated by the suspiciously 'old' girl/model, her make-up, the way she is strategically lit and the amount of thigh she is showing to us. One reading therefore runs: this is a set-up, an opinion masquerading as a fact, an assertion disguised as a truth. What if the 'problem' of under-age sex is not a moral but a practical problem? What if this demonising of girls with 'inappropriately' womanly bulges (and the girl is the principal focus) is part of the problem?

These are the kinds of reading which Communication Studies will ask you to consider – not to convert you from a moral to a pragmatic view of under-age sex, but rather to get you to understand the potentially polysemic character of communication at most times in most places in your life. All meaning is thus 'up for grabs'.

▼ 3 DECODING AND DE-CODING

In this section we will consider two basic approaches to the study of communication, the semiotic and the process approaches.

- We will provide broad definitions of the two schools of thought.

- We will consider a simple but useful process model.

- We will set out the foundations of semiotic analysis.

How can it be that different people make different readings of the same text? Why is it the case that people who think in the same way about communication group together to support each other in their interpretation of what communication is, how specific texts should be read, and how they view the world?

As stated in Part 1, there are two main schools of thought of communication theory. The process and the semiotic schools constitute two different approaches to the study of communication. They offer us tools with which to systematically analyse communication texts. Let's look at the process and semiotic schools and, in so doing, further explore key ideas of representation, genre and convention.

As the only real test of explanations is through their practical application, let's examine another text. This text is a still from the 1998 film *The Truman Show*, directed by Peter Weir and starring Jim Carrey.

Figure 3.7 *Still from* The *Truman Show* (Paramount *1998*). *Courtesy of the Kobal Collection*

How are we to understand it? What might it mean? Let's use process and semiotic approaches to try to understand what it means and how it makes its meanings.

PROCESS SCHOOL

- Sees communication as the transmission of messages
- Is concerned with how senders and receivers encode and decode
- Sees communication as a process by which one person affects another
- Is concerned with matters such as efficiency and accuracy
- Evaluates the success of communication in terms of 'delivered signal'

SEMIOTIC SCHOOL

- Sees communication as the generation and sharing of meanings
- Is concerned with how messages and texts interact with people
- Sees the study of communication as the study of text, context and culture
- Does not see misunderstanding as evidence of communication failure

Put simply, the process explanation of our film capture would see it as the encoded version of a desire by Paramount Studios to publicise their film among a specifically targeted audience who would then decode this message and either comply with or reject or ignore their efforts. The significant issues here are the assumption that the text is a version of some predetermined intention, that the message is therefore essentially singular, and that the effects of communication can usually be quantified.

The significant elements – intention, sender and audience – are often obvious, but it is sometimes necessary to tease them out. Process models of communications, like Lasswell's Formula below, can serve as useful prompts for this exploration. In 1948 Harold Lasswell offered a five-point plan for identifying the significant features of communication processes. Lasswell's Formula asks five questions:

- Who?
- Says what?
- To whom?
- In which channel?
- With what effect?

This formula is immediately useful since it clarifies areas of investigation which we recognise as the sender, the message, the receiver, the channel (and medium) and the outcome.

CHANNEL/MEDIUM It is important to distinguish between these sometimes confused concepts. Whilst a medium is a means of communication, a way of communicating (a technological medium like television or film or a human medium like speech or gestures), a channel is a physical connection between communicators, a route (like sound waves or the electronic type that is carrying this message to you).

Lasswell insists that we find a specific context for communication texts and then implies that the narrow context he has identified is the only one that counts. We will see later that the semiotic approach also privileges context, but in a very different way, to describe those wider cultural, social, political and historical conditions within which texts might be located and made meaningful.

Let's apply the Lasswell Formula to, for example, the video cover of *The Truman Show*:

- **Who?** Paramount/Peter Weir/Jim Carrey
- **Says what?** This is a film called *The Truman Show* with . . .
- **To whom?** Those who saw it and those who missed it
- **In which channel?** A publicity photograph
- **With what effect?** It is seen, touched and, it is hoped, bought

The Lasswell Formula has served its purpose in efficiently identifying the text, its context and its intention. As an instrument for further analysis, however, it is limited – beyond a discussion about who the sender is. What's more, different texts produce different sets of results, with varying degrees of usefulness – even within the same genre.

Apply Lasswell's Formula to the text below (the video cover of *The Italian Job*) and compare your results with those given above for *The Truman Show*. What differences do you notice?

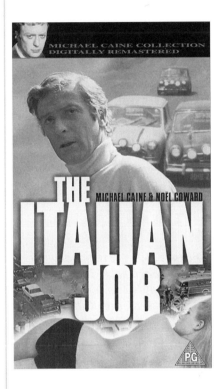

Figure 3.8 *The Italian Job*
(Paramount 1969; video cover)

The problem here is partly caused by a more sophisticated text, or at least a more open text (or a text that is differently closed). Whilst the preferred reading/dominant discourse of *The Truman Show* text runs along the lines of 'Jim Carrey, he's a funny man/top star/guarantee of quality', *The Italian Job* text is much more diverse. It is clearly offering explicitly alternative readings which may be modified to suit the reader's interests: to do with Caine as an actor/cultural item; to do with the film as a classic of sorts; to do with those other classics, the Minis; to do with the 1960s and certain kinds of chic or cool; to do with technical qualities never seen before.

It is possible that the combined effect of these 'alternatives' in fact ironically makes oppositional readings less likely, that they are all in fact in their ways preferred readings.

If you are opposed to the premise that Jim Carrey is a kitemark of quality, you are liable to reject the whole package, whereas if you reject Caine's claims you are offered alternative reasons to respond constructively – the text is in active negotiation with you.

KEY TERM

NEGOTIATION This concept is at the very heart of the semiotic approach to the study of communication, implying as it does that texts do not have meaning except through the process of negotiation between text and reader.

Very much in the manner of the logical approach we used in the previous section, the semiotic approach is concerned to consider systematically those elements that constitute communication texts. This process is sometimes referred to as deconstruction because, simply speaking, what is being done is breaking texts down into their constituent parts. For example, we might recognise that the following film still is constructed from elements including setting, costume, lighting and actor performance.

Figure 3.9 *Still from Trainspotting (Figment/ Noel Gay/Channel 4 1996). Courtesy of the Kobal Collection*

KEY TERM

CODES consist of signs. Signs are anything that has the potential to generate meaning, to signify. When a sign has generated meaning, it is said to have achieved signification. This is fundamental to the semiotic approach to the study of communication.

Identifying the contributing codes of communication is a very useful step in the analysis of any text; it is very like discovering the spectrum of colours from which all others are made. Codes are the languages of communication; they are the systems through which communication operates. John Fiske (1990) argues that it is important to distinguish between two types of code, which he calls representational codes and presentational codes. Representational codes are those that produce texts like the one above; they are used to create messages with an independent existence. On the other hand, presentational codes are used to provide information about senders and contexts; they are primarily concerned with self-presentation. Clearly, the still from *Trainspotting* theoretically has examples of both types of code, though its very presentation as a still makes it essentially representational rather than presentational. The presentational elements – notably the non-verbal communication offered by the above character's posture, appearance and facial expression – are all explored in detail later in this text.

It is enough here that we take on board that at the heart of the semiotic approach to the study of communication is the recognition of codes as the organising systems of communication. Implicit to this understanding is the notion that all communication is encountered and interpreted in a social and cultural context, in other words through interaction with other human beings. Systems and structures, like the conventions of a language, make the generation of meaning possible, but it is at the level of interaction and context that individual meanings are made.

Codes are, in essence, convention-governed systems that are agreed to by members of a community or culture or society. Codes may be behavioural, signifying, technical or cultural; in other words they might be used to determine how we behave, make meaning, use media or even maintain our way of life. They organise what we do, what we see and what we say. They constitute our lives and are the various languages in and through which our lives are expressed.

ACTIVITY . . .

Identify and list the codes likely to be active in a simple activity like walking to a local shop to buy groceries. Classify these codes in terms of (a) those that condition or control our behaviour and (b) those that affect the way we make meaning or communicate. You may wish to start by considering the code that determines which bits of the built environment we walk on and which bits we generally avoid.

If our lives are literally described by a network of codes, the next useful step might be to look at points of intersection. Codes are all very well as organising principles of communication, but to us as students of communication, interested in the interaction of text and reader, the particular will always be more important than the general.

Let's think about the CD, the cover of which is reproduced overleaf. Although it is quite interesting to see the CD pictured overleaf in terms of a set of coded conventions – representational and technical – we are always likely to be more interested in what it particularly is and, in this case, how it particularly sounds. What is encoded here is a piece of communication that works through a number of codes, some of which we are unable to access in this format, except in our auditory memories if we have the knowledge and inclination. The CD on the following page is not a CD but rather it is a representation of one. It is an idea given concrete form. It cannot be played.

Figures 3.10 & 3.11 *SClub7, Bring It All Back CD. © Polydor Ltd. Courtesy of Polydor Ltd*

A code is a system of signs agreed by the users. Given signs are selected from within given codes. There is, therefore, clearly a code within which 'Bring It All Back' can generate meaning and another, which can distinguish between the 'S' sign and 'CLUB 7'. The background, too, is a significant sign, a foundation on to which other signs are locked.

Without needing to access the musical content, we are aware that communication is taking place: an encoded message is being offered for decoding; an invitation to negotiate meaning has been posted; a collection of signs is doing all it can to signify. Whichever way you choose to describe this situation, this is the essence of all text-based work.

Before we go any further, it might be important to register your first impressions of and personal response to this basic text.

S CLUB 7
Bring It All Back

What is communicated by the S CLUB 7 CD? Look at every component and comment.

While the approach we are adopting here is essentially semiotic, it does not differ that much at this point from the process approach. Do not see these approaches as mutually exclusive (as a matter of either/or). At a practical level, let them both inform your critical work. Process simply puts much greater store by the role of the encoder and what his/her intentions are, whilst semiotics tends to privilege the receiver.

If we move now from the CD to its cover, we can take another step towards understanding how codes operate and how signs are selected and combined.

This arrangement of signs (group members, facial expressions, costumes, setting) is clearly a selection from a vast number of possible selections and combinations. The number of different ways seven people can be arranged in a straight line is staggering. The signs that appear can only be understood in terms of their relationships both with one another and with all the selections that have not been made (the choice of a light background, for example, precludes the choice of a dark one). These relationships are what the Swiss linguist Ferdinand de Saussure (1983) called the syntagmatic (or horizontal) relations and the paradigmatic (or vertical) relations of a code, a language, a set of signs.

KEY TERM

SYNTAGM   In semiotics a syntagm is a chain of signs, a unique combination of sign choices. Units may be visual, verbal or musical. The scale of the units and syntagms may range from the very large (the nine planned episodes of the *Star Wars* triple trilogy might constitute a syntagm) to the very small (as in the syntagm 'small' which consists of the signs 's', 'm', 'a', 'l' and 'l'). The important point is that syntagms invite negotiation as a whole; they are bigger units of potential meaning.

KEY TERM

PARADIGM   a set of signs from which one might be chosen to contribute to a syntagm. Paradigms define their individual members with reference to all others in the set. To select from a paradigm is at that moment to reject all other signs in that set, just as by selecting something (or nothing) to cover your feet today, you have rejected all other possibilities; this choice from a paradigm of 'foot coverings' has contributed to the syntagms which constitute the things you are wearing today. When Peugeot's 'lion' went 'from strength to strength', it got its strength partly from the paradigm of 'elite animals' from which it was chosen and partly because that paradigm does not include 'weasel', 'frog' and 'sloth'.

ACTIVITY . . .

Look at the S CLUB 7 cover and identify SIX significant paradigms which have been used to create the syntagms offered.

■   Which of these do you consider to be the most important to the meaning of this text?

■   Which choice turned out for you to be the most significant?

■   What are the dominant signs in these syntagms?

The important thing to remember is that, as students of communication, we are interested specifically in engaging with texts in an attempt to work out their meanings. It is not technical terms which unlock texts but rather the issues these concepts and methods raise. The two-dimensional grid which Saussurian linguistics imposes on any text is useful only, ultimately, if it delivers more than the lay and naked eye.

In the case of S CLUB 7, a very conventional text is further clarified by reference to such paradigms as 'settings for bands', which here directs attention to the cleanness and/or blandness of a photographic backdrop and from there to the banal realisation that it's sand they're in and that the backdrop is clearly meant to represent the sky and/or sea. For an 'enjoy-it-while-you-can' teeny-pop sensation, this is a snapshot of their best summer ever with as much sincerity and irony as the sender and receivers will allow. Given that all the human figures are taken from that specialist paradigm 'members of the pop group S CLUB 7', it is their arrangement and presentation that are important. Here, in fact, is an excellent example of the overlapping of representational and presentational codes, where the self-presentation of individuals is set firmly within the representation of the group itself. The individual syntagms that represent the seven individuals are in themselves part of a larger syntagm whose meaning is 'S CLUB 7'. The male figure at the top of the cover, for example, is communicating discretely through various non-verbal signs, such as his facial expression and his posture, but he is also himself a significant component of the representation of the whole group.

In all of this, broader issues of representation are also being addressed; for, although such factors as gender, ethnicity and even sexual orientation are clearly inscribed, the meanings assigned to and through them are very much open and available. At a superficial level, for example, we notice that three of the 'girls' are sitting upstage (in the foreground) at the base of a pyramid that has a black male and a (too-conveniently-contrasting and slightly subordinate blonde) white female at its apex, as a kind of symbolic master and mistress. In seeing some of this, we are allowing ourselves the opportunity to explore the very idea of convention, or rather ideas of it, and to see the levels at which formulas work. It also reminds us that blandness and conventionality are neither necessarily neutral nor harmless. Too much public communication plays these games and carries a significant ideological impact simply because it goes unnoticed and unchecked. This is the point the writer George Orwell was making when he remarked of advertising that it 'hits below the intellect'.

▼   ## 4 WORDS AND PICTURES: SIGNS AND SIGNATURES

In this section we will further examine the semiotic approach to the study of communication.

- ■ We will look at the composition and operation of signs.
- ■ We will examine the different levels at which signs can have significance.
- ■ We will consider Peirce's ideas about the sign categories icon, index and symbol.

Now that we have established the two principal approaches to the study of communication, we can begin to look more closely at their claims to explain the character of communication in practice. This section will further explore the semiotic approach to texts whilst the next section will take the process further.

INTENTION

When we are examining texts in which the sender, message and receiver are clearly identifiable, it is a relatively easy job to frame a response. However, it can be a very different matter if the text is a little elliptic or enigmatic. The A6 flyer that follows was

Figure 3.12 *Cambridge Youth Project 'Ordinary'*
flyer. Courtesy of Selina Dean of Cambridge

ACTIVITY . . .

Examine the flyer depicted here.

■ What might the purpose of it be?

■ Who might send this text? Give two or three possible options.

■ Who do you think the intended audience might be (in terms of age profile, personality, etc.)?

discovered in a Cambridge library and attracted with its Japanese cartoon-style aesthetic. It features, almost uniquely in advertising, the word 'ordinary' and a striking image.

As far as the process approach to communication is concerned, the answers to the above questions are found on the flyer's reverse side:

- **Purpose:** 'why not write . . . for *Gunge* newspaper'
- **Intended audience:** 'between the ages of 14 and 25'
- **Sender:** The North Cambridge Youth Project

However, what they add up to is a list of intentions, a notion of what the designers or compilers or sponsors hoped they were communicating to their target audience. They do not necessarily do justice to the quality of the design or to that of the companion piece (below) in which the man is replaced by a woman and 'ordinary?' is replaced with 'quiet?' These may be male and female versions or perhaps versions for males and females. They share reverse-side texts and have clear generic links: the floating background texts, the style of illustrations and the arrangement of elements. Despite the clearly stated intentions,

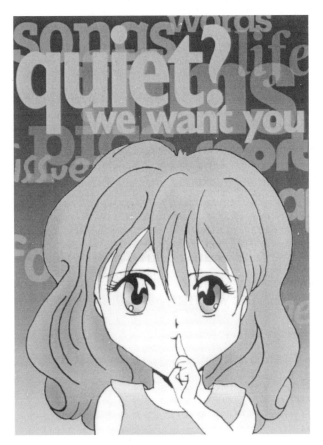

Figure 3.13 *Cambridge Youth Project 'Quiet' flyer. Courtesy of Selina Dean of Cambridge*

the reverse side clarifications do little to identify a preferred reading of either of these striking designs.

In the majority of print advertising, readings of largely visual texts are prompted, supported, privileged, even prescribed by a variety of verbal arrangements: headlines, captions, slogans, titles. Roland Barthes, the French semiotician, devised the term 'anchorage' to describe the ways in which texts, or parts of texts, are anchored to particular meanings (Barthes 1967). In this way the creator of a communication text can steer the reader to the meaning that they prefer them to make of the text. In the crudest sense, this process can be exemplified with reference to the following simple illustration.

ANCHORAGE   The process by which the meaning of a text is fixed, usually by means of a caption or voice-over to visual images.

Figure 3.14   Dog/Cat/Horse?

In the above example, assigning any of the animal titles to this drawn animal is tantamount to investing this crudely made sign with meaning. While it is fair to say, with process theory, that at the point of conception, this collection of marks had a conscious intention, its polysemy (its capability for different meanings) is also difficult to dispute. In fact, the issue is made more problematic and interesting by its context as an illustration from a textbook in a chapter addressing explicitly the ways in which words work upon visual material and in so doing limit the possibility of multiple meanings. Its genuine intention (and therefore one of its readings) is thus 'something drawn that might be variously interpreted' or more specifically 'something drawn that might plausibly represent "dog", "cat" and "horse"'.

Perhaps the crudest example of this is the visual joke, where words, a punch line, allow readers to discover something in an image they have not seen. When we were young we might have been presented with this visual puzzle:

What is this?

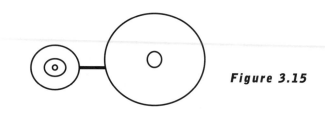

Figure 3.15

COMMUNICATION STUDIES: THE ESSENTIAL INTRODUCTION

The answer – a bird's-eye view of a Mexican frying an egg – is a classic anchoring statement because it literally activates the given sign and answers our need for explanation, for a meaning. On the page is a series of circles and a line. Words link this to a situation, if somewhat stereotypically and surreally. What we are seeing here – in a very stark way – is the relationship Saussure identified between the two parts of a sign – the signifier and the signified.

KEY TERM

SIGNIFIER/SIGNIFIED According to Saussure, the basic unit of communication is the sign. The sign is composed of two elements – the signifier and the signified. The signifier is the label that people attach to objects when they want to communicate about them. The signified is the object or the mental concept of the object to which the signifier refers. The signifier and the signified unite to form the sign, but the relationship between the two elements is an arbitrary one, that is, there is no logical or necessary relationship between them. That's why it's possible to change which signifier relates to which signified; there are no absolute rules connecting the signifier and the signified.

In the Mexican gag the signifier is anchored to its comic purpose by the words of the punch line and at the same time other explanations (other signifieds) are downplayed or eliminated. The circles and line might, for example, have had a scientific, paranormal or anthropological significance. Anchorage lessens or even removes the 'might' given that its function is, in Barthes' words 'to fix the floating chain of signifieds'. This fixing is clearly evident in the cover design of the FilmFour listings magazine, which features a still from the British film *Elizabeth*, together with a couple of substantial 'anchors'. This is obviously a publicity shot for the film. The photographic backdrop suggests this, but FilmFour has fixed its meaning in a particular way. This is a potentially open representation of a complex historical character, partially closed by the twin captions: 'KILLER QUEEN' and 'ELIZABETH RULES OVER A MONTH OF BRITISH FILM'.

ACTIVITY . . .

What readings of the image are being suggested by the captions? What alternative readings become possible if the words are taken away? (What has been done to the image to make it more effective?)

As we begin to consider the potential readings of any image, it is noticeable that images are capable not only of different meanings but also of different types of meaning. Put simply, and with direct reference to the *Elizabeth* still, there is a significant difference between the designation 'Cate Blanchett in the film *Elizabeth*' and the designation 'Killer Queen' or even 'a woman who needs to have her wits about her'. Barthes addresses these different kinds or levels of meaning in his notion of 'orders of signification'. These are levels at which signs might be significant or signifiers may connect with signifieds.

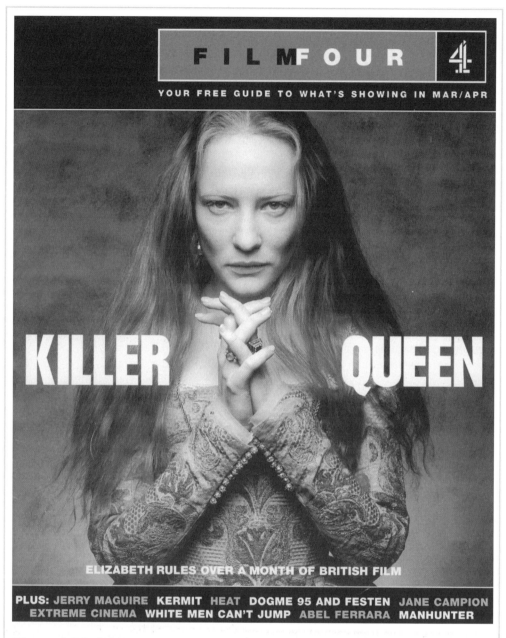

FILMFOUR 4

YOUR FREE GUIDE TO WHAT'S SHOWING IN MAR/APR

KILLER QUEEN

ELIZABETH RULES OVER A MONTH OF BRITISH FILM

PLUS: JERRY MAGUIRE KERMIT HEAT DOGME 95 AND FESTEN JANE CAMPION
EXTREME CINEMA WHITE MEN CAN'T JUMP ABEL FERRARA MANHUNTER

Figure 3.16 '*Killer Queen' poster. Courtesy of FilmFour*

The first order of signification is *denotation*. Connections are made between signs and objects. It is agreed that specific signs will signify specific objects at a general societal level. In the *Elizabeth* example, what is denoted might include 'the actress Cate Blanchett', 'a woman in period costume' or 'the film's central character Queen Elizabeth'.

The second order of signification is *connotation*. If denotation describes the way in which signs signify at a general societal level, then connotation describes the way in which signs signify at a specific individual level. Connotations describes the way in which groups of people share meaning at an associative level. By virtue of the groups we are members of, we share in the connotative use of signs. In the *Elizabeth* example, the particular ways in which this image has been presented might provoke particular sorts of personal response, connoting aspects as diverse as vulnerability and danger.

Myths are, according to the authors of *Key Concepts in Communication and Cultural Studies* (O'Sullivan *et al.* 1994), a culture's way of conceptualising an abstract topic. A myth consists of a collection of concepts bound together by general acceptance and significant in our understanding of particular kinds of experience. The image we have been examining contains within it a very specific kind of myth, that of Elizabeth herself, however she is represented, and the age she names. This is connected to notions of national identity and pride as well as the perpetuation of another significant myth, that of monarchy as a natural repository of the nation's hopes and dignity.

The third order of signification is *ideology*. Fiske and Hartley (1978) have suggested that myths and connotations are in themselves evidence of a deeper, hidden pattern of meaning which they label ideology. This is ideology as a description of the various ways in which society, or those controlling it, organise and control the ways in which meanings are generated – what Marxists would call the intellectual means of production. A final visit to our example will reveal that part of the meaning system in which the text is active has to do with gender. It is hard to avoid understanding this image of a woman without reference to the connotations of the female, not to say myths about femininity, and this is partly a response to the text's implicit ideology. Here the woman is strong but only in the ultimate context: that women are weaker, more vulnerable and conventionally not like this.

ACTIVITY . . .

Looking at the images on page 86, demonstrate your understanding of denotation, connotation, myth and ideology by suggesting at least FOUR supporting captions.

It is clear that some signifiers, by their character, need far less anchoring than others. This has partly to do with the open or closed character of texts but it is also related to two other ideas, one from each of the process and semiotic approaches, which it may be useful to introduce at this point.

The first idea is that of *redundancy* which derives from Shannon and Weaver's process model of communication (1949). Shannon and Weaver, in a development of the Lasswell Formula we used earlier, proposed a model of communication which, while linear (a straight line), addresses the issue of inefficiency in communication, here described as noise source.

Figure 3.17 *Norman Parkinson, New York, New York (1955). Courtesy of Hamiltons Photographers Ltd*

Figure 3.18 *Cartoon*

REDUNDANCY/ENTROPY A communication that is low on new information and which is highly predictable is said to be redundant. A communication that is high on new information and that is highly unpredictable is said to be entropic.

If we meet someone every day and they always say the same thing to us, that communication can be characterised as redundant. Our knowledge of the conventions of film in general and of specific film genres in particular makes much of film narrative being easy to predict, that is to make them redundant. Astute communicators will try to wrap up the entropic elements of a communication with redundant elements to make it more easily understood. It could be said that the objective of an effective communicator is to make the entropic redundant, that is, to make the unpredictable, the difficult to understand, easy to understand.

Diagram 3.1 *Shannon and Weaver's Mathematical Theory of Communication*

In recognising the potential for interference between the intended message encoded by the transmitter and the received message, Shannon and Weaver (1949) are partly acknowledging the polysemic character of texts. However, within the process tradition to which they are significant contributors, polysemy is not really an issue. Shannon and Weaver are concerned only to establish those inefficiencies which might limit the transmission of intended meaning to the receiver, and through this to suggest ways in which these inefficiencies might be countered. They are concerned with accurate decoding and how it might be achieved. The Shannon and Weaver model is often referred to as the Mathematical Theory of Communication. They were trying to devise a system to eliminate the deterioration of communication using telephones. They discovered that if a mathematical value could be placed on the noise source, then the telephone engineers would know by how much the signal would have to be increased to overcome the noise source.

Redundancy refers to the level of predictability that can be built into a message or a text. Genre, for example, assists redundancy in that it offers a series of expectations which are to a large degree predictable. When we choose to see a horror film, we do so in the secure knowledge that significant parts of the text will be already familiar to us from our experience of other horror films. This familiarity makes us secure and confident.

BROADCAST/NARROWCAST To broadcast is to transmit highly predictable (redundant) information to large, heterogeneous (i.e. having nothing in common with each other in terms of age, gender, sexual orientation, income, geography, disposable income, lifestyle or interests) audiences. To narrowcast is to transmit highly unpredictable (entropic) information to small homogeneous (i.e. having much in common in terms of age, gender, sexual orientation, income, geography, disposable income, lifestyle or interests) audiences.

In order to communicate with a general public audience, most broadcast communication has a large degree of redundancy, in that it conforms to predetermined conventions. New situation comedy on television, for example, will be keen to reference its original comic situation, its cast of soon-to-be-familiar characters, and its cumulative punch lines in the context of the genre as a whole. Redundancy, rather than anchorage, is the key to identifying intended meanings and preferred readings in this case. Redundancy is, in effect, an implication of generic or even formal conventions, a sort of insurance policy taken out by the sender to guard against potential audience misunderstanding or bewilderment.

In contrast, unpredictability in the content or form of a message is described as entropy. Entropic content concentrates information in a demanding way, whilst entropic form usually breaks existing conventions. Entropy opposes redundancy and calls for a plurality of response rather than a conventional singularity of response. In time, of course, as broken conventions become the new conventions, the entropic becomes redundant and the process begins again. An example of this process would be Channel Four's *The Big Breakfast* which set out systematically to break all of the conventions of breakfast television and ended up being successful and greatly imitated.

Conventions are also at the core of the relationship between signifier and signified, as one of the principal influences on the ways any reality can be represented. For example, if we want to communicate the idea 'baby', we might choose a conventional way of representing this by speaking or writing the English word that is formed 'b-a-b-y' or 'B-A-B-Y'. In fact these are only two of the vast number of ways this word might be represented in written or printed form. Others include 'baby', 'Baby' and 'BABY', each of which carries its own particular connotations. What must be grasped, however, is that, whatever the typeface, there is no logical or necessary connection between this sign (these signs) in its physical form as signifier and any idea or reality we might associate with it, that is, any signified. The connection is artificial and arbitrary, a matter of agreement. Language then is highly conventional in the same way that it is highly redundant.

ACTIVITY . . .

Collect or compile TEN different ways or forms of representing the concept sometimes represented by the word 'baby'. These representations may be made by you or collected from outside sources. Arrange them in order of greatest convention, in terms of the degree to which their meaning is dependent on 'outside' knowledge of the language, society and culture in which they were made. A word is therefore highly conventional whereas a photograph has a low degree of convention.

Clearly, you will have found representations (signs and syntagms) in which the relationship between the signifier and signified is other than arbitrary. Photographs of babies, for example, do not represent 'baby' simply by a matter of agreement, but rather through a closer (albeit technologically aided) relationship between signifier and signified. These representations take their form largely from the character of the signified. In the case of baby photographs, the shape and size of the baby pictured is largely determined by the shape and size of the baby photographed. The signifier is thus said to be motivated to some degree by the character of the signified: the more significant the determination, the higher the *motivation* is said to be.

Figure 3.19a
Baby drawing
(Paul Mendez)

Figure 3.19b *Norman Rockwell, detail from 'The Tantrum', cover of the Saturday Evening Post, 24 October 1936*

Figure 3.19c *Baby photograph. Courtesy of www.digitalvisiondownload.com*

MOTIVATION In semiotics this refers to the relationship between a sign and what it represents. Specifically it describes the degree to which the form a sign takes (word/symbol/drawing/photograph) is determined by) the subject being represented. Thus the horse in a colour photograph is said to have high motivation simply because, as a sign, its form (what it looks like) is very like the horse it is representing. Similarly a word sign has very low motivation because its form/shape/appearance usually has next to nothing to do with whatever it is representing.

This is not to say that any representation is free from convention, for no sign is totally motivated (though some are totally conventional). In any representation, even photographic, there is room for the sender to impose perspective, focus, distance; in other words, there is room to conventionalise the representation. The more consciously the images are being produced for specific contexts, the greater the degree of convention bearing down on the motivated image.

The three images opposite appeared in a brochure for a day nursery/crèche (Figure 3.20).

ACTIVITY . . .

These three images/signs/syntagms are clearly highly motivated (they were originally glossy, full-colour representations). Examine the degree of convention in each of these and suggest what sorts of meaning are delivered in this way. Another way to do this is to look at the level of redundancy or predictability of them as messages.

If we now look at the front cover of the brochure which featured these images, we can see more precisely – owing to the anchorage provided by words – the context for these images. We can also identify a number of significantly conventional signs to support and contrast with these significantly motivated ones. This is useful up to a point, but it does leave a rather large grey area somewhere between highly motivated and highly conventional. Whilst Saussure was content with the dichotomy of signifier and signified, of motivation and convention, Charles Peirce went further. Rather than a dichotomy, Peirce (1966) proposed a trichotomy – three elements in the composition of the sign, three different types of sign. He labelled these three types of sign as icon, index and symbol.

The cover opposite contains good examples of Peirce's three sign categories which, he stressed, were tendencies and not mutually exclusive designations.

Peirce firstly identified those signs that communicated their signified through resemblance, in other words by looking like their signified, or in certain cases by sounding like or smelling like their signified. These are essentially motivated signs and he labelled them *icons*. The representations of the children and the toy box clearly fit into this category.

Second, Peirce talked of *indexes*: signs that communicate their signified by association; in other words, because one thing exists, another thing is assumed to exist. We see smoke,

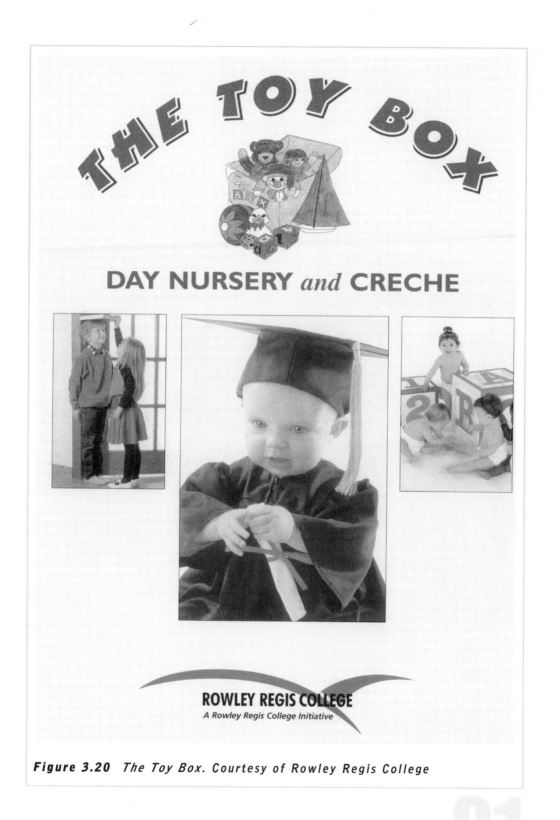

Figure 3.20 *The Toy Box.* Courtesy of Rowley Regis College

we assume the existence of fire. Therefore the character of the relationship between indexical signs and their objects is said to be existential. The above cover provides a range of examples – from the mortar board and gown as indexes of education to the toys and toy box as indexes of childhood and fun. A mortarboard does not resemble education; rather it is in some sense a part of education as a broad concept. Notice also that the toy box has been described as both iconic and indexical, reflecting the different ways in which it is communicating.

Peirce's third sign category, *symbol*, was reserved for signs where the relationship between sign and object was a matter of agreement. There is no logical or necessary relationship between the signs 'toy box' and the object we recognise from the picture; it is a matter of social convention. If we follow the social convention, we will get along with fellow human beings. If we don't, we will not get along, we will most likely be shunned by them. All the words on this cover and the college logo are typical examples of symbolic signs.

Family Afternoons at The Barber Institute of Fine Arts

In uncovering the categories of sign we find we are, in fact, engaging with the very act of signification, examining how signs mean even before we examine what they mean. In the whole of this section we have been trying out explanations of the way texts work in order to find out more about what they might have to say. Our next text carries with it a significant challenge: to communicate your understanding of sign categories with reference to a specific live text.

Figure 3.21 *Art Alive!* flyer. *Courtesy of the Barber Institute of Fine Arts, University of Birmingham*

Plan, in note form, a five-minute presentation entitled 'Icons, indexes and symbols' aimed at your fellow students. Exemplify your explanation with detailed reference to the above leaflet cover, paying particular attention to:

■ the attractive exclamation mark

■ the three shaded blocks

■ the man in the false beard

■ the choice of typefaces.

▼ 5   TAKING THE PROCESS FURTHER

In this section we will examine the process approach to the study of communication.

■ We will look at Gerbner's model of communication.

■ We will examine the character of the sender in communication in terms of status and in terms of a gatekeeping role.

We have looked at the semiotic approach to the study of communication where meaning is a matter of negotiation within a specific cultural context. We will now attempt to address some of the issues thrown up by the process approach. Let's start with the significantly more sophisticated process model of George Gerbner. Gerbner moves the basic linear model offered by Lasswell and Shannon and Weaver into a second dimension, making a distinction in the process between the act of perceiving the world ('seeing') and the act of communication itself ('saying').

Gerbner's model is an attempt to provide a general-purpose model of communication, and as such it is perhaps doomed to failure. However, it does provide a useful context in which to discuss aspects of the communication models and ultimately the limitations of models. Gerbner's model works best for communication that is genuinely informative, which provides the receiver with information, of which he/she is previously unaware. To

Diagram 3.2 *Gerbner's model of communication*

understand Gerbner's model, let us look at Pete's story as presented in the case study that follows.

CASE STUDY

In December 1980 I was awoken, as an undergraduate student, in my hall of residence by my roommate to the news that John Lennon, the former Beatle, was dead; in fact, he had been killed. My roommate, Mike, had heard this 'news' on early morning radio. In Gerbner's terms he had made a selection from the range of potential news available to him in his context as a radio listener for whom only one radio channel was available at that time; the one to which his radio alarm clock was habitually tuned. In fact the event was so newsworthy it would not likely have mattered which radio station he was receiving. This news selection (in Gerbner's terms this perception of an event) had most likely been prompted by a number of factors: the insistence of the radio announcer that this was *the* news story; the peculiar social and cultural relevance the Beatles had to anyone like the two of us, who were born at the very beginning of the 1960s; the fact I was, to him, 'a long-haired hippy'; the fact Lennon was only 40 years old. None of this plays a significant part in Gerbner's version of communication, save in a stretching of context to a much broader 'where we're at (man)'; emotionally, socially, culturally. Gerbner suggests we select what we 'see' (hear, think, taste) from a range of available stimuli and that, when we have selected, we deliver this perception to our receiver(s) in the most appropriate way; for us, for them and sometimes for both.

As Mike moved that day from his bedroom to mine, through the shared living space, he probably was converting an idea/surprise/shock into a communicable form, just as I now in this retelling am finding appropriate means. Mike was entering Gerbner's 'means and control' dimension, and my bedroom, awaking me with a noisy door, a phatic shoulder shake and a clear message: 'John Lennon's dead'. There was no room for misunderstanding, little for selection. My context as receiver probably made the message more believable, the very fact that I'd been woken up was an index of the importance of this news. What was available to me was partly this fact dawning on me and partly the urgency of the communication: the voice, the face, the words. The follow-up was, 'He's been killed', but by then the message had been received, perceived, understood. In this case, Gerbner's model, if necessarily imprecisely, does offer a meaningful account of communication in practice. The world is perceived, and that perception is passed on to a receiver, at which point the act of communication is over.

How different it is, then, if we examine a very similar message in a very different context – largely pictorial, public, political and nearly a thousand years old. The most famous section of the Bayeux Tapestry contains the following words and images:

Figure 3.22   The death of Harold. Detail from the Bayeux Tapestry

Applying Gerbner, the event is clear – an incident from a battle in 1066. However, this is the point at which the model begins to break down. It is fair to say that this section of the tapestry is an attempt to represent the death of King Harold, the English leader; this is anchored by the Latin text, 'Harold Rex interfectus est' (King Harold is killed). There are probably interesting things to say about the 'means and control' dimension, given this is the victor's version of the event and was constructed some 30 years after the battle, ironically by English seamstresses under the commission of William's half-brother, Odo. Nevertheless it is difficult to see Gerbner's model as usefully clarifying this process, which was prolonged, celebratory and clearly propagandist. In fact, it is difficult even to argue for the tapestry as a coherent perception, then representation, of a far-off event: it reads much more like the conscious coining of a new mythology. Its bias and perspective are clear, it certainly has intention, but its form and style expect a much fuller response. This openness is partly shown in the above section which the Bayeux-bought guidebook describes, appropriately in French, as 'Harold est tué d'une flèche dans l'oeil' (Harold is killed by an arrow in the eye). This is prompted by the figure straddled above by the word 'HAROLD', who appears to be removing an arrow from his face or head: it is the stuff of legend. Scholars, however, with other ways and more experience of reading texts like this, inform us that the convention is to depict the victim at the point of death, crudely, under the word 'killed' or 'dead' or whatever. This would make Harold the victim of the stooping, mounted Norman knight to the right and would neuter the joke that has Harold's last words as 'Careful with that arrow; you'll have somebody's eye out'. This is not a History lesson, but rather a lesson in the precariousness and potential inefficiency of communication, even communication of a very contrived, considered and artificial kind.

In the case of Pete's learning of John Lennon's death, the immediate sender was both obvious and identifiable, though in a more profound way he was the last in a chain of gatekeepers, which stretched back to those who witnessed Lennon's fatal wounding. Mostly this was a matter for mass media news organisations, save at the final stage when it became a stimulus for interpersonal communication. There is a theory that the more important the news item, the more likely we are to receive the news from an interpersonal source – a friend, a family member, a colleague. A more contemporary example might be to think of how you found out that Diana, Princess of Wales, had been killed. Was it from a mass media source? King Harold's death is told in a much less immediate way and it is highly unlikely that any of its intended audience would have had to wait until 1096 to find out what happened at Hastings. The relationship between the teller, the tale and the audience is less than straightforward and yet in many ways it has immeasurably more in common with the modern mass media than did Pete's friend's important news of 8 December 1980.

ACTIVITY . . .

Identify the sender(s) in the following communications:

■ The *Sun* newspaper

■ The film *Mission Impossible 2*

■ The campaign of TV advertisements for Budweiser beer

■ The Oasis album *Standing on the Shoulder of Giants*

■ The book *Harry Potter and the Goblet of Fire*

■ The television cartoon series *The Simpsons*

Identifying senders is significant in the sense that it has an impact on the way we respond to messages. This is why when advertisers choose to write advertising copy in the style of newspaper or magazine journalism, the words 'ADVERTISEMENT' or 'ADVERTISING FEATURE' declare this to be the case. Mass media communications are usually produced by complex teams but the industry is forever asking us to individualise and personalise its communications. Promoting films by means of their directors and stars is an example of this. It is easier to relate to Stanley Kubrick as sender than to the large numbers of people who were responsible for making *Eyes Wide Shut*.

Senders, in terms of their status and authority, are one factor that contributes to the building of audiences. Status here has a phatic function; it attracts attention. There are clearly types of text that are sold on the basis of the sender's identity. Advance orders of the latest release from popular bands, popular novelists or a film featuring a particular star are proof that sender status is a vital ingredient in mass media marketing.

PHATIC COMMUNICATION Aspects of language which serve to reinforce social relationships rather than to communicate information (e.g. 'Have a nice day').

Audiences are also built around certain kinds of message. We have previously discussed genre as an example of this, but the ways in which messages are composed work at more subtle levels as well. The process approach is always concerned to explore how communication can be made more efficient. For example, Gerbner's model focuses on the relationship between two aspects of a message: its form and its content. This explicitly acknowledges that there are a number of ways of communicating a given content, at the level of both medium and channel. What process theory is keen to suggest is that some forms are in specific cases better suited than others, and therefore that the job of the communicator is to find the best formal match for a particular content to a particular audience.

When evaluating the effectiveness of any piece of communication, we are partly engaging in this debate, placing the particular text in a paradigm of appropriateness for a particular context. It is clear that most communication texts are targeted at a specific (although not always specified) audience and equally clear that this is a contributing factor to the way in which texts and messages are composed. Equally clearly, this cannot be the last word on a process that is human and creative. Process models are used to evaluate communication in terms of its intentions and the degree to which those intentions are fulfilled. This may function as a useful starting point but it can all too easily limit both our response to texts and our understanding of their impact and effectiveness. What is intended is often clear or is easy to guess but what is achieved in and by a text is very often both more and less than its intention. There is a character in Ian McEwan's novel *A Child in Time* (1987) whose first novel becomes a surprise success just because it ends up on the wrong desk at a publisher and is released as a novel for teenagers and not, as intended, for adults. This is the problem with assuming that what was achieved in communication is what was intended to be communicated. Communication is invariably achieved, but there's often a big difference between the desired objective (intention) and the achieved result (outcome).

Consider the intended meaning of the promotional postcard below, issued by the National Union of Students. What do you think about this as a piece intended for students? What do you think the creators of this advertisement wanted to achieve?

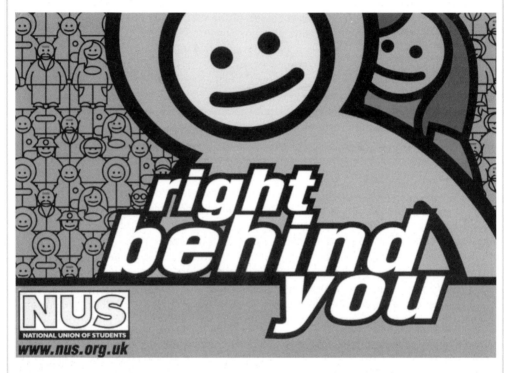

Figure 3.23 'Right behind You' postcard. Courtesy of the National Union of Students

Clearly, the audience are being asked to identify themselves with the images offered, either literally or in terms of a style to which they can relate. In its original form the text was brightly coloured, glossy and boasted high production values. The background images are regimented whilst the two foregrounded figures are close in an almost intrusive way as though they can't fit into the frame. All of these factors increase the interactivity of the text, the way in which the text encourages the receiver to actively engage with it. The degree to which this engagement is the norm in media communication gives the lie to arguments about audience passivity. In many adverts, for example, the audience is asked to find the desired meanings for themselves.

The increasing popularity of phone-in competitions and popular referendums on all manner of subjects is further proof of the activation of the mass audience. Because feedback is being built in here, there will be a crude increase in the effectiveness of communication. Within the terms of reference of the process school, feedback gives encoders information on how their messages are being received and therefore notionally the opportunity to improve them.

Feedback to print-based texts can be expressed in two main ways: the direct way which takes the form of filling in reply slips, donating money, or buying a book (for example); and the indirect way which sees the text as a starting point for various kinds of interpersonal and medio communication. This is partly the reason why shock and scandal are so effective because they stimulate indirect publicity. The advertising for the clothes firm Benetton has often courted such publicity, offering controversial campaigns which prompt massive amounts of indirect (and some direct) feedback. Moreover, developments in technology, and particularly the emergence of the Internet, have offered much greater opportunities for texts to be interactive because of the very fact that even with mass media texts the feedback can be almost instantaneous.

The phenomenon of *The Blair Witch Project* is a case in point, where a campaign begun by an Internet film reviewer almost unwittingly hyped this low-budget film to notoriety and international success. Here was a film which explicitly involved its audience in its promotion, its merchandising and its communication.

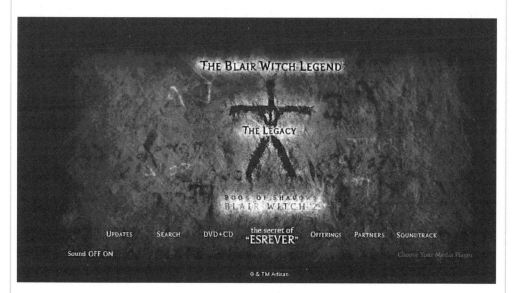

Figure 3.24 *Blair Witch website. www.blairwitch.com*

ACTIVITY . . .

Consider the specific ways in which the above website identifies and communicates with its audience. Who are they and how are they addressed?

For Gerbner the whole Blair Witch 'project' is a classic case of operations in the 'means and control' dimension. In Gerbner's terms the film's producers are simply selecting the most appropriate channels in the same way that any film is marketed. Gerbner's model cannot allow for (nor should we expect it to) the ability, granted largely by an unlicensed new medium, of the film's audience to 'hijack' this process and do it for themselves. Partly the audience for this reading comes from the difference in register between the website quoted and the conventional language of film promotion. They are almost different languages.

Halliday (1978) defines a register in three dimensions:

■ Formality/ informality
■ Technicality
■ Character as an essentially written or spoken 'dialect'

The register of the *Blair Witch Project* website is somewhat informal but significantly technical; it demands specialist knowledge. While it is in a real sense written, it is more properly a version of a spoken register, copying the patterns of speech. The extract below, taken from the video cover of the film *Titanic*, might stand as an example of a more conventional film promotion:

> Nothing on earth can rival the epic spectacle and breathtaking grandeur of *Titanic*. Winner of eleven Academy Awards® including Best Picture, this sweeping love story sailed into the hearts of moviegoers around the globe, ultimately emerging as the most popular motion picture of all time.
>
> International superstar Leonardo DiCaprio and Oscar®-nominee Kate Winslet light up the screen as Jack and Rose, the young lovers who find themselves on the maiden voyage of the 'unsinkable' R.M.S. *Titanic*. But when the doomed luxury liner collides with an iceberg in the frigid North Atlantic, their passionate love affair becomes a thrilling race for survival.

ACTIVITY . . .

Define the register of this piece in Halliday's terms. What differences are there between this and the earlier website register?

Register is intimately connected with the notion of mode of address, or the recognition that texts 'speak' to readers from predetermined positions using specific codes and registers. In choosing a register or even setting a register, a certain kind of relationship is being established, a set of conventions is being activated around which the text invites us to respond, even to judge. In the case of *The Blair Witch Project*, the mode of address is related to a documentary tradition of home-made film and thus our otherwise critical eyes are drawn away from technique and towards content. Its register is a strange mixture of the extremely informal, not to say amateurish, and highly technical in that the film is in fact engaged in a sophisticated discussion about the techniques and conventions of the horror genre itself.

REFLEXIVITY This describes what it is to be self-conscious, to be self-aware, and to reflect on who you are, what you're doing and how you present yourself in the world. It is a feature of much of contemporary communication that it is similarly conscious and aware. It is self-reflexive. In this way, for example, we are used to seeing films about the making of films, advertisements that play with the conventions of advertisements, and comedies that refer to the 'rules' of comedy.

In a process sense the film simply (and luckily) hit upon the most appropriate form for its treatment of its content. In a semiotic sense its reflexivity and openness as a text allowed a significant range of readings which in turn built an audience. One model that goes some way to integrating these positions is that of Roman Jakobson. Jakobson (1962) identifies six elements in communication. He arranges them in a primarily linear fashion:

	CONTEXT	
	MESSAGE	
ADDRESSER	CONTACT	ADDRESSEE
	CODE	

Diagram 3.3a Jakobson's elements of communication

He then goes on to link these six elements to the functions of communication by suggesting that within each communicative function a different element is dominant. He then arranges his six functions to correspond to the dominant element in the arrangement above.

	REFERENTIAL	
	POETIC	
EMOTIVE	PHATIC	CONATIVE
	METALINGUAL	

Diagram 3.3b Jakobson's functions of communication

- **The emotive function** communicates the sender's emotions, attitudes and status.
- **The conative function** prompts the receiver's response to the act of communication and encourages participation.
- **The referential function** communicates the relationship between the text and the wider reality, truth and fact.
- **The poetic function** communicates the text's formal and stylistic qualities.
- **The phatic function** establishes and maintains channels of communication.
- **The metalingual function** identifies the significant codes of the text.

Jakobson argues that whilst all of the above functions are co-existent in any act of communication, their importance varies according to the character of the individual act of communication being considered. A chat show guest's reminiscences of their childhood would be principally emotive; a stand-up comedian would hope to be chiefly conative; our experience of the news is likely to be referential; our enjoyment of an adaptation of a classic novel ought to be poetic (otherwise described by Jakobson more broadly as 'aesthetic'); much embarrassed communication on public transport with strangers is

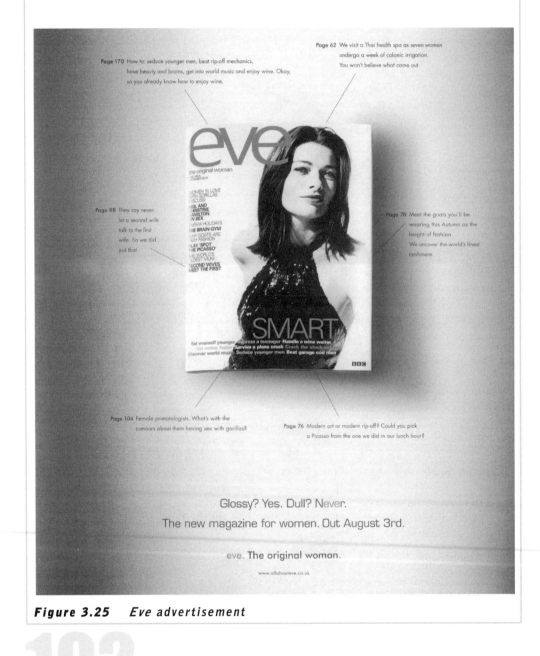

Figure 3.25 *Eve advertisement*

phatic; whenever we enquire of the geographical origin of an English speaker we are engaged in the metalingual function of communication. Jakobson offers a structuralist insight into the character of communication in a linear context and offers us as readers a useful and, in terms of the two approaches, a largely non-partisan approach.

ACTIVITY . . .

Identify Jakobson's six elements and six functions within (the *Eve* advertisement opposite). Which do you personally consider especially significant in this example?

▼   6   **PUTTING IT BACK TOGETHER**

In this section we will be demonstrating the use of techniques of textual analysis on actual texts.

- We will take you through an in-depth analysis of a couple of print texts.
- We will give you advice on planning and writing responses to texts.

We have broken down the communication process into its component parts. It is now time to start putting it all back together again. This section will offer you examples of the sort of analysis you will be asked to undertake as a student of communication. This section is principally about demonstration – of a method, of a way of thinking, of a critical process. It will deal with a range of texts and the principal tasks you will face.

The process of looking at, engaging with, and ultimately analysing texts is a logical and straightforward one. It requires you first of all to examine what you are offered in an open, honest and personal way and then to use that information along with the specific knowledge and experience provided by your course of study, and/or this text, to push that response further. It is a subjective and objective approach, usually in that order but most often in an integrated fashion. Having asked 'What do I think about this text?', you are expected to consider 'How else could this text be considered or interpreted?' Sometimes this 'how else' makes you reconsider your own initial position, sometimes not. It is perhaps useful to see this process in terms of a series of actions:

- **Look**: What is it? How does it impact on you?
- **Read**: What does it say? What does it consist of?
- **Explore/analyse**: How is it structured? How does it work?
- **Review**: What do I think of it now? Is it as I originally thought?
- **Respond**: Here are my considered thoughts, feelings, opinions.

FIRST IMPRESSIONS

It is vital to record your first impressions of the texts you are asked to work with. In most cases this initial engagement is all a text has in its original, 'real world' context. Because much of the material produced by the mass media is genuinely ephemeral (i.e. here today and gone tomorrow), first impressions are sometimes all that a text is intended to receive. The article opposite appeared in *Q* magazine, taking up approximately one third of page 28 within an issue of 164 pages. What is your first impression?

It is likely that your first impression was some kind of response to the striking, full-length image of an attractive young woman. This is clearly the intention of the article's designer, given that the girl's picture takes up more than half of the allotted space, is head and shoulders above the accompanying text, and is photographed in a way that accentuates her prominence, dominance and her literal length. You may also have been struck by the reference in the headline to Ted Hughes, the former Poet Laureate. Stereotypically we are perhaps being asked to be surprised at the juxtaposition of this attractive young woman and poetry.

At this point it is useful to be able accurately to classify the text with which we are dealing. Lasswell (1948) is useful in this respect, inviting the identification of sender, message, receiver, channel and effect. In the case of the *Q* article, the responses could be:

Who?	*Q* Magazine
Says what?	Jewel's book of poems is out in May
To whom?	*Q* readers, contemporary music enthusiasts
In what channel?	A news/feature article
With what effect?	They know about, are amused by, or have received opinions about Jewel's poetry

These responses can then be supported or challenged with reference to conventional communication practice within the identified medium and/or channel. The confirmation question runs something like 'What makes this an article in a music magazine?' (If we didn't know, on what basis would we guess?) In this case our evidence might include: the relationship between images and text; the way in which the central image breaks the border; the bold text headline; the hierarchy of types; the caption image; the youthspeak vocabulary; and the energetic and economic register of the text.

It is not always this straightforward, but the process is always about looking for those aspects of a given text which it shares with other texts you have looked at. Moreover, it is important to remember that the sort of critical analysis you are engaged in is not about producing correct answers but rather about producing meaningful responses. Dealing with anonymous texts is a matter for intelligent deduction not hopeful guesswork. To identify

Who Needs Ted Hughes?

When a ropey pop star poetry book sells two – yes, that's right – *two* million copies.

A Night Without Armor, Jewel's book of poetry, has now sold over two million copies in United States.

According to the preface, the Alaskan-born singer "explores the fire of first love, the fading of passion, the giving of trust, the lessons of betrayal and the healing of intimacy" in the book. A sample poem is A Couple Sitting On A Beach which consists of four simple lines: "He's the skinny one of the two/He reminds her of it constantly/He's a very funny guy that way/Ha-ha as she wobbles-to-walk wobbles-to-walk."

A Night Without Armor is published by Harper Collins in the UK in May. Meanwhile Jewel is also making her acting debut later this year in a new Ang Lee film, Ride With The Devil.

Jewel: Shall I compare thee to, like, a really nice leaf?

Figure 3.26 'Who Needs Ted Hughes?', *Q* magazine, no. 151, April 1999, p. 28. Courtesy of *Q* magazine

the precise source is not the issue; to appreciate the characteristics of a text is far more important.

We are now becoming interested in this *Q* article, given we have engaged with it both in terms of the initial impact and in terms of how it fits into a genre. The next stage is to consider in detail what we are in fact being offered. It is useful here to think in terms of the dominant signifiers, the dominant syntagms and the significant paradigms, and codes that are at work in the text.

In an almost arithmetical way we are considering the different ways in which the meaning of the article might be calculated or totalled. This process might start at a formal level in the equation:

$$IMAGES + WORDS = TEXT$$

In the text in question, this bears considerable fruit, for it asks us to see a relationship between the dominant image (full length, colour, half article size), the secondary image (close-up, black and white, miniature inset) and the words. A single reading of the article is enough simply to reveal this relationship.

This is, in essence, a narrative – a story that transports us from image A to image B, or crudely from a state of ignorance to a state of knowledge. Having got the formal structure worked out, we can get into the detail: of the significant syntagm which is the first image; of the text in terms of its register, its vocabulary, its mode of address, its bias; and of the book cover as a conventional representation of 'serious' writing and 'serious' writers. This stage, however, is simply setting the agenda, uncovering interesting issues of representation, of narrative and of genre. It is also appropriate at this stage to identify the dominant codes, which in this case are largely non-verbal and verbal.

KEY TERM

NARRATIVE   The way in which a text reveals information to the audience in order to create a 'story'.

HOW SHOULD I MARK UP (ANNOTATE) THE TEXT?

Clearly, this preparatory work on texts requires significant annotation of the texts themselves. Start on a separate sheet and sketch the general relationships, for example the proportions of text and the positions of images. Once you approach the details of a text, the most appropriate place to work is on and around it, exploding general points to either side, above and below.

DECODING WHAT'S THERE

Paradigms are those collections of signs from which we make selections. The signs chosen are then ordered into chains that we call syntagms. Identifying these paradigms is therefore a useful way of revealing something of the process of construction. In the *Q* article

COMMUNICATION STUDIES: THE ESSENTIAL INTRODUCTION

two images are used which are taken from the same paradigm – the paradigm of available images of the singer Jewel (this paradigm is in itself part of a broader paradigm of representations of women).

Clearly, these images, be they of Jewel or of women generally, come from very different parts of these respective paradigms. In fact, the preferred reading is probably to see them as opposites, a fact that is reinforced by the use of technical codes (colour versus black and white; medium shot versus close-up). It is our job, however, to explore beyond the dominant discourse, to refuse to take the stereotypes at face value. For while the cover of Jewel's book is a study in understated convention (serious facial expression, face cleared of unruly hair, dark clothing, wordy backdrop, title positioned to avoid any hint of cleavage), the full length 'Girls just want to have fun' shot has more to say if we are prepared to look.

Unanchored this could easily be a fashion catalogue shot or even part of a sequence for a Lads magazine. In the context of an article amazed at the success of Jewel's 'ropey pop star poetry book', it is simply meant to describe the antithesis of 'poet'. The caption ('Shall I compare thee to, like, a really nice leaf?') makes this clear. Jewel is just an ordinary girl – vain, superficial and unsophisticated. What this anchor activates is one set of dominant signifiers which adds up to 'silly girl out to have fun' or worse. At the same time it de-activates any part of the image which might contradict or oppose this reading, any factors which might in fact empower Jewel or suggest she is in control of her own communication. Yet these elements are present if we care to look for them and the conversation between 'Jewel as fool' and 'Jewel as cool' can be referenced in practice in this way:

Jewel as fool:	Jewel as cool:
Flick of hair across the face is flirty	Hair unkempt suggests refusal to conform
Blondish hair connotes stereotype bimbo	Facial expression is defiant, confident; challenging gaze engages reader
Open coat reveals breast	Clothing is deliberately and ironically trashy
Navel is exposed	Disguised thumbs-up is indication of knowingness
Short skirt has stereotypical connotations	Slouching posture: refuses to be pin-up
Plastic mac is sexy in an obvious way	Long legs are accentuated
Posture is open-legged, available	Posture is confident
Active foot indicates playfulness, coyness	Trainers are a key signifier, denying the stereotypes of girls in short skirts: they are practical, enabling
Jewel is just another pop bimbette	**Jewel knows what she is doing**

Thus we can see that the image is in fact potentially more problematic than the preferred reading will allow, and we are learning a little more about mass communication. At this point you usually have a couple of sides of notes and hopefully half the time allotted for the task left for presenting your response. The starting point for this phase should be your review of the evidence you have uncovered, from first impressions onward, arriving ultimately back at your considered impression of the text. Sometimes your opinion has not significantly changed; either way this kind of general response is a sound place to start your written critique.

Rather than labouring a point, let's review the process by quickly responding to a new text illustrated opposite. Here are the key questions or prompts with some suggested responses (these responses are not exclusive; they are not the only valid responses).

LOOK: What are my first impressions? What is it?

It's brightly coloured and attractive, even jolly. It's an organised collage of images. These are and this is The SIMS. It's a package design for a CD-ROM computer disc. The sender is whoever makes The Sims.

READ: What does it say? What does it consist of?

Formally, some computer graphics, some design work and some words. In terms of content it is saying 'Here it is, come and get it!' to a youngish/not too old audience. It wants us to buy the CD. Colour is clearly important: clear, bright, well defined.

EXPLORE/ANALYSE: How is it structured? How does it work?

The dominant signifiers are the words and the human figures. A dominant code is characterisation, we are being asked to see these human figures as a cast of characters (or rather a small part of one).

Much of the intended meaning of the cover depends on the degree to which you are able to read the character types, or stereotypes. Stereotypes are moulds into which we pour our experiences: in this case they are exploited to communicate a more general effect. Here are representations of men and women, young and old, which are deliberately easy to read. They do have a range from The Robber, complete with swag bag bottom left to the unspecified man centre right or woman at top left.

Essentially the represenations are iconic, though with limited motivation, and this allows a range of visual humour and an informal register and mode of address. The costumes are recognisable, the facial expressions are dramatic but in this context amusing. They appear to be in on some kind of joke that we're not quite aware of.

REVIEW: What do I think of it now? Is it as I initially thought?

An attractive and amusing text, whose function is principally phatic. This is The SIMS, a people simulator, but also these are the Sims, potentially new friends. The strap-line under the roofed title offers us a sort of kitemark with 'from the Creator of SimCity'. The copyright symbols also offer a suggestion of value and quality.

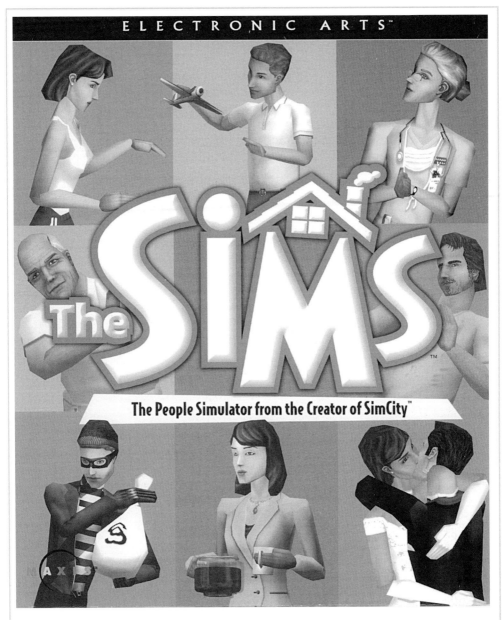

Figure 3.27 *The Sims, courtesy Electronic Arts*

RESPOND: Writing it up

Having made a structured response to any given text, you will be required to present this in a specific way. Conventionally this will have one of the following complications.

■ A word limit of, say, 300 words

- The need to submit your response in note form
- A specific form and/or audience (for example, prepare as a hand-out for A Level students)

In all of these cases it will be important to plan your response so that you offer your reading in the most convincing way and so that you miss out nothing important. It will be important to read the task carefully to discover what precisely is required. The best way to do this is physically to underline the key words of the task and then write down the implications of each of the words or phrases you have underlined. In other words, write in your own words what bearing each of these words should have on your response.

In terms of the relatively straightforward word-limited critique, the important thing to do is to avoid mere description and to ensure significant analysis is offered. This can be aided by the way you structure your response, which will of course be into a series of paragraphs. The first and last paragraphs largely take care of themselves. The first paragraph should provide an overview and/or an account of your initial impressions; the last paragraph should leave the examiner with a summary of your considered opinions on the qualities and effectiveness of the text. In between the body of the analysis you need to detail the three significant stages of analysis – classifying the text; deciding what's communicating; and decoding/exploring meanings. If you work on 50 words at each end and 50 to 100 words in each paragraph in between, you'll get a feeling for the proportions of your piece. Our response to the Sims cover would have the following plan, working towards 300 words.

1 **First impressions**   humour, colour, computer graphics

2 **What's there?**   syntagms: words and pictures
                            representation: gender, age, ethnicity-icons
                            setting: index of abstract design
                            anchorage: sets agenda

3 **What does it mean?**   dominant code: representation
                            paradigms: stereotypes
                            signification: connotation/myth

4 **Final thoughts**   relationships within visuals/between characters
                            relatively sophisticated text, skilful, successful

Another way of demanding a lot of analysis in a fairly short time is the recourse to note form. It is vital that you understand that this is what the game's about. The essence is your analysis of the text, the note form is an examination mechanism for you to express yourself in a quicker and hopefully clearer way. The function of your note form, therefore, is to 'showcase' your analysis clearly and economically. The hope is that you will cut through the verbiage to the key critical and technical vocabulary, not that you will limit the analysis by limiting the vocabulary. Clearly, note form requires techniques and devices (for example bullet points, sub-headings, variety of type, underlining, use of space and layout), but in this context it principally requires analysis, detail and depth.

Note form analysis of CD-ROM cover

First impressions: colourful, engaging (phatic device)
                               title is pun (play on words)
                               humorous (words and pictures)

What is it?   Who?: Electronic Arts
                               Says what?: Here's a new computer simulation
                               To whom?: the great PC-owning public
                               In what channel?: a CD-ROM package
                               With what effect?: we see it, we buy it

What does it consist of?

   SYNTAGM 1:   some words (anchors and advertises)
                               some figures (iconic Robber to young man)
                               a background (index of 'showcasing'/windowdressing)

The third sort of task is more difficult to predict but it is once again an examiner's trick for testing your skill in analysing texts and your knowledge of how texts work. Here you are asked to present part or all of your analysis in some creative way for some designated audience, for example the summary sheet for students we discussed earlier. In this kind of task there are potentially two sets of considerations: (a) the conventions of the designated form must be addressed; and (b) the specific needs of the specified audience must be considered. In the case of the summary sheet, given there are no agreed conventions, it is simply a matter of making sure that what you produce is:

■   a sheet (and the example task specified this as A4)
■   a summary of the material

Audience is a slightly more problematic variable, as it is likely to dictate the register of the whole response, the choice of language, and the sophistication of the content. One way to ensure that audience is considered substantially is to try and imagine the response from the audience's point of view and to then write down what kind of response you think they would want. You might do this by suggesting adjectives, say five of them, which would best describe the kind of response the audience would want. For example, if you were asked to devise a revision sheet on 'the categories of sign' based on evidence from the Sims CD box video cover for your fellow students, you might come up with a list like this:

What kind of sheet will they want?

1   easy-to-follow
2   technical
3   well-evidenced
4   confident
5   attractive

This then becomes part of your brief for the revision sheet, a sort of blueprint. While the likeliest audience for such a task would be your peers, you could be asked to produce work for children of all ages or maybe adults keen to learn about semiotics. In all cases remember that what is being tested is your knowledge of critical techniques and your ability to respond to texts.

▼ 7 SOME PRINT TEXTS AND SAMPLE TASKS

In this section you will have the opportunity to respond to a range of print texts for yourself. Each text is accompanied by a set of prompts.

In the final section you will have the opportunity to try out your developing critical skills on a range of print-based texts. In each case you will be provided with a series of prompts to stimulate your response and then one or more examination-style tasks.

What you will realise, looking across a range of very different texts, is that it is experience of the method, of the specific tools, that is needed and not necessarily experience of the potentially vast range of texts. In other words, it matters that you have looked at texts, not that you have looked at a specific variety of text. What you also need is genuine and honest engagement with texts and this is clearly helped by them being unseen and unprepared.

Figure 3.28 *Egg Card advertisement, www.egg.com*

Prompts:

- What is the dominant signifier?
- What is the relationship between the upper and lower parts of the advertisement?
- How does the design of the bottom half work?
- Who is the intended audience?

ACTIVITY . . .

Prepare an Overhead Projector Transparency (OHT) which sums up the strengths and weaknesses of this advertisement as a piece of effective communication.

ARTEFACT B: COMIC BOOK PAGE

Prompts:

- How does this text work?
- What are its chief components?
- Comment on representation in this text.
- Comment on the register of this text.
- What are the functions of colour here?

ACTIVITY . . .

Prepare a set of notes for a five-minute presentation to your fellow A Level students entitled 'Comic Book Communication' which uses page 115 as your only source of evidence.

A very different kind of cartoon communication is provided each day in all newspapers – the political cartoon. Here the issue of representation is made more interesting by the fact that many of those represented are 'known'. The first task of the cartoonist is therefore to create a likeness or exaggerated caricature of the public figure which the audience will recognise. This is often achieved by a combination of iconic and indexical features, wherein the exaggeration of key features (e.g. the ears of Prince Charles) and the use of significant props (e.g. the Queen's crown in an inappropriate context) combine to create a signifier that is identifiable with its intended signified at the level of denotation but which also carries with it implicit connotations.

Figure 3.29 *Illustration from Alan Moore and Dave Gibbons,
The Watchmen* (Titan Books Ltd, 1987)

ARTEFACT C: POLITICAL CARTOON

Figure 3.30 'The Four Stages of Royal Life' by Scrank from the *Independent on Sunday, 6 August 2000*

Prompts:

- Comment on the presentation of each of the four 'royals'.
- What is the 'meaning' of the pea pictured bottom right?
- What is the effect of the caption?
- What attitude to royalty does this cartoon have?

Note: this cartoon appeared in the week the Queen Mother reached the age of 100.

ACTIVITY . . .

You have been asked to explain Peirce's three sign categories (icon, index and symbol) for a Communication Studies textbook like this one. You have been allowed 150 words in total, and the above cartoon has been provided as evidence. You should take your illustrative examples from here only.

ARTEFACT D: PROMOTIONAL POSTCARD

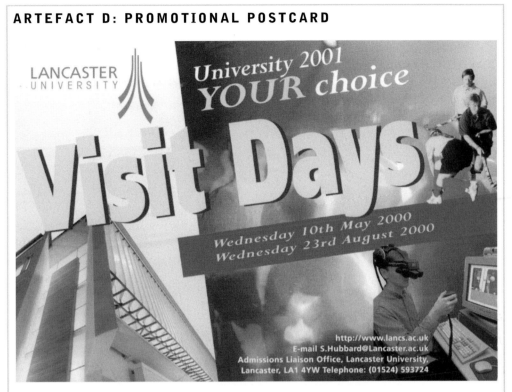

Figure 3.31 *Lancaster University flyer. Courtesy of Lancaster University*

Prompts:

- Comment on the title 'Visit Days'.
- What is the purpose of the division of the card?
- What is the meaning of the computing image?
- What are we being offered here?

ACTIVITY . . .

In 250 words justify the design of this postcard, pointing out the ways in which it positively represents the university and the experience of university life.

ARTEFACT E: GREETINGS CARD

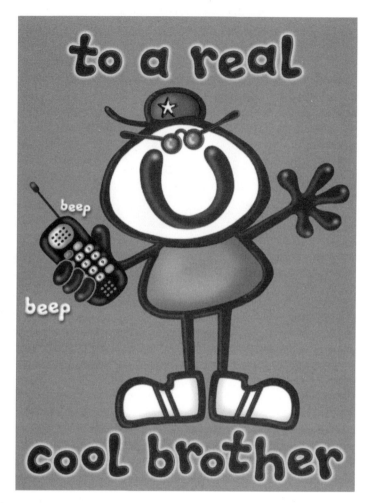

Figure 3.32 *Planet Happy card*

Prompts:

- Comment on the way the words are arranged on the page.
- What sort of representation are we being offered?
- What is the function of the mobile phone?
- What is the register and function of this cover?

Prepare a design for a 'real cool sister' card and annotate semiotically to demonstrate the nature of the communication you are conducting. Identify the significant paradigms, the character of the signs used, and the preferred reading. Present your design and analysis within a single A4 side.

ARTEFACT F: SCREENPLAY

The following is the first page of the published teleplay of *Karaoke*, the first of Dennis Potter's final two pieces for television written just before, and with the knowledge of, his impending death in June 1994.

PART ONE

KARAOKE SCREEN

Against montages of images with some relevance to the music (teenagers kiss, jive, drive chrome-fendered-and-finned cars, etc.) the words of the song come upon the lower half of the screen, in English, sandwiched by Japanese.

> **Why must I be**
> **A teenager in love?**

At the same time, from the start, a male voice is singing, badly, with an East End accent, the same words as they march across the screen, darkening on cue.

Pull out and pan across.

INT. WEST END KARAOKE AND HOSTESS CLUB. NIGHT

Panning past other karaoke screens showing the same patterns and text, past a big table of grinning Japanese businessmen, to find the singer, ARTHUR ('PIG') MAILION, a bald, bull-necked heavy in his late forties, bellowing ludicrously inappropriate words with no sign of irony or any hint of loss of an obviously high self-regard. He wears a gaudily striped tie, in bad taste.

MAILION: [Singing]

> **Each time we have a quarrel**
> **It almost breaks my heart**
> **'Cos I am so afraid**
> **That we will have to part —**

continued

INT. A TABLE. THE CLUB. NIGHT

As MAILION *continues to bellow, a middle-aged (English) businessman pulls a comic face, addressing* SANDRA, *a young and sexily clad* HOSTESS. *They have champagne.*

BUSINESSMAN: God in heaven. Must be *yonks* since he was a teenager. In or out of love.

[SANDRA *is either bored or unwell*]

SANDRA: [*Flat*] Yeah. Well. There you go.
BUSINESSMAN: If he keeps this up, he'll empty the place.
SANDRA: [*Same tones*] He can do what he likes, can't he?

Prompts:

■ Comment on the ways in which typography distinguishes between different kinds of text.

■ Examine the language heard by the audience.

■ Comment briefly on the three characters presented in this extract. How are we given information about them?

■ What is a 'montage'?

ACTIVITY . . .

Comment on the different kinds of language and typography used on this page. What is the relationship between language and typography?

ARTEFACT G: WEBSITE HOME PAGE

Figure 3.33 *Routledge Media Arena website*

Prompts:

- In what ways is the experience of the web page different from that of this book?
- What are the primary conventions of a website home page?
- In what ways does the text establish its authority?
- What are the weaknesses of this format?

ACTIVITY . . .

Select a website home page and consider the different ways in which it attempts to target its audience. Consider also the barriers it might be putting up to those it does not wish/intend to target.

FURTHER EXAMPLES

It seems corny to say so, but if you want examples just look around. Communication texts are around you and among you – from the cereal packets you absentmindedly read at breakfast to the books or magazines you read before you go to sleep. All have their messages, their devices, their conventions and their idiosyncrasies. All await the careful reader. A list of places to start might include:

- Leaflets: look at a range from those which inform you about sexually transmitted diseases to those which offer you *English Heritage* or *The National Trust*
- Flyers: from adverts for Dial-a-Pizza to local band promotions
- Brochures: from college prospectuses to luxury car specifications
- Magazines: from *F.H.M.* to *The People's Friend*
- Newspapers: from free papers to 'The Free Press'
- Advertisements: from matchbooks to billboards
- Posters: from Che Guevara to Baby Spice
- Book jackets: from Harry Potter to Dennis Potter
- CD covers: from Westlife to Parklife
- Websites: from *The Blair Witch Project* to Tony Blair.com
- Scripts: from screenplays to school plays
- Storyboards: from *Chicken Run* to *Logan's Run*
- Postcards: from college promotions to seaside humour
- Greetings cards: from 'It's a Boy!' to 'With Deepest Sympathy'
- Packaging materials: from cereal packets to shop liveries

This is not a list to alarm you but rather to remind you of the vital part played by communication texts in our lives. To be aware of this is in itself a step towards being an effective critic.

1   Consider the ways in which an organisation with which you are familiar (e.g. your school/college, place of work or worship, your preferred nightclub) presents itself in terms of the texts it offers wittingly and unwittingly to be read. Contrast the formal/direct communication (prospectuses, open days, slogans) with the informal/indirect communication (relationships, premises, reputation). Suggest ways in which your chosen organisation might improve its communication.

2   Using any medium or combination of media, present a guided tour of a specified part of your local area. Present the material in the manner of a reading, offering interpretation that might be historical, cultural, political and/or aesthetic, that is, choose what you want the guide to do – inform, entertain, persuade, advertise, or all of these. Present your new text to an audience of local people and evaluate its impact.

3   Responding to and interpreting practical texts is an essential way of drawing together the various elements of a Communication Studies course. By considering the variety of communication, you are implicitly responding to the cultural question 'What is communication?' Which definition of communication best fits the experience you have of the range of texts we have considered, from the built environment to body modification?

4   The writer Virginia Woolf claimed that 'what a female writer writes is always feminine: the difficulty is in defining what is feminine'. How far do you think it is useful to talk about communication texts as masculine and feminine?

5   The whole pattern of social life is being radically altered by developments in Communication and Information Technology, particularly in terms of the Internet and e-mail. To what extent has this changed the character of our experience of communication texts? (What difference has it made to our social lives, working lives and relationships to traditional mass media?)

FURTHER READING

Fiske, J. (1990) *Introduction to Communication Studies*, 2nd edn, London/New York: Routledge.

Guiraud, P. (1975) *Semiology*, trans. G. Gross, London: Routledge & Kegan Paul.

Hawkes, T. (1977) *Structuralism and Semiotics*, London: Routledge.

O'Sullivan, T., Hartley, J., Saunders, D., Montgomery, M. and Fiske, J. (1994) *Key Concepts in Communication and Cultural Studies*, 2nd edn, London/New York: Routledge.

Williams, R. (1962) *Communications*, Harmondworth: Penguin.

PART 4: COMMUNICATION PRACTICE

In this part we will attempt to put the communication skills and effective communication advice into a practical context.

- We will work through a sample AS-style project.

- We will look at the skills of research, planning, writing and reviewing in the context of a coherent practical investigation

Here we're going to look at how you can prepare to take part in, to observe and to analyse 'live' communication. You will be able to bring these skills of participation, observation and analysis to the preparation and development of your own communications – verbal, written, presentational and representational.

For example, in AQA's AS Communication Studies specification, students are required to conduct an investigation into an aspect of communication skills. The unit has four elements of assessment:

1 A 500 word research 'essay' (for 'essay' you should read 'report')
2 The preparation materials and visual support materials for a ten minute oral presentation to interested other people (fellow students)
3 The oral presentation itself
4 A 500 word review

GENERAL ADVICE

In a sense the first piece of advice has been given implicitly: look first at what you have to do, clearly identifying what's required of you, what the tasks demand of you. These task demands will define the scope, character and substance of your research. Five hundred words at AS level is a significant challenge, if only because there will not be the room to write at such length that you might arrive at the required standard. Five hundred words should act as a cue, a prompt. It may be saying:

- Be modest in the choice and scope of your investigation; what you find out cannot use more than 500 words to explain.

- Carefully draft and redraft your essay: economy and concision are valued; so carefully choose your words.
- Remember the standard is AS; it is based on what a 17-year-old student can be expected to achieve after one year (or less) of study.

These are important messages, and understanding them can make a significant difference to your achievement. As students of communication, you are always being asked to communicate about communication. We live in a world of communication texts and coursework assignments are classic, formal examples of decidable texts. Questions, tasks and assignment titles are written to allow candidates to demonstrate their knowledge and understanding of communication principles but they are not always entirely transparent. They do not set out to trip up candidates but with wit and experience you can learn to read them for the support they often give. By looking for the implications of what is said and the particular words used, you can often get a feeling for a task.

GETTING STARTED

It is useful to appreciate the spirit of a piece of assessment, for in this you might find clues as to how the assessment should be approached. For example, if the audience for the task is young, then an implication might be that the approach you require is a lively and adventurous one. To see the emphasis of a piece of assessment, we need to know its context. In the case of AS Communication Studies unit 1, the context is the module's content, which might usefully be summarised as:

- Knowledge and understanding of communication skills
- Perspectives and techniques
- Skills of investigation and research
- Note-making and oral presentation skills
- Exploration of conventions of communication and communications
- Importance of non-verbal communication
- Skills of evaluation

This part focuses on skills, methods and techniques. The Communication Practice module prioritises skills and the unit test (a coursework 'portfolio') rewards both practical work and theoretical perspectives. Fifty per cent of the unit marks are given directly to practical work, to the preparation for and delivery of an oral presentation. In spite of the fact that investigations can be 'theoretical or practical', the clear emphasis enshrined in the module title is on 'introducing communication practice'. It might be possible to research academically the best way to haggle over the price of a pair of jeans with a market trader. It would be more relevant to the spirit of this unit to observe the process at first hand and to draw some conclusions about what is going on.

The module offers a wide range of choices and the difficulty comes in heeding our earlier advice – be modest. You are asked to consider skilled (or unskilled) communication wherever you may find it. The list of example skills here is both general and only a starting point. So, when looking at this list, treat the advice 'be modest' as 'be focused' or 'specialise'.

- Speaking, listening and empathising
- Reading and observing
- Identifying and using sources of information
- Drafting and writing
- Planning and structuring a presentation
- Oral presentation skills
- Dealing with questions
- Reviewing own performance
- Using IT to communicate

This is a general list of communication skills rather than a list telling you precisely what to investigate. This is positive as, in the best traditions of coursework, it throws both choice of content (the human text) and task open to you the candidate. Clearly, an investigation of 'speaking' as a skill could hardly be condensed into 500 words. On the other hand, the study of an individual speaker in an individual context or an investigation into strategies by which conversations are joined or started would be focused, individual and thus ideal. The emphasis here is on the specific, on the observed, the experience of communication and the skills and methods of the researcher. Sometimes it is best to start with a context and work back to a skill. The examples of context given in the specification are quite predictable and not particularly unusual:

- Classroom
- Interviews
- The workplace
- The family
- Leisure activities
- Shops
- Media texts

If one takes these as starting points, infinite possibilities begin to reveal themselves. 'Leisure activities' includes all manner of genuinely interesting communication locations: night clubs, sports grounds, concert venues, even the back seat of your car. All of these in all their permutations have their own dynamic. 'Media texts' also turns out to be a goldmine. The opportunity offered here is to open up film clips, television episodes, even newsreel to a communication skills analysis. What were the problems with Robert De Niro's character's communication with the Cybil Shepherd character in Martin Scorsese's *Taxi Driver*? What are the key communication skills required by a vampire slayer given the evidence of Buffy?

REAL LIFE CONTEXTS, REAL LIFE TEXTS

In keeping with the whole of AS, the starting point must be to start from where you are. AS Communication Studies is essentially about your immediate experiences of communication; as sender and receiver of messages; as a member of a modern society surrounded and bombarded by communication texts; as a student of communication, investigating its forms and functions. A key to understanding communication practice is to make the connection between real life contexts and real life texts. Two sets of 'real life' experiences are privileged here:

- **Real life contexts**: places and situations in which communication takes place
- **Real life texts**: the extra, McLuhan would say 'extended', experience we have of communication, both directly and indirectly, as a result of our interaction with texts: films, television, music CDs, virtual reality, various forms of advertising

Marshall McLuhan (1964) incisively described the mass media as 'an extension of our senses' and it is in this spirit that texts are here engaged. We consider them not as text but rather as repositories of communication data, as stores of communication experience. We consider them not as representations but rather as presentations. In this sense a film like *Titanic* can be used in the same way as a family home video, or as CCTV footage can be used as a means of looking at people in town centres making out or fighting.

Clearly, there is some difference between communication in our lives and communication in media texts. Partly it is a difference between undirected and directed performance. However, the essence of this difference is not easy to identify and, as we shall see in Part 5, a leading account of 'self-presentation' (the processes by which we bring ourselves to the world) suggests that when we communicate we are always staging a 'performance'. The theorist Erving Goffman, whose work is discussed in detail in section 5 of Part 5, expressed it as follows: 'All the world is not, of course, a stage, but the crucial ways in which it is not are not easy to specify' (Goffman 1990).

The stimulus of 'real life' leads you in two directions: to a method that is genuinely investigative and exploratory (which really wants to find something out) and to a content that is found in your life and your experiences. If you are wondering where precisely to look, the following 'lives' might prove useful:

- **Home life**: what do you do when you're home alone; the things you watch and think about and listen to and write; the games you play
- **Family life**: your immediate home context; your primary group; those people with whom you live and to whom you are connected
- **Working life**: where you go to do what you have to do; the work you do and the people you do it with
- **Social life**: where you go to do the things you like to do; the people you like to see; the places you like to go; the things you like to do

ACTIVITY . . .

Make simple lists of possible investigations into each of the following lives, alongside ours:

Home life

- What are the communication skills needed to use a PC effectively?
- Which communication skills, if any, does playing computer games develop?
- What skills are demonstrated by successful television presenters?

- What is the difference, skillwise, between an effective performance of a song and an ineffective one?

Family life

- How effective are members of your family at listening to one another?
- What techniques does your brother/sister use when avoiding or arranging dates on the phone?
- How could you communicate more effectively with all or any of your family members?

Working life

- Examine the different ways your teachers use questions.
- What communication skills does an effective teacher/student need?
- How does the way in which you speak differ between work and home (both in what you say and in how you say it)?

Social life

- What communication skills do you need to attract potential partners in a crowded nightclub?
- What sorts of communication skill do bands employ between and around performing songs?
- What do you need to become an enthusiastic and committed sports spectator?

TITLES, QUESTIONS AND HYPOTHESES

Having arrived at some kind of focus, the investigation can begin. The AS specification suggests that candidates will 'formulate an appropriate title, question or hypothesis'. It may be as well to hedge your bets and go for all three, given that they can each be potentially used to tighten the focus of the investigation. The title is simply a signpost which tells of the general area of concern, for example 'communication in nightclubs' or 'my mum's phone technique'. The question, in keeping with much of this part's advice, takes this a step further by first asking you what you want or need to know. It then provides an answer in the form of an avenue of enquiry: 'How important are verbal skills in the nightclub context?' or 'Is my mum's telephone technique skilful?' The hypothesis is a step further still in that it asks you to make public your expectations for the investigation and to offer them to be proved either sound or mistaken. A hypothesis is a theory offered in the form of a proposal put forward to be examined for its validity. In the quoted examples, sample hypotheses might be 'verbal communication in nightclubs is almost entirely phatic in function' (it opens channels and maintains them) or 'my mum is a very skilful communicator by phone'.

Formulate questions and hypotheses for the following investigations:

- A teacher's questioning skills
- Skills for interviews
- Mr Bean's communication problems
- Listening as a skill for students
- Computer games and communication skills

It is important to know why you are working and what you are working towards. This coursework project is concerned with observing communication in practice, so it is vital to know what you are looking for and where you are looking from. Like much of communication practice, the key is good preparation. If you need to observe communication, you need to be prepared to record the available evidence effectively and at the same time be aware of the limitations of any such observation.

OBSERVATION: THEORY AND PRACTICE

Every investigation will be different and each investigation will require its own specific approach. However, there will be general principles that apply across most cases. The first is an ethical issue concerning the obligations you, as a researcher, have to the subject(s) of the investigation. The British Psychological Society has a code of practice which relates to psychological research and which states that 'Psychologists shall normally carry out investigations . . . with the consent of the participants.' It goes on to suggest that participants should have 'adequate knowledge of the nature of the investigation or research'. Even where it is not possible to give full information about the work in advance (for example, where this would interfere with the research), researchers are expected to 'provide such full information retrospectively'. Research into people's communication skills is unlikely to be as sensitive but these are sound principles from which to work.

Working with your subject(s) is a good place to start your plans for observation. Having participants who are at their ease being observed is likely to make the observation more comfortable and thus more successful. Clearly, your methods of observation will be determined by your subjects and context, but all methods have their advantages and disadvantages. We must start by recognising that observers do have an influence on what is observed and then think of ways in which this can be minimised, controlled or taken into account. Here are a number of ways you can improve the quality of your observations:

- **Become a participant in the observed activity**. Participant observation puts you into the thick of the action and allows you to see the demonstration of skills first hand. It also potentially puts the subject at ease in that the observer is not a conspicuous external presence. The disadvantages have to do with the difficulty of trying to observe an activity whilst taking part in it (this might be helped by recording the activity on video or minidisc or audio cassette).

- **Allow the subject to site the observer**. 'Where do you want me to sit?' is often a productive starting point. It allows the subject to deal with their own difficulties in their own way (and being observed is always to some extent 'difficult'). This might not allow the best view of the activity but it will help to create a conducive atmosphere.

- **Observe over a long period**. Even if your intensive observation is to be over a short period, an extended attendance at the observed activity will break down barriers. Hopefully you will become a fixture of the situation and thus less of an obstacle.

- **Record your activity**. A recording is a useful prompt to memory rather than something to analyse in itself. A minidisc or Walkman recorder is an unobtrusive way to collect evidence of verbal communication and the sequence of events. Video cameras seem especially intrusive at first, but if left on they tend to 'disappear'. However, it's worth recognising that video cameras only see what is in front of them, so you do get a significantly limited view.

Obviously this is not a problem if you have chosen to analyse behaviour displayed in a film or video, though you are of course watching communication that knows in an obvious way it is being observed. With or without these interventions, the other significant factor in the quality of observation argument is the preparation you make for the kind of evidence you need to collect. An observation will need an observation sheet, a purpose-designed piece of stationery that will help you collect good-quality information. Partly it is a matter of knowing what you are looking for and partly a matter of allowing yourself opportunities to record what's actually going on. What this means in practice is allowing yourself a set of prompts which includes 'other'.

The purpose of the observation sheet is to collect data or evidence on which you can base your research essay or report. It is useful to differentitate between two different types of evidence that might be collected during an observation which are themselves the results of two different kinds of response to the experience of observing. Both are equally valuable:

- **Statistical evidence**: This results from analysing the content of the activity. How many questions were asked? What kinds of questions were asked? How often was eye contact found with members of the audience? How often were the subject's arms folded and unfolded? These are important facts if you hope to come to conclusions which can be proved. As far as any data collected by human beings may be considered to be objective, these will tend to be objective.

- **Critical evidence**: This is the result of considering the meanings and motivations of the observed behaviour. What is the function of eye contact in this context? What is the effect of open questions on this audience? What does folding arms mean in each case? This is the first stage of analysis, which must begin while the subject is still warm. It is a reflection of how it seems to you at the time and is thus honestly subjective.

These two kinds of data should ideally support each other or at least provide a check which will prevent you from drawing bizarre conclusions from what you've actually observed. The feeling you have that your subject finds it difficult to hold or maintain eye contact might be confirmed by a low tally of observed eye contacts. A high tally might similarly confirm your experience that your subject was working hard to engage with audience members individually. The relationship is mutual and therefore provides a double test for any hypothesis; it asks 'where's the evidence?' twice.

Do not attempt to observe too broadly. The essence of this investigation is 'focus' and your observation should reflect this. Observation sheets should not normally exceed an A4 side. To make this format usable means limiting the number of observation categories or fields. It is important to begin by recording the details of the context of the observation efficiently and then to keep track of the sequence of events. An observation sheet might usefully start with a set of prompts which addresses the key elements of what you're observing ('Who? When? What? Where? How?' are as good as any, together with an implicit 'Why?').

Sample Observation Sheet Header

Subject (who):	Context (where):	Method (how):
Activity (what):	Observer:	Start time: End time:

It may seem tempting to fill the sheet with prompts but it is much better to layer your observation. You might, for example, begin by looking for and at non-verbal elements, then move on to identify linguistic features before finally concentrating on strategies (those rehearsed routines of communication we use on a day-to-day basis). This would allow you to use a sort of scrolling A4 to cover the various stages of an observation. The following example was used to observe (the interview was conducted over the telephone) the verbal communication of a university teacher, who was acting as an expert for a Communication Studies student's A Level project on 'children and TV violence':

Subject (who):	Context (where):	Method (how):
Activity (what):	Observer:	Start time: End time:

Content	Comment
Phase:	Start time:
Register/mode of address (how are we being spoken to?):	
Vocabulary (what sorts of words were used?):	
Paralanguage (tone, pitch, volume, etc.):	
Phase:	Start time:
Register/mode of address (how are we being spoken to?):	
Vocabulary (what sorts of words were used?):	
Paralanguage (tone, pitch, volume, etc.):	

There is nothing particularly surprising about this sheet, nor should there be. Essentially we are looking to identify the key elements of interpersonal communication and then see what influence they have in particular situations. See how the observation sheet offers a grid for you to work in. The vertical axis is divided into five minute phases and the horizontal axis is divided into statistical and critical modes (you collect data on the left and you make comments on the right). Perhaps it would be useful to see this sheet after use:

Subject (who):	Context (where):	Method (how):
Jane	'Home' (both)	Telephone
Activity (what):	Observer:	Start time: 6.30 pm
Expert interview	Me	End time: 6.45 pm

Content	Comment
Phase: opening	Start time: 6.30 pm
Register/mode of address (how are we being spoken to?): friendly, engaging, informal, very relaxed teacher–pupil.	Jane was pleased to hear from me and very supportive. The conversation began with pleasantries.
Vocabulary (what sorts of words were used?): Sophisticated and academic. Restricted code in the sense of a technical language (social science). 'Uses/gratifications', 'magic bullet'.	Jane is clearly well educated and intelligent; her use of language is precise and self-confident (in the same way that she is).
Paralanguage (tone, pitch, volume, etc.): Accent is very 'posh', intonation is musical and pleasant on the ear, there is plenty of variation.	Jane's accent signifies her social class (she is a colonel's daughter). She makes good use of an attractive and flexible vocal range.

This observation sheet can also be used when addressing examples on video or tape/CD. The facility offered by these formats to pause, to slowly advance, and to rewind gives greater scope for detail on the sheet and considered comment. Clearly, a single observation is of little use and any findings will need to be checked by at least one further visit. If a subject is performing in a media text, a second extract from the text would serve this purpose. There is an unwritten rule of proportion in these cases which considers the length of observation alongside the intensity or concentration of the action. Media texts, as conventionalised representations, will work in fairly short extracts, whereas the less precise character of live communication requires significantly longer periods of observation. Real world observations should be limited, except in exceptional cases, to an upper limit of 30 minutes.

If you had decided to observe your teacher to determine if they were a skilled communicator, three 20-minute observations will be of far more use than a single 90-minute marathon. Don't be afraid to bring your previous experience to bear on this or any other case or to imagine your common sense has no role to play. Communication Studies is always reminding you of the importance of context and yours is of utmost importance here. Your investigation begins and ends with yourself: what you know, what you believe, what you have found out. As a student of communication, it is inevitable that you will want to make reference to available theory, either in terms of what you have been taught here or elsewhere or in terms of further reading and academic research.

The key to using 'theory' is that it must inform your investigation and ultimately understanding of communication in practice. What merits the title 'theory' is after all the result of investigations much like yours and the drawing of conclusions from these. Nietzsche claimed 'There are no facts, only interpretations' and this is nowhere more true than in social science research. We can offer only our 'treatment' of material, supported by detailed reference to available evidence and research, which is in itself a treatment based on similar grounds. This is the spirit of investigation – at best it is open and flexible and sure of itself.

WRITING IT ALL UP

When you come to write up your findings, it is likely that you will find 500 words limiting and that you will need to edit down to the required number. Drafting is therefore essential. While there will need to be a degree of formality in the style of this essay, a greater need will be for the writing to have a balance and a shape that reflect both its status as an essay and the priorities of the mark scheme. In the mark scheme for AQA's Unit 1 the key phrases are 'critical, analytical thinking', 'range of appropriate examples', 'focused' and 'conclusion'. This is describing a well-structured piece of writing which gives priority and thus space to a detailed and analytical account of the work undertaken and which draws conclusions from this work. The five-paragraph essay, a format which is detailed later in Part 6, will likely serve as a blueprint here:

- **Introduction**: State your case and methods briefly; include your working hypothesis [50 words]
- **Main point 1**: Try to make a point (in this case draw a conclusion from your investigation) and then support it with evidence from your research and reading [100 words]
- **Main point 2**: As above: quotation from and reference to primary sources is valuable (your actual observations) [100 words]

- **Main point 3 and other comments**: As above, but you've only got 500 words so any other comments will be welcome [150 words]
- **Conclusion:** Given that the mark scheme refers directly to a conclusion in the three highest mark bands, make sure yours is formal and evident; reflect on your investigation as a whole in terms of its strengths and weaknesses; summarise what you have learned and, by implication, what the audience can learn from this [100 words]

Given that the assessment objective tested in this task refers to the ability to 'demonstrate knowledge and understanding of key concepts, conventions and theories', your writing style is a secondary issue. It might be best to address the matter of style in terms of efficiency. You need a way of writing that allows you to pack the maximum amount of analysis and comment into 500 words. But you must not lose clarity or comprehensibility. The case study below may help to point the way.

CASE STUDY: BASIL FAWLTY AS THE 'HOTELIER FROM HELL' LISTENING SKILLS INVESTIGATION

My investigation was into the communication skills required by a competent hotelier by examining John Cleese's presentation of 'the hotel manager from Hell' across two series of *Fawlty Towers*. My hypothesis was that servicing the needs of customers depends on appropriate motivation, a strong sense of empathy and active listening: Basil Fawlty proved to have none of these. I watched Fawlty 'live' with an appropriate set of observation sheets, detailing his verbal and non-verbal communication along with his relationships with others. These are my findings. [*85 words to set the scene*]

Birtwhistell (1970) has suggested that some 65 per cent of meaning in dyadic (two-person) communication is carried non-verbally. If this is so, then Basil Fawlty is giving out all the wrong signals. His non-verbal leakage is so 'heavy' as to suggest a kind of communicative incontinence rather than competence. His orientation is often distancing and contemptuous, his paralanguage is dismissive (with an intonation which signifies sarcasm) and aggressive (inappropriate volume and emphasis) and his use of his height and a lack of understanding of Hall's (1959) notion of 'personal space' means guests are too often intimidated. Clearly, his physical appearance is an aspect of this problem but it is aggravated rather than alleviated by his behaviour. [*110 words on my first major point: use of NVC*]

He equally lacks sensitivity in his use of language to guests, rarely finding an appropriate register. He was found to range wildly from the ridiculously self-deprecating and fawning for those he considers his 'betters' (such as the self-styled aristocrat in *A Touch of Class*) to the downright abusive (telling guests to 'Shut up!', even shouting this or at one point ordering all the guests out of the hotel). His language is sophisticated, if a little ostentatious, a wide-reaching elaborated code, which in itself often functions as a barrier to communication. Guests are more often put off by the torrent of words than engaged by them. [*106 words on my second major point: use of language*]

However, the singular skill that Fawlty most lacks is that of empathy, the ability to see and feel as others do, to put oneself in another's shoes. Fawlty is ill at ease with himself and thus with other people. His attempts at social one-upmanship suggest a fragile self-concept and this is directed against his hapless guests, who are made into 'riff-raff' by his failure to understand himself, a classic case of 'projection'. To genuinely get on with the guests of this modest hotel, Fawlty would need to recognise it as being modest. Without this he will always lack the necessary social skills. [*102 words on my final major point: empathy*]

By deduction it is possible to construct something like a model of the ideal, or at least a potentially successful, hotelier. It would probably start with motivation, having a clear idea that managing a hotel is what you really want to do; this probably outweighs any consideration of skills. Wanting to be effective in itself ought to inform your non-verbal communication and help to promote a positive impression. Given the primacy effect (that first impressions count), this should allow verbal communication a constructive context and further encourage engagement and empathy. Fawlty lacks appropriate motivation (he is concerned only with himself) and, as a result, all the skill he has is pitifully misdirected. [*110 words in conclusion*]

[Total words: 513]

This essay will form part of the basis for the oral presentation, but do not think that this is merely a translation exercise where you squeeze the essay into the presentation. The oral presentation is about the investigation and not the research essay. The key here is *audience*. The essay is written for an examiner, therefore it will be written in a kind of formal written style. The presentation is for your peers – fellow students and learners. Not only will this probably mean you modify your style to go with the modification in form, but it will also mean you modify the content. What is selected for one audience will be very different to that selected for another. Your essay is likely to have little room for the flavour of the observation or the humour whereas in the oral context features such as the character of the observation or humour will be useful ways to alleviate tension and thus making your audience more appreciative of your message.

We have dealt with oral presentations in Part 2. This oral presentation requires you to invite an audience and rewards you for your necessary preparation and visual aids. Both of these dimensions need a mature response. The oral presentation is a practical examination, an assessed performance. You must select people in front of whom you are happy to perform. You simply can't afford to be shy in this context so don't invite those audience members who will make you shy (or in front of whom you will be too 'cool' to perform). Similarly, this is a Communication Studies examination in which you will need to be asked intelligent questions. There is no room for sentiment, for an 'I'll be in your presentation if you'll be in my presentation' approach. Choose those who can, not those you fancy.

In terms of rewarding preparation, there is again a need for an awareness of context; this is real but it is also academic. It may well be true that many excellent presentations have been done without recourse to either notes or visual aids and that many presentational catastrophes are accompanied by a sheaf of notes and impeccable OHTs. This is not the point; marks cannot be given for the quality of nothing. Put simply: you are actually being asked to prepare notes for a talk with visual aids.

REVIEWING YOUR PERFORMANCE

Finally you are asked to review your presentation and investigation in the light of your performance as a communicator. This is an important stage educationally and, as a bonus, you are given a 30 mark incentive to do it. Essentially the review asks: 'What have you learned?' This question can be broken down into three more precise questions:

- What have you learned about communication skills?
- What have you learned about research?
- What have you learned about yourself?

The mark scheme is once again our first port of call with identifiable key points as 'relates to both research and presentation', 'recommendations/ proposals for improvement', 'evidence of evaluation and critical thinking' (for the highest band) and 'conclusion'. Five hundred words in five paragraphs would plan out like this:

- **Introduction**: Opening comments reflecting overall success/failure of investigation [50 words]
- **Review of research methods**: What worked and what did not; assessment of the reliability of evidence (honestly) [100 words]
- **Review of research conclusions**: How valid are your conclusions? What factors did you miss or neglect? [100 words]
- **Review of oral presentation**: How useful were the materials? How responsive was the audience? How did the questioning go? [100 words]
- **Conclusion**: What would you have changed? What have you learned about communication? What would you do next? [150 words]

The case study below helps to illustrate how to do this.

CASE STUDY: REVIEW OF BASIL FAWLTY INVESTIGATION

My investigation was based upon observation of that classic of British television comedy, not as a text but as the recorded evidence of the 'life' of one Basil Fawlty, a frustrated and largely unsuccessful hotelier. It was a good choice in the sense that the evidence was substantial (running to more than six hours airtime, which Fawlty largely dominated), focused (the comedy revolves around Fawlty's lack of significant communication skills such as empathy) and richly enjoyable (which helped to keep me motivated). [*82 words to set the scene*]

On balance the observation work might have been a little more detailed. I watched a good deal of Fawlty communication but perhaps in not enough detail to pull out the finer points. Familiarity was also a problem (a sort of comfortable psychological barrier): I knew the material so well before I started that I sometimes found it difficult to look at it again in a different way. Objections may be raised about the fact that this is a directed 'performance' and thus manipulated, but Goffman has explained how so much of our interpersonal communication is also performance based. Anyway hotels are public and always have audiences. [*105 words on research methods*]

The results of my observations and critical analyses were hardly surprising: a character designed as an object lesson in inappropriate public relations was in fact inept when it came to 'people' skills. However, my research did clarify these problems and helped me to see their importance. Fawlty lacks empathy, a basic emotional understanding of his guests. This is the centre of many of his problems, since it informs everything he says and does. This is an observation which has practical implications for Hotel Management courses and for our day-to-day communication. [*90 words on research conclusions*]

Obviously Fawlty was a great icebreaker when it came to the oral presentation. I was able to project a short segment onto a screen as a largely phatic opening move and this worked well. The presentation itself was greatly helped by the audience's familiarity with the material and love of it. This in itself was a kind of barrier since it ruled out genuinely critical material. I struggled early on to find an appropriate register, to find the right compromise between formality and informality, between the language of writing and the language of speech. The questioning phase of the presentation provoked some good questions and was genuinely engaged and surprisingly enjoyable. I injected humour to keep the 'first person talk' element buoyant, which partly worked. [*125 words on doing the oral presentation*]

As this review implies, I have learned both general and specific things. The general lessons have been largely to do with organisation, or sometimes the lack of it; my observation sheets were a little poor, my visual aids lacked 'polish'. More specifically I have greatly benefited from seeing communication theory evidenced in practice. In a sense my study of Fawlty emphasised the dangers of taking basic communication skills too lightly. In analysing communication practice, many of the theoretical discussions we have had in class have been illuminated – about the verbal/non-verbal relationship; about the importance of active listening; and about the nature of communication itself. [*104 words on what has been learned*]

[Total: 506 words of review]

Bibliography

Goffman, E. (1990) *The Presentation of the Self in Everyday Life.*
McLuhan, M. (1964) *Understanding Media.*

PART 5: THEMES IN PERSONAL COMMUNICATION

In this part we are going to look at a wide range of themes, ideas, concepts and issues in personal communication. We have grouped them together under three broad headings: Verbal and Non-Verbal Communication; Intrapersonal Communication; and Group Communication.

▼ 1   VERBAL COMMUNICATION

In this section we look at verbal communication.

- We consider what language is, how it can be defined, and how human language is different from animal communication systems.

- We look at the formal study of language.

- We consider language in relation to gender.

Without language, human beings would probably lead less complex lives than they do. The capacity to use language is one key factor that separates the human animal from other animals. Imagine a world in which language did not exist; consider all the things that we would be unable to do (for example, this book could not exist). It would be impossible to express our ideas. The range of feelings that we could express would be much more limited. The seemingly simple process of communicating with other people would be much more time-consuming and imprecise. Passing on our experiences to other people and to the generations that follow would be impossible. Similarly, our awareness of the experiences of previous generations would be quite limited.

There can be little doubt that language is a central part of our experience as human beings and has contributed to human animals dominating planet Earth. Of course, there are people who would question whether this domination is a good thing. Civilisation might well be an elaborate dead-end in the process of evolution, but the fact remains that the capacity to use language as a means of communication is largely responsible for the development of the peoples who occupy planet Earth.

WHAT IS LANGUAGE?

Language is a complex sign system. The signs it uses are composed of either sounds or symbols in the form of letters. These sounds and letters are put together to form words. Words in turn are combined together to form sentences.

As you saw in Part 3, where we looked at textual analysis, the function of a sign is to signify an object or concept that has an existence in the real world. The sign stands in place of that object or concept and is used to represent it.

Language is composed mainly of symbols. A sign that is symbolic is one that has no direct connection with the thing it stands for. The word 'cat' has no real link to the furry animal that it represents. We could just as easily use the word 'wood' to describe the furry quadruped. The use of the word 'cat' is arbitrary. It represents a cat because everyone agrees that that is what it represents. Unless of course you live in France, where you would call it a 'chat'. It's when you think about the fact that there are thousands of languages in the world which all have different signs to represent the furry quadruped that you realise that there is no essential, logical or necessary connection between objects in the world and the signs that we use to represent those objects.

Most written and spoken signs are symbolic. A few words that we speak are in fact iconic. They work by being recognised as similar to what they represent. These are called onomatopoeic words, where the sound of the word imitates what it represents. 'Squelch' or 'quack' are iconic rather than symbolic. Some languages are written in an iconic fashion. Chinese employs ideograms which are a type of word picture.

In his *ABC of Reading* (1951) the poet Ezra Pound explained how simple ideograms function, for example

人　man

木　tree

日　sun

Here we can clearly see how these iconic signs relate to their objects. Pound then explained how simple ideograms could be combined to form more complex ones, for example

　sun tangled in the tree's branches, as at sunrise, meaning now: the East

WHAT DO WE DO WITH LANGUAGE?

So what is the value of this complex sign system that allows us to communicate with one another? What are the uses to which human beings put this great skill? After eavesdropping on a few conversations or listening to people on their mobile phones, you may be tempted to reply 'not a lot'. It is possible, however, to categorise some of the functions of language to identify how it is used. These functions would include:

- **The communication of our experiences of the outside world**. Using language is an important way of letting other people know about the world and our experiences of it. For example, we can tell people of dangers that exist as well as the pleasures to be had. In this way, language allows us to explain our emotional response to our experiences of the world.
- **The capacity to communicate ideas**. You will see that this is linked to the previous function. However, language does not limit us to describing our experiences of the concrete and tangible. It allows us to talk about abstract concepts, such as love and truth. It also allows us to speculate on the very purpose of our existence.
- **The capacity to be creative**. We can sing songs or recite poetry using language. This is sometimes referred to as the aesthetic function of language.
- **The capacity for making reassuring noises to each other**. This is called the phatic function. It implies that many of the utterances that we make carry little information. They are designed simply to help with social interaction. They have been described as ritualised exchanges. For example, the question 'How are you?' requires the ritualised answer, 'Fine. Are you OK?', rather than a detailed audit of the receiver's state of mind and body.

ACTIVITY . . .

Spend some time listening carefully to someone else speak. Try to identify examples of each of the above functions in their conversation. Which of the functions do you feel predominates? Do you think this is likely to vary from person to person?

You can see from the above examples that language is important to human beings in determining how they communicate their experiences. If language is such an important factor, it follows that to some extent the view that we have of the world is likely to be determined by the language that we use. Indeed, an important philosophical debate is concerned with the relationship between thought and language. Put very simply, the question is how does language affect the way in which we think? Do we in fact use language to think with? If so, then language obviously must determine and define what we are able to think.

The term used to describe this concept is linguistic relativism. In essence it means that the language we have learned to speak determines the way in which we see the world. So for example, if we have grown up using German as our first language, we will interpret the events that take place in the world differently to a person who has grown up using French or English.

Language in this way positions us to take a particular view of the world and our experiences in it. This theory was put forward by Edward Sapir (1956) and Benjamin Lee Whorf (1956) and is called the Sapir Whorf Hypothesis. A hypothesis is a theory and, like many theories about the human mind, it is hard to prove whether it is true or not. However, it may be useful to look at an example of how the hypothesis might work.

English people have a reputation for being embarrassed about sex and bodily functions. It may well be that this embarrassment is in part due to the fact that the words we use to describe these activities and the related bodily parts are all taboo words in English culture. Indeed, most of them are swear words and many are used as a means of verbally abusing people we do not like. If we look back to the medieval period in this country, a poet like Chaucer was happy to use such vocabulary, in its original meaning, in a poem like *The Canterbury Tales*. It was in the Victorian era, famed for its hypocritical prudery, that such language was outlawed.

The question is the extent to which social prohibitions on the use of this language have created this furtive attitude to sex and bodily functions among English people. Certainly our European neighbours seem to be far less inhibited about these issues, as a glance at their television programmes will reveal.

Another example of the way in which language can be said to frame our thinking is in the issue of race, where 'white' is assumed to have positive connotations and 'black' to have negative connotations. Many English people still use forms of or synonyms for 'black' to connote negative ideas. For example, people use a phrase such as 'giving someone a black look' to describe an intimidating or threatening gesture. 'Black sheep' is used metaphorically to describe someone who does no good. White, on the other hand, has connotations of purity and cleanliness. A white Christmas is much hoped for. White weddings are symbols of chastity and purity. At funerals people are expected to wear black. On the other hand Chinese culture associates white with death. (If nothing else the fact that different cultures employ the same sign in different ways reinforces the notion that there is nothing essential about the signs we use to represent objects; there is no essence of cat about the sign 'cat'; there is no essence of purity to the sign 'white'.)

It can be argued that the connotative power of black in our language serves to determine our thinking about blackness in a negative way.

You may like to consider the way in which language is also said to reinforce attitudes to gender. This issue will be discussed at greater length later in the section.

SOME USEFUL TERMS IN LINGUISTICS

The study of language is called linguistics. It is useful at this point to introduce some of the terms that are commonly used in linguistics.

Semantics

Semantics is the study of meanings. One of the complexities of language is that the same word can have different meanings. In the same way, similar sounding words can be spelled differently and also have different meanings. Moreover, the meaning of words can change over a period of time.

KEY TERM

SEMANTICS   The branch of linguistics that is concerned with the meaning of words and how these have changed. It is concerned with the relationships between signs and meaning.

As we have already stated, the meaning of words is arbitrary. Words mean what they mean because of agreement within a culture as to their meaning. Of course, in reality, semantics is not quite such a precise science. If, for example, we use the word 'dog', we all have a mental concept of a mammal with four legs and a tail. However, each of us is likely to have an individual picture of a dog. Perhaps it is our own pet dog of which we are particularly fond, a small black poodle for example. As you saw in Part 3, words, like other signs, carry with them denotative and connotative meanings. The word 'dog', while representing the concept of the animal, will carry with it meanings that will be interpreted in different ways by individual members of a culture. Not only will each have a different mental picture of a dog but also the word will carry emotional connotations for many people. For example, some will experience great feelings of warmth and affections towards the pet waiting to greet them when they arrive home. For others it may be fear, hatred and anxiety after an unhappy experience with an aggressive dog.

For this reason many people see words as imprecise tools for conveying meaning. In the above example, we considered an example of a word that is a concrete noun. Such words refer to objects that have a tangible existence in the real world. A dog is something that you can perceive with your senses. Many words that we use are, however, abstract. They refer to ideas. Truth, love and beauty are examples of abstract nouns. If it is difficult to fix the meaning of words that relate to real objects; it is clearly even more difficult to agree on the meaning of words that describe things that exist only as ideas.

Syntax

Syntax is a way of describing the conventions of how words are combined to form meanings. Syntax is in fact the rules of language or its grammar. We tend to observe these conventions much more carefully when we are writing than when we are speaking. For example, it is quite common in speech to miss out the verb from a sentence. In writing this is traditionally assumed to be a serious omission.

Phonology

Phonology is the sound system of language. The basic unit of sound is called a phoneme. This represents an individual sound, such as that made by the letters 'th' in English. Although the sound 'th' exists in English, it is not found in other European languages such as French. Consequently, one way of identifying a person speaking English with a French accent is that they will pronounce words containing these letters awkwardly.

Phonetics

We call the study of the sounds of language phonetics. Systems for writing shorthand such as Pitman use phonetics. In Pitman shorthand the symbols for 'sea' and 'see' would be identical because they sound the same. Of course, when reading back shorthand notes, the actual word would be determined by the context.

Discourse

Discourse is another term that you will find useful in your exploration of the nature and use of language. In fact this is a good example of a word that has taken on new and different meanings to meet a range of different needs. In *Key Concepts in Communication and Cultural Studies* (O'Sullivan *et al.* 1994) its meaning in linguistics is defined as 'verbal utterances of greater magnitude than one sentence'.

KEY TERM

DISCOURSE ANALYSIS is a branch of linguistics that concerns itself with conversations between two or more people.

The term is more generally used in Communication Studies to describe a particular type of speech used by a group of people. Lawyers, for example, are said to use the discourse of the law. This is a vocabulary and way of speaking specific to legal circles. Media forms such as television have their own discourse or way of speaking.

Each of us is likely to be able to use a range of different discourses in our daily life according to the context in which we are speaking. The discourse of the Communication Studies classroom is likely to be rather different to the discourse of love, for example.

RESTRICTED AND ELABORATED CODES

In an important study of the use of language published in 1971, Basil Bernstein suggested two categories that are used according to the situation in which we find ourselves, namely the restricted code and the elaborated code.

The restricted code is used mostly in group situations when we are speaking to people who are likely to share our interests and experiences. It is characterised by a limited vocabulary and a basic use of syntax. Restricted codes are also likely to have high levels of redundancy (or predictability) in the words that are used to encode a message. Bernstein argued that restricted codes reinforce the sameness of people communicating within a group. One way in which you can readily identify the use of a restricted code is if you are listening in to a group of people and find yourself feeling excluded by the way in which they are speaking. For example, if you listen to a professional group such as lawyers or doctors, they will employ a restricted code to discuss issues relating to their work which many of us would find hard to understand. Similarly, a lawyer or a doctor might feel excluded if he or she were to listen to a group of Communication Studies students discussing semiotics or even restricted and elaborated codes.

Elaborated codes use a wider range of vocabulary, more complex syntax and are much harder to predict (they are more entropic). The elaborated code is less concerned with group relationships and more appropriate to the expression of individual ideas. In fact using an elaborated code is in many ways an assertion of a person's individuality by identifying differences between speaker and listener. Just as the restricted code assumes a background of shared interests, assumption, even a common view of the world, so the elaborated code is about uniqueness and individuality.

Clearly, an individual is not limited to the use of just one of these codes. A surgeon who might spend much of his or her day speaking in a restricted code to colleagues about clinical matters may well go out for a social drink in the evening and employ an elaborated code to express views on the current political situation or the appointment of the new England football manager.

In Bernstein's original research his focus was on the language of children and identified how social class directly affected the use of these codes. In general working-class children were found to use restricted codes, largely because working-class communities are characterised by social relationships that are close-knit and inward looking. Middle-class children, however, employ an elaborated code because social relations within this group are more mobile and more outward looking. In fact a characteristic of middle-class language use is the capacity to move between restricted and elaborated codes in response to the demands of the social situation.

ACTIVITY . . .

It has been suggested that the words 'restricted' and 'elaborated' imply a value judgement about the language codes people employ. Do you think there is evidence to suggest that we value the use of elaborated codes more highly than restricted codes?

Compare and contrast the use of language by characters in the British situation comedies *The Royle Family* and *Keeping Up Appearances*. Pay particular attention to such aspects as education, family background and social position.

The study of language is obviously a complex and difficult business. This study is further complicated by an important distinction made by Ferdinand de Saussure (1983). He used the term 'langue' to describe the rules of language, or more accurately the system of language that allows us to communicate with one another. The term 'parole' is used in contrast to this to describe individual use of language, or the single utterances that people make. However, it is only possible to study the notion of langue by looking at individual uses of it in the form of parole.

Most people have the competence to use language. By this we mean that they can construct sentences in order to communicate with other people. An important question in linguistics is where does this competence come from. Or, put more simply, how do we learn language?

As we have stated, human language is a sophisticated means of communication that separates human beings from other animals. An obvious question to ask is how this ability evolved. The work of Noam Chomsky (1968) is particularly important in this context. Chomsky's work spans many academic disciplines, but his particular contribution to Communication Studies is his exploration of how language is learned. In the process of researching this issue, Chomsky attempted to teach language to chimpanzees – with somewhat limited results.

The arguments that he puts forward are both complex and difficult. In a simplified form his basic argument is that we are all born with an innate or inborn ability to learn language. This innate ability might be compared to our walking on two legs, in that it is a skill that distinguishes us from most other mammals. The question that may have sprung into your mind might well be why different nations speak different languages. To explain this, Chomsky makes an important distinction between syntax and vocabulary.

It is a capacity to learn the conventions of language (of grammar and syntax) that we are born with. Research indicates that these conventions are basically very similar for all languages. The differences between the conventions of different languages are trivial in comparison with their similarities. Chomsky uses this fact to argue that the capacity to learn language is an ability that we are all born with. What distinguishes one language from another is the vocabulary that we learn. If you grow up among people who speak English, you will learn an English vocabulary. In France, you will learn French. Children growing up in bilingual households generally learn both.

Speakers of a first language are sensitive to the conventions of their language. Someone for whom this language is a second (or third) one will often be identified when they don't observe the conventions of that language. If someone says 'I have been in England since five years' we know what they mean but we also appreciate that they have literally translated from their first language (in this case French) into their second language, English.

Our working knowledge of syntax allows us to use vocabulary to generate sentences. The number of sentences we can generate is potentially limitless. Of course, not all of them will make sense, although they may conform with conventions of grammar.

Chomsky's argument is a complex one but one of his prime concerns is the issue of what he calls 'deep' and 'surface' structures in language. These allow us to do the same thing in two different ways or to create a sentence that contains two different meanings. For

ACTIVITY...

Chomsky gives the example of the following sentence which, although grammatically correct, makes little sense:

Colourless green ideas sleep furiously.

Try to generate sentences of your own that have this quality.

COMMUNICATION STUDIES: THE ESSENTIAL INTRODUCTION

example, a sign outside a pharmacist's shop that reads 'we dispense with accuracy' is capable of two different interpretations. On the other hand we can create two sentences (e.g. 'The child kicked the ball' and 'The ball was kicked by the child') which both convey the same idea. For Chomsky this competence in generating language that contains both of these structures is the basis of how we communicate. In fact, it can be argued that creating meaning is a feature of the human condition and a function that we are all predisposed to do.

Interestingly, a lot of research into the acquisition of language has centred on the use of sign languages. There is a commonly held belief that sign language is a basic iconic language that is a poor substitute for spoken language. However, studies of signing have shown it to be a complex system of communication with its own syntax as well as its own vocabulary. Although the United Kingdom and the United States generally share a common verbal and spoken language system, they have completely different sign languages, neither readily comprehensible to a native signer from the other country.

People using sign language are capable of engaging in the same abstract debates and discussions as those who use verbal means of communication. Clearly, sign language has freed itself sufficiently from relying on resemblance to express such complex and abstract ideas.

Patterns of language learning are also regional as well as national. In the same way that we learn the vocabulary of the culture in which we grow up, so we also learn to imitate the speech patterns and pronunciations of the people in the area in which we live. We learn to speak the dialect of the place where we develop our language skills. In this way, in the UK we can identify people by their accent. People from Yorkshire, Merseyside and London all have specific patterns of speaking that help us to place them geographically.

There are also specific variations in vocabulary between regions used to describe everyday items. Small pieces of bread, for example, can be called rolls, cobs, balm cakes, breadcakes or batches, according to the area of the country in which you find yourself.

For the first 60 years of the twentieth century a regional accent was considered a distinct obstacle to advancement in certain careers. 'Received pronunciation' or RP is the term used to describe English spoken without any trace of regional accent. It is the type of English spoken traditionally by BBC newsreaders and for many people it is a voice that connotes authority. Most of the films and television programmes made before the mid-1960s feature lead actors and presenters speaking RP; indeed, regional accents tended to be reserved for people of a socially inferior status, for example the chirpy Cockney private you'd always find in British films about the Second World War. Up until the 1960s, whatever region of the United Kingdom young actors came from when they went to drama school, they would be trained to speak RP. It was only the popular acceptance of naturalistic drama that enabled actors such as Albert Finney, Rita Tushingham and Michael Caine to keep their regional accents (although in *Zulu*, Caine's first film in a leading role, his accent was distinctly RP).

Nowadays an RP accent doesn't have anywhere near the value it once did. A number of regional accents (such as those associated with Yorkshire, Lancashire and Scotland) and adopted accents (such as Estuary English) are now felt to be a distinct advantage when trying to gain employment as, for example, a British breakfast television presenter or British children's television presenter.

ACTIVITY . . .

How important is dialect in modern British society? Do we value people with regional accents as highly as those who speak RP?

■ Examine TWO serious news/documentary programmes (e.g. *Newsnight, Panorama, News at Ten*) for the accents/type of language used by the presenters/interviewers. Does this affect their image and the importance that we as the audience attach to what they are saying? Who is likely to be the target audience of this sort of programme?

■ Examine TWO long-running soaps and note the accents and language of the main characters. What does it tell you about the social class of the characters and their likely education/jobs/etc.? Who do you think is the target audience for this sort of programme?

HUMAN BEINGS AND ANIMALS

You will of course be aware that many animals have complex methods of communicating with one another. Dolphins and whales, for example, are known to communicate in quite complex ways. No animal, not even our close cousin the chimpanzee, as Chomsky proved, is capable of communicating in quite the same way as the human animal. So what is it that makes human language unique?

One important characteristic is our creativity. Language allows us to make things up. As we see from the example of Chomsky's meaningless sentence, we can be creative in using language. Indeed, we can be creative to the point of telling lies.

We can also be creative in making up new words for our language. The world of Information Technology has meant that we have needed to create a whole series of new words to describe this method of communication. Internet, e-mail and megabyte are examples of newly created words designed to allow us to communicate about communications technology.

Language also allows us to talk about things that are far away either in space or time. This capacity is called displacement. Transmitting information about events, places and cultures we have not encountered first hand is a capacity given to us by our use of language. It is central to our capacity to share and collect ideas and information about the world at large. Our own experiences of the world may be limited by the language we inherit from how other people speak about the world. In consequence we can have quite detailed information about places we have never visited and times in which we were not alive. In fact our capacity to be creative in the use of language means that we can talk about the future, despite the fact that none of us has yet experienced it.

LANGUAGE AND GENDER

Gender, it has been argued, is socially constructed. This idea implies that, although we are born male or female biologically, we learn to behave in a male or female way because of social pressures. Sex and gender are, therefore, two different issues. Sex is biological and anatomical; gender is created by our cultural experiences.

One of the chief ways in which we experience our culture is through the use of language. It follows that language is likely to be a key factor in differentiating the way in which gender is constructed and ultimately how males and females will learn to behave.

In her important book *Man Made Language* (1998), Dale Spender argues that language reflects the dominance of men in our society. The notion that the power relations in our society favour men is called a patriarchy.

Just as we suggested earlier in this section that language is a tool used in the oppression of cultural minorities, so it can be argued that language is controlled by men and used to support the dominance of men over women. A good example of this is the use of the word 'man' or 'mankind' to signal human beings of both sexes. Another example is the way in which the social status of a woman is often defined by her relation to a man. An unmarried woman is called Miss; a married woman called Mrs, and then takes on her husband's family name. Feminism has achieved significant objectives in the broad acceptance of the term 'Ms' as a title that doesn't signify a woman's social status and in women retaining their own family names rather than taking on their husband's or partner's family name.

Female behaviour that men disapprove of is often spoken of using pejorative or negative words.

Women are far more likely to be described in terms of their physical attributes. A tabloid newspaper is hardly likely to write about an attractive blond man with a gorgeous pair of legs. Such descriptions of women are common. Indeed, the dumb blonde stereotype is exclusively reserved as a way to describe women, despite the number of male celebrities who fit this description. This use of language, a feature of much journalism, suggests that the world is perceived from a male perspective in which women are objects whose desirability is to be evaluated and determined by men.

ACTIVITY . . .

Consider the following pairs of words:

Master: Mistress   Host: Hostess   Wizard: Witch

In what way does the feminine version carry connotations that do not exist in the male equivalent? Can you think of any more examples where the female version carries with it pejorative meanings? How do you think this influences our attitudes to gender?

In this section we consider the significance of non-verbal communication.

■ We look at the different categories of non-verbal communication, including paralanguage.

■ We consider the relationship between verbal and non-verbal communication.

As you will have realised, our verbal behaviour is an important way in which we communicate with one another. However, we also use another large repertoire of skills — non-verbal behaviour.

KEY TERM

PARALANGUAGE   Communication which is in the form of utterances other than the words themselves, e.g. the volume of one's voice.

When we communicate we are offering data to the world. In the process of doing so, we also offer information about ourselves, our feelings and attitudes and our relationship to the people we are addressing.

KEY TERM

DATA AND INFORMATION   The terms 'data' and 'information' are often used as if they were interchangeable; they are not. Data are raw, unprocessed facts, figures, etc. Once data have been processed, information results. When we make a specific enquiry of data, information is produced. The fact that you are 17 is a piece of data, as far as you are concerned. But should a police officer ask your age, and you reply '17', that is information to him. This is because he is asking your age for a specific purpose.

A simple greeting such as 'How ya doing?' or 'Wassup?' can carry with it much more about ourselves than seems possible in such a simple utterance. Much of the additional information is transmitted through non-verbal channels. Our tone of voice, the look on our face, or even the way in which we position our body can reveal to the receiver of our message our feelings as we transmit the message. For example, it is possible that the message 'Nice day again' is intended to be a deeply ironic comment on yet another day of bad weather. A sardonic grin or world-weary shake of the head may communicate that the message is intended to be a despairing comment on such depressing weather.

Clearly, verbal and non-verbal communication are closely linked. In the above example we see that the non-verbal message can, and often does, contradict the verbal one to invert the meaning of the message.

But, before we explore this in depth, let us consider the main types of non-verbal signal that people transmit. There are many ways in which people communicate by non-verbal means but the ones we'll focus on here are:

- Proxemics
- Orientation
- Eye contact or gaze
- Facial expression
- Gesture, especially use of hands and arms
- Dress
- Posture
- Paralanguage

There are other forms of non-verbal behaviour, for example, changes in our skin pigment such as blushing when we are embarrassed. An interesting issue is raised here. How much control do we have over the non-verbal signals we transmit? Blushing is generally seen as an involuntary action that gives away information to another person about our emotional state or even our motives.

We might arguably add smell to this list. In the non-human world smell is a powerful mechanism to send out signals that both attract and repel. The same is true of humans who have created a whole industry to produce synthetic odours that will attract other human animals.

Let's look at each of the forms of non-verbal communication we've identified. From here on in we'll refer to non-verbal communication as NVC.

PROXEMICS

Proxemics, a word coined by E. T. Hall in 1959, is the study of how we handle the space around us, especially in relation to other people. Like most animals, human beings are territorial. Just like a domestic or a feral cat, we create for ourselves spaces that belong to us and to which we try carefully to control access. Our homes and our spaces at work or school or college are examples of these. Consider the rooms in your house. Some are shared by the family, others are 'owned' by specific members of the family. Going into someone else's room is potentially to invade their space.

ACTIVITY . . .

Consider how spaces are occupied within the classroom.

- How is the teacher's space marked out?
- How are the other spaces occupied?
- Where would a newcomer or visitor to the class sit?

One issue to emerge from your consideration of how space is occupied is about how territory reflects the power relations within groups of people. The more powerful a person, the larger and more impressive the space they will occupy.

There is, however, another, more important type of space; this is the space that we carry with us. Each of us has this individual invisible space that we protect from outside intrusion. It might be compared to an invisible bubble around our body. In a crowded place such as a bus or a train, we can feel uncomfortable if a stranger encroaches on this space. On other occasions, we may welcome certain people to enter this space. Our feelings about this are determined by the situation and by the relationship we have, or might like to have, with the person or people who are near to us.

There are, however, important cultural differences in our attitudes to the proximity, or nearness, of other people. Some people argue that it is typical of British people that they do not encourage physical contact with other people. 'Don't touch' is an admonition we all remember from childhood. We are taught that touching things, other people, or even our own bodies, is socially undesirable. We may be wary of other people who are tactile and touch us. For example, some people like to hold on physically to the person they are talking to, as though to ensure that they have their full attention. In some cultures physical contact with relative strangers is openly encouraged. Watch how continental teenagers greet one another by kissing on both cheeks. In Britain kissing in this way tends to be reserved for close family members and intimacy between sexual partners.

So proxemics can provide us with important information about communication acts between people. It can shed light on the following:

■ **The situation that they are in** – whether they are whispering intimately to one another or making a public speech
■ **The relationship between two people** – whether they are relative strangers or intimate friends
■ **The relationship they might like to have with each other** – for example, if one person invades another's personal space, the reaction of that person may well suggest whether this is welcome or not
■ **Their cultural background or even their social attitudes** – some people will use the invasion of personal space as a means of intimidating another person. For example, a police officer questioning a suspect will often stand uncomfortably close

ORIENTATION

Closely linked to the concept of proxemics is the idea of orientation. This means the way in which people place themselves relative to one another. When someone comes to sit next to you, it is generally seen as a much friendlier orientation than someone who sits directly opposite you. The latter position is potentially confrontational while the former suggests closeness and support. Such a technique may well be used by a boss or a teacher wishing to indicate a non-threatening or supportive relationship with a colleague or a student.

Consider the significance of orientation at meal times within a social group.

- Does sitting at a table create a relaxed atmosphere and encourage conversation more than eating off a tray?

- Do we trust people more if they sit in certain positions in relation to us?

- Why do we feel uncomfortable when people stand behind us?

EYE CONTACT

Eye contact is one important way in which we communicate our feelings towards other people. Just as we are warned when young about touching, so we are also told that it is 'rude to stare'. Much of our behaviour in terms of eye contact with other people betrays our animal origins. We need to make initial eye contact to assess a stranger, as Erving Goffman (1963) points out. Prolonged staring in the animal world, however, is usually identified as a threatening form of behaviour. Averting the eyes and avoiding someone's gaze can also be seen as a means of avoiding conflict.

In human terms eye contact is obviously not as simple as this, but you may recognise elements of animal behaviour in the way people look at one another. If, for example, you find yourself inadvertently staring at someone, you will notice that their behaviour will change, often becoming either defensive or at the other extreme aggressive towards you. Similarly, we tend to be deeply suspicious of people who 'cannot look us in the eye'. They are seen as shifty or people with something to hide.

Gazing is also to some degree gendered. Men gaze at women, sometimes in an intimidating way. To gaze at another person, or to hold that person in your gaze, may well reflect the power relations between two people. Perhaps men in a patriarchal culture feel freer to gaze than women.

As with proxemics, eye contact, as Michael Argyle (1983) points out, can be an index of the closeness of a relationship that people share. Lovers, at least according to popular music, gaze into each other's eyes. Indeed, there is a popular belief that you can detect the truth in people's eyes. Although people may hide the truth with words, their true feelings will be revealed in their eyes.

It seems clear that, as with many non-verbal signals, eye contact has at least some degree of ambiguity about its meaning. Like many other acts of communication, a lot can depend on the context in which it takes place. For example, we may use eye movement seemingly to negate a verbal message. Take for example an instance where we use our eyes to indicate that a statement we have made is ironical, i.e. has the opposite meaning of the one that might normally be received. A teacher who says 'You obviously have a profound grasp of communication theory' but accompanies it with a despairing look upwards is most likely telling an unfortunate student just the opposite.

You may also like to consider the way in which people disengage from eye contact. What is the significance of looking away from someone? What signals are being passed when people glance away like this? Later in this section we will consider the role of eye contact in the way in which people make conversation.

Not all NVC that contradicts a verbal message is necessarily deliberate or voluntary. Indeed, non-verbal behaviour may on occasion give away a person's true intentions or state of mind. The term 'leakage' is used to describe the process by which this happens. In interview situations, for example, we may wish to appear relaxed and unconcerned about our chances of getting a job. However, certain aspects of our non-verbal behaviour may reveal the internal tension that we are feeling. Wringing our hands or gripping the seat tightly both indicate stress.

ACTIVITY . . .

Is it possible to control such tell-tale signs? Is it possible to prevent leakage?

■ Think of other instances when someone might try to hide their emotions (a) in a work situation and (b) in a social setting.

■ What might give them away (in terms of voice, orientation, eye contact, etc.)?

FACIAL EXPRESSION

Eye movement or contact is part of the larger system of non-verbal communication of facial expression. Much of the communication we participate in takes place in a face-to-face situation. In general we face the people we are addressing whether it is a formal or an informal situation. Obviously facial expression is bound to be an important indicator to other people of our attitudes, state of mind and relationships to them.

The human face has a complex arrangement of muscles that allows us to produce a whole range of different expressions, most of which are an index of our feelings. Through our facial expression we can indicate whether we are happy or sad or in pain. We can tell them if we are glad to see them or are angry with them or even afraid of them.

One of the most important signals that we can issue through our facial expression is the smile. Smiling is an important facial gesture that indicates to other people that we are ourselves happy and content. It is also used to indicate that we are pleased to see the other person and, most importantly, that we mean them no harm.

Desmond Morris (1994) suggests that two of our most important facial gestures, the smile and the frown, are linked to the facial expressions that we adopt during conflict. When we are angry and feeling aggressive, we tend to tighten our lips around our mouth and lower our eyebrows. This latter action is a means of protecting our eyes in an ensuing fight. We accompany these gestures with an unblinking stare, which we have seen is very much an attempt to intimidate another person.

However, when we become afraid after having committed ourselves to a conflict, we tend to pull back the corners of our mouth exposing the teeth. Morris calls this a typical 'fear face' which is a submissive gesture to suggest to an opponent that we are not a threat. This facial expression is very similar to the smile, which is a uniquely human gesture. A smile, therefore, is in at least one sense a submissive gesture indicating to another person that we are friendly and do not pose a threat to them.

There are many occasions when we may have to smile in a forced way. We are told to say 'cheese' as a way of creating a smile specifically for the camera when a photograph is taken. We may also fake a smile to pretend we are pleased to see someone when we are not. Generally people can detect a false smile – for example, when the camera lingers too long on a smiling television presenter. It seems that we can distinguish between a spontaneous smile and one that is generated for effect. Obviously there are other situations when we may wish to give off false signals with our use of gesture. In a situation such as a card game (e.g. poker), where we do not want an opponent to know what we are really thinking, we will often endeavour to suppress our spontaneous gestures. Indeed, we may even try to give off false signals to stop people reading our body language.

It has been argued that, when people are lying, this can be detected through their body language. For example, it is said that we touch our faces and blink more frequently as though try to cut ourselves off from the lies we are telling.

Desmond Morris's work is important because he used real life situations to classify the postures and gestures that human beings use. He notes that simple gestures such as the handshake have countless variations. He even argues that there are actual frontiers where different gestures begin and end. Similarly, he suggests that gestures, just like language, are also capable of changing their meanings over a period of time.

ACTIVITY . . .

The handshake may have its origins in the idea that people meeting are able to demonstrate to one another that they are unarmed by offering an open palm. Clearly, the handshake has developed subsequently as a social greeting, but still is an important means of reassuring both friends and strangers of our friendly intentions towards them.

Observe the handshaking and other greetings rituals that take place between people. Consider how these vary in terms of:

■ gender

■ ethnicity

■ region

■ age

What judgements do you think people make about each other on the basis of handshakes? Why do captains of opposing teams shake hands before a game?

The fact that human beings have adapted to walking on their hind legs has freed their hands, among other things, to be used for making gestures. On occasions these gestures are a replacement for speech. For example, if you are in the quiet working area of a library you may put your finger to your mouth in a gesture to tell someone to be quiet.

Similarly, when your voice is otherwise engaged, for example talking on the phone, you may use hand gestures to tell another person to come in and sit down. You may even be able to indicate that they can help themselves to a drink.

ACTIVITY . . .

Think about situations where gestures are used to achieve objectives that cannot be achieved by language. For example, in sport hand gestures are often used as a code for relaying information without the opposing team being able to decipher it. Financial markets and race-tracks, two gambling arenas, employ extensive use of hand gestures for conveying information.

- Why do you think hand gestures are so important here?
- How do they relate to spoken language?
- What other situations are there where hand gestures can be important?

Some gestures work alongside the words that we utter. It is argued that these hand gestures reveal a good deal about our emotional state as we utter messages to other people. It is interesting to observe that we often make hand gestures even when the receiver of the message is unable to see them, for example when we are speaking on the telephone. Obviously many of the gestures are automatic. They function to reinforce the message that we are uttering by means of language.

We all have a range of typical gestures that we make for pushing people away, or drawing them towards us. Consider what these gestures usually are. What gestures do we use when we want to indicate to people we are pleased with them or we are admonishing them?

ACTIVITY . . .

Watch a politician or other person addressing a public meeting either on television or, better still, by attending yourself. Make a list of the different types of gesture they use.

- How does each of these gestures relate to the message being spoken?
- How do you, the audience, respond to different hand gestures?
- Are there any gestures that make you more inclined to accept the verbal message?

DRESS

Dress is often identified as an example of a code. As with all codes, there are certain conventions that apply to they way in which things are done. These conventions have to do with the way in which we combine items of clothing and the appropriateness of certain types of styles of dress to specific situations. If we fail to observe the conventions, then we risk giving offence. By the same token, if we choose to ignore these conventions, we may have set out deliberately to challenge convention, perhaps by even by seeking to give offence. On the other hand we may just have got it wrong. Imagine a situation in which a good friend invites you to a fancy dress party. You turn up dressed as Batman or Robin to find that everyone else is in normal casual party dress. Your fellow partygoers might enjoy a comic interlude at the sight of your discomfort in failing to conform to the dress code for that occasion.

An extreme example might be to dress in loud and colourful dress for a funeral. Convention demands that people wear black or dark coloured clothes as a symbol of mourning. To break such a convention might be seen as a provocative act showing disrespect to the dead person and the family of the dead person.

In the same way, most people wear clothes that have at least some kind of congruity. A 'well dressed' person will wear outfits that match. This will be achieved by avoiding colour clashes and usually by avoiding combining formal and informal garments. However, once dress codes are established, people can choose to ignore, invert or play with those codes. Accordingly some people successfully combine tee-shirts and formal suits, or trainers and formal suits.

ACTIVITY . . .

- How do you decide what to wear?

- Do you always have a choice?

- Are there clothes that you hate wearing?

- Is your wardrobe organised into 'outfits', that is, clothes that you know work well together?

- Think through how you might describe your wardrobe as a paradigm and particular outfits as syntagms.

The clothes we wear make a statement about ourselves. Even if we are not the type of person who worries unduly about our dress, people we meet and interact with will still interpret our appearance as though we had deliberately constructed a message. As we have seen, one way in which this is done is through the wearing of clothes inappropriate to a particular situation, by accident or by design.

An interesting example of dress code is the use of uniform. Uniform is used to signify the role or function that a person performs. It distinguishes the wearer from other people.

Police officers wear uniform as a means of establishing their power and status as well as making them recognisable to members of the public.

Some uniforms are also signifiers of the rank and status of the person who wears them. In the police and armed forces this may take the form of symbols such as stripes and crowns that can be read by those who understand the code. Generally, the more elaborate the symbols, the higher the rank. Some uniforms may be colour-coded to distinguish people of higher rank.

Uniforms usually have some impact on the behaviour of both the wearer and those with whom they are in contact. A uniform provides a person with a sense of belonging to a group. It also bestows on people a sense of authority. It is interesting to note how the uniforms of security guards imitate those of police officers.

It can be argued, however, that we all wear some sort of a uniform. A uniform is an important method of establishing our allegiance to a group. It can be used to establish to the world that we belong to a particular group and share that group's values. Although less formal and homogeneous than a military uniform, the clothing of different subcultures has served to act as a uniform to identify people with shared values. Hippies, skinheads, punks, crusties, goths and grungers are examples of such subcultures. More recently the vogue for designer labels, sports clothing and trainers has been used to signify allegiances, especially the wearing of football shirts of a particular team.

It can be argued that we are all subject to a pressure to conform and to demonstrate allegiances to different groups within society. Our dress code is an important mechanism by which we signal this conformity to a group.

ACTIVITY . . .

- Is it possible to dress in a wholly 'individual' way? What are the 'rules' that, even unconsciously, influence our choice of clothes (e.g. situation, time of day, gender)?

- Do the clothes we wear make a statement about us? Give examples of three very different types of attire and the reactions they are likely to provoke.

A uniform is an extreme example of formal dress. The business suit with its conservative dark shades is worn to distinguish people who have 'important' jobs that require them to meet people and make important decisions. Casual clothes are often seen as inappropriate in a business environment as most companies are keen for employees to reflect a positive, clean-cut image of the firm through their own appearance (efficient, smart and reliable). In some offices, where there is no direct contact with actual customers, management has introduced weekly 'Dress Down Days' when employees can leave their suits behind and are encouraged to wear jeans and tee-shirts or other casual clothes. This practice was first introduced by computer companies in the US and was designed to help break down barriers between different levels of workers and to encourage teamwork and improve communication on an interpersonal level.

Dressing formally for an interview or even a court appearance is clearly important in the same way. We wear formal clothes to tell the world we have made an effort to look smart. We are also signalling our willingness to conform to the demands of authority, an important gesture to make in both the job market and the magistrates' court.

ACTIVITY . . .

- What is your attitude to school uniform?
- What function do you think it is intended to serve?
- How effectively do you think it serves this function?
- Is uniform generally popular or unpopular with students?

There are situations where dressing casually is more appropriate, such as when we are relaxing or socialising. Casual clothes are generally more comfortable and this may make us feel and behave in a more relaxed way. On occasions, however, a person may wear casual clothes in order to present a reassuring image to another person or group. Some teachers, for example, decide to dress informally perhaps in order to signify a less authoritarian relationship with their class.

It is obvious that we make a lot of initial judgements about people because of their clothes. In the same way the clothes we choose to wear invite other people to think about us in certain ways.

Dress is just one aspect of the physical appearance that we present to the world. We might also consider such aspects as hairstyle, jewellery, make-up, body adornment and body modification. Each of these is open to interpretation by the people with whom we come into contact. Collectively they make a statement about ourselves and our system of values. Hair length or facial hair in men, for example, can determine the assumptions that people make about the person beneath. The type and style of jewellery worn by men and women is open to interpretation. Similarly, body adornment and decoration in the form of tattoos or face and body piercings can all act as signals to other people. Of course, like all signals they are open to being read in a variety of different ways according to the attitudes, values and background of the 'reader'.

POSTURE

Closely allied to the impact of dress is the impact of our posture. Posture is about the way in which we position our bodies. Much of our early socialisation has taught us the importance of an erect posture, which means holding ourselves upright and straight to our full height. On the other hand slouching is associated with poor posture and by implication laziness or slovenly behaviour. 'Sit up straight', 'shoulders back' or 'chin up' are instructions regularly heard at home and at school.

We associate an upright posture with people who are confident about themselves. The armed forces and the police are drilled into adopting this posture which, in the same way as their uniform, gives them an air of confident authority. Their posture is another sign of the status and role within society.

Contrast this military bearing with a homeless person begging on the streets. Their posture is one of sagging, with their body almost being allowed to collapse into a heap. Their low self-esteem, perhaps combined with cold and hunger, is reflected in their posture. Their body sags to indicate their lack of status and confidence. Indeed, it is common to see people bending their bodies into a foetal position, as though seeking the reassurance they once had in the womb.

Certainly we use posture as one means of indicating to another person our feelings of friendship or hostility. Certain postures such as standing with hands on hips can be construed as confrontational and hostile.

ACTIVITY . . .

Make a list of postures that might be considered hostile. Make a second list of postures that might be considered friendly.

Good posture is something that can be learned. A technique was invented last century by an Australian actor, Frederick Alexander. He argued that adopting good posture by becoming sensitive to the way in which we hold our bodies is beneficial to our physical and mental well-being. Certainly spending time look at yourself in a full-length mirror from a variety of angles will indicate a good deal about the postures you adopt. It might also provide a useful area of study to consider some of the different postures people adopt when they are communicating with us. Often a person's bodily posture can provide an indication of how comfortable or otherwise they feel about the person they are next to.

Posture is also another aspect of our behaviour when we are together in a group. It is often possible to observe that people unconsciously imitate the postures of the people they are with, sometimes as a couple in larger groups. This process is known by a number of names, but most commonly is called mirroring or, more grandly, postural congruence. An example of this is the way in which people often cross their legs or fold their arms to mirror the postures that people in their immediate circle have adopted. Part of the function of such actions is to reinforce group identities and to suggest conformity within the group. Just as dress can be used to reinforce the cohesion of the group, so too can posture. This is perhaps another reason why drill is such an important element of training in the armed and the police forces.

COMMUNICATION STUDIES: THE ESSENTIAL INTRODUCTION

Consider the ways in which people walk, perhaps using some of the verbs that we use to describe different kinds of walking. What assumptions do we make when we see people

- strut

- saunter

- swagger

- mince

- march?

PARALANGUAGE

When we speak, we don't just communicate with words: we also make noises that aren't words. We raise and lower our voices. We pause. We stress some words (almost like underlining words when writing by hand or emboldening words when word-processing). We call this paralanguage. It can be defined as those utterances that we make when we are speaking that are not in fact identifiable as language.

If you listen carefully to people speaking, the words they say are punctuated with noises such as 'um' or 'ah'. We also punctuate our speech with pauses, hesitations, little laughs or coughs and splutters. In paralinguistics these phenomena are considered, alongside the words themselves, as an important aspect of the message we are communicating. In addition people tend to have quite individual speech patterns which can make their voices distinctive and memorable. Such factors as pitch, stress, accent and pace are other aspects of paralanguage that can determine how the messages that we utter are interpreted.

The importance of paralanguage in determining the way in which people respond to our spoken messages is evident from the following example. Imagine you hear the following words:

'The house is on fire'

If this sentence is spoken, in the absence of any visible punctuation marks, it could be interpreted as a statement or as a question. What would determine the way that we might interpret such an utterance is *how* it is spoken. When we ask a question, the pitch of our voice tends to rise as we near the end of the sentence. This rising pitch is generally interpreted by listeners as an indication that we are asking a question, rather than making a statement. Tone of voice, as it is commonly known, is an important indicator of the intention of the sender in uttering a message. You might like to consider the significance of irony here, where a sender may actually mean the opposite of what is being said. Some people find it almost impossible to detect when other people are being ironical.

Pitch is just one aspect of paralanguage that helps a listener fill in the detail of what we say. If, for example, we were to shout the sentence loudly, it would be readily perceived by anyone in earshot as a warning, an alarm and a plea for help. The volume of our utterances can clearly impact on the way the message is interpreted. We tend to shout when we get angry or excited. Speaking at a particularly low volume, or whispering, usually indicates that we do not wish the message to be overheard. In the same way our speech will tend to speed up when we have a message that is emotionally charged. If someone speaks particularly slowly, we might draw the conclusion that they are patronising us.

ACTIVITY . . .

In the section on language we looked at the issue of accent and dialect. These are also an important aspect of paralanguage as they determine they way we sound to other people. Different regional accents are spoken with unique intonations and rhythms. Many of these accents carry with them connotations of the attitudes behind the voice, many of which are obviously quite stereotypical. You may like to consider what your initial reactions are to the following regional accents, all of which are associated with working-class communities:

East London

Liverpool

Glasgow

What judgements are you likely to make about the messages that are uttered by people who speak in these accents? You may also like to consider your own sense of linguistic community.

- Do you have an accent?

- How does this make you react to these accents?

- How do you think people from these communities are likely to react to the way in which you speak?

- Are the assumptions they might make correct?

As we suggested in the section on language, 'received pronunciation' is often considered to be the 'correct' way in which to speak the English language. It is interesting to note that elocution lessons are designed to make people speak RP, presumably because this is more desirable than a regional accent.

The function of the sounds that we make in addition to verbal utterances is an important aspect of our exploration of paralanguage. A question that clearly needs to be answered is why we use these sounds and how they contribute to the meaning of our messages.

One function they serve is to stop the flow of speech. This is particularly noticeable when we are listening to someone speak whom we expect to be fluent. A newsreader, for example, rarely hesitates in reading a bulletin. Any hesitation usually indicates that

COMMUNICATION STUDIES: THE ESSENTIAL INTRODUCTION

something has gone wrong – the autocue is stuck or a studio director is shouting through the earpiece.

In conversation, however, such hesitation is commonplace and often passes unnoticed. Indeed, we might be suspicious of a person who was too fluent in their speaking. We might think that they had rehearsed it, rather like a salesperson might have practised a pitch to persuade us to fit new double-glazing. In conversation, we hesitate and interject ums and ahs for a number of reasons. Not least of these is to give us more time to consider what we are saying. Typically, if someone asks a difficult or embarrassing question, our immediate response is quite likely to be 'um', not least to give us time to think of an answer or excuse.

If we ask someone a direct question, these hesitations can be interpreted as important signals indicating to us the amount of trust we can put in the response that follows. In a court of law a hesitation may be deemed to tell rather more than the words that follow it.

Figure 5.1 *Truth Machine advertisement*

THE LINK BETWEEN VERBAL AND NON-VERBAL COMMUNICATION

As you will have seen from the above example, there are clear links between verbal and non-verbal communication. Most of the time when we communicate we use a whole repertoire of skills to construct messages. There has been a good deal of debate about the relationship between verbal and non-verbal communication (NVC). One issue that has been frequently revisited asks which of the two is the more important in the construction of a message. You may like to consider your own responses to this complex question and perhaps undertake some research of your own. You can do this by careful observation of how people use both verbal and non-verbal signals in different situations and how other people respond to them. At a more complex level, you may wish to explore the way in which non-verbal and verbal signals relate to one another in the process of conversation.

It is appropriate here to explore this last area. One of the functions of NVC in its different forms is as a regulator. A regulator is a mechanism that helps us to control the flow of conversation. When two people speak to each other, they generally do so in an ordered fashion. Each takes a turn at speaking and contributing to the conversation. This ordered method of communicating is largely achieved as a result of our learning to read different signals that indicate to the other person whether we are intending to continue speaking or wish them to speak.

In conversation with someone, we will indicate that we want them to, for example, listen to us or to react to what we've said. We call these indications cues. Many cues are signalled paralinguistically. Others are achieved by non-verbal behaviours such as eye contact. This is one way in which we invite the person we are addressing to join in conversation. Similarly, they may use eye contact as a method of declining the opportunity to converse. In the middle of a conversation we also use eye contact to signal that we have finished speaking and that we wish them to contribute. Eye contact and facial expression are important methods of encouraging and supporting the person who is speaking. They provide clear feedback signals that help regulate the way in which the person continues to address us.

ACTIVITY . . .

What sort of signals, verbal and non-verbal, do we use to close a conversation? How do these differ from those we use to initiate one?

It has probably occurred to you that one feature of interpersonal communication is that much of what goes on is predictable largely because it is governed by convention. Patterns of greetings tend to work to established formulas. 'How are you?' as a greeting is generally followed by 'Fine, thanks. How are you?' Other responses are of course possible, but social convention determines that this is the most likely exchange. In Part 3 we identified this predictability as redundancy. In interpersonal communication *redundancy* serves at least two key functions.

First, it is an important way of strengthening social bonds. In the example given above, the mutual concern exhibited by both parties suggests that each takes an interest in the other's well-being. Similarly, saying 'Take care' to a departing friend or acquaintance strengthens the relationship by indicating a similar concern.

Second, redundancy is a means of ensuring that a message is accurately received. A good example of this is teaching. Effective teachers use redundancy in a number of ways:

- They plan their classes so they have very predictable shapes to them.
- They use repetition, synopsis and summary to ensure key ideas are understood.
- They wrap up entropic communication with redundant communication (like a sandwich) to ensure students are not disorientated.

In *Key Concepts in Communication and Cultural Studies*, O'Sullivan *et al.* (1994) point out that redundancy is best not seen in a Communication Studies context as 'something unnecessary'. People who send messages with a high degree of redundancy are demonstrating a high degree of concern for their audience in wishing to ensure their messages are accurately and easily decoded.

▼ 3   INTRAPERSONAL COMMUNICATION: SELF AND SELF-CONCEPT

In this section we begin to look at intrapersonal communication.

■   We consider key ideas such as self-concept, self-image, the ideal self and self-esteem.

We have looked at some of the ways in which we communicate with each other by verbal and non-verbal means. We now move to examine what is, for many commentators, the source of all our communicating, our self. Communication within, with and to the self is called intrapersonal communication.

Clearly, intrapersonal communication is vital because it defines who we are.

The existence of the 'self' (the 'inner monologue') may seem self-evident and beyond doubt. We are surely all aware, at some level, of the difference between our inside and outside voices, of the voice that makes the decisions and the one that carries them out. When we look in a mirror, we are immediately aware of two 'selves' – the one seeing, the other seen. Thinking is similar if less obvious. When you are asked a question like 'When was the last time you lied?' or 'What was the most shameful thing you have ever done?' you are immediately aware of a kind of processing going on in your head. This will be partly concerned with recalling various examples of shameful behaviour and rating them for their shamefulness. It is also about examining your sense of self in relation to the context, the audience and your emotional state and gatekeeping the information; modifying or even holding back the 'truth' in order to protect your sense of yourself .

KEY TERM

GATEKEEPING   A process by which information is selected and modified for inclusion within communication messages. White's Gatekeeping model offers a useful visual representation of this process:

Diagram 5.1   *White's Gatekeeping model*

Gatekeeping is a concept which can be useful at both ends of the communication scale; from helping to explain how our own thoughts become messages to understanding the content of a national newspaper.

Stopping to think about what to reveal about yourself to others is a classic example of what intrapersonal communication is in practice. Non-humans may be conscious of sensations, such as hunger, thirst and pain but they lack this self-consciousness, this sense of self within the self. Murphy defines the self as 'the individual known to the individual'. This known individual probably consists of a number of identifiable, if not provable, components and processes, which may include:

- Thinking (cognition)
- Perception (both sensory [with the senses] and cognitive [with the mind])
- Memory
- Feelings/desires
- Motivation
- Personality
- Consciousness (that which you are aware of)
- Conscience (your moral sense)

Some people would like to add some traditional concepts such as 'heart' and 'soul' or even 'spirit'. These are really answers to the biggest philosophical question 'Who am I?' However, we should equally be aware that above all it is workable definitions we are after; definitions that will help us to understand how communication works. This section will largely provide this by exploring the above list and looking at the impact of these ideas on communication in practice.

SELF-CONCEPT

Let us first look at the ways in which we, as individuals, respond to our individuality. The best place to start is with 'self-concept', the idea we have of ourselves as individuals. Self-concept consists of three elements, each of which makes an important contribution. The first of these is self-image, the opinion or picture we have of ourselves.

Self-image

ACTIVITY . . .

EITHER (a) answer the question 'Who am I?' 20 times, in each case responding in the form 'I am . . .'.

OR (b) answer the following list of self-probing questions:

- Who are you?
- What do you do?

- What do you do well?
- What do you do badly?
- What is your strongest feeling?
- What is your strongest belief?
- What is your strongest desire?
- What is your oldest memory?
- What is your most shameful lie?
- What has been your greatest triumph?
- What has been your most wretched disaster?
- Who do you love?
- Who do you hate?
- Who do you like?
- Who do you dislike?
- Are you too tall or too short?
- Are you too thin or too fat?
- Are you too clever or too stupid?
- Who would you like to be?
- Which question would you like to be asked?

If you responded to (a), the interesting thing to do is to try to spot trends in the results. If you chose (b), it is valuable to go back and calculate how many of the answers you gave are genuinely honest and thus useful. How many of your answers are really a response to the need to have an answer and/or the need to have a potential audience?

Kuhn and McPartland (1954) conducted this experiment, asking option (a) above, on both 7-year-olds and undergraduates and they reached some interesting conclusions. First they were able to see responses to the 'Who am I?' question falling into two categories which they related to:

- **Social roles**: the parts we play, either 'ascribed' (or given) rather like daughter or son or 'achieved' roles (such as student or part-time worker)
- **Personality traits**: statements about what we think we are like, such as 'I am very easy-going' or 'I am very hard-working'

Kuhn and McPartland also found that the main difference between the 7-year-olds and undergraduates was in the proportions of 'social roles' and 'personality traits'. On average 7-year-olds recorded five social role statements while the undergraduates recorded ten. This suggests that as we get older we progressively describe ourselves in terms of the jobs we do or status we have. This has a convincing ring to it, for on meeting people for the first time the thing adults most often offer, after their names, is what they do.

The other aspects of self-image relate to the various versions of the self which are being imaged. We can distinguish between the intellectual self, the emotional self and the body self (or body image), though we could also add social and physical or physiological selves. Body image is a particularly important factor in growing up in a society where stereotyped body images are common. This is the point at which self-image becomes influenced by the other components of self-concept, in particular, the ideal self.

Ideal self

ACTIVITY . . .

Note: this activity is not intended to be a traumatic experience where you put yourself down. Loosen up – education should be fun!

Ideal self is the kind of person you would like to be at best. Examine the three designations:

- Intellectual self

- Emotional self

- Bodily self

Sum up the ideal male or female according to society or the media. How far is your ideal self similar or different to these?

Ideal self is an easier concept in theory than it often is in practice. Trying to probe the ideal self in any kind of public context results in the same kind of gatekeeping we spoke of in relation to shameful secrets. In expressing our ideals, we will often resort to projecting these on to other, often public people. To conceive of your ideal self in terms of another person is usually to get role models and ideal selves confused.

ACTIVITY . . .

Who are your role models and heroes/heroines? What qualities do you admire in them? If you would like to be more like these people, what more than their success (money, fame, sex etc.) do you want?

Rogers would see in role-modelling evidence that we have a number of layers or levels of self-consciousness. The modelling of ourselves in terms of other, often public and famous people, is part of a process that creates, presents and maintains our own 'public self'. This 'public self' is a significantly more superficial version of the self than the one we 'show' to close friends and family, let alone the 'core' self that remains with us at all times. His concentric circle model shows the interconnectedness of these 'selves'.

Diagram 5.2 *Roger's Concentric Circle model*

Self-esteem

Rogers (1961) suggests that the gap between self-image and ideal self is likely to be a measure of an individual's self-worth or 'self-esteem', as the third component of self-concept is usually known. Coopersmith (1967) defines self-esteem as 'a personal judgement of worthiness'. In other words self-esteem is a currency of self-regard: it measures and records how good you feel about yourself. High self-esteem is obviously aided by such socially valuable attributes as physical athleticism and/or attractiveness, but it is most significantly helped by the respect of others.

Of the four key factors identified by Dimbleby and Burton (1998) in the creation of a sense of self, three are directly concerned with the relationships we have with others:

- Reactions of others
- Comparisons with others
- Identifications with others
- (the fourth is the roles we play)

ACTIVITY . . .

'Identifications'

- Who are the significant others for you?
- Whose reactions matter to you?
- Whom do you compare yourself to?
- Who are you compared to?
- With whom do you identify?

We have already to some extent dealt with identifications when we talked about role models. Much research has been done, particularly in the fields of education, management and sports psychology, into the beneficial effects of positive feedback. This is sometimes called the 'Pygmalion effect'. (This is a reference to the play by George Bernard Shaw where Professor Higgins makes a bet that he can turn a Cockney flower girl into the RP-speaking toast of London society. In other words, he believed he could change someone.) Researchers might, for example, privilege schoolchildren according to illogical criteria like eye or hair colour. Most often these children would end up heading the class academically. This suggests that our expectations are a powerful tool for changing attitude, behaviour and perception. This is usually referred to as the self-fulfilling prophecy, a vicious or sometimes beneficial circle.

Here the established expectations cue behaviour, which further supports the expectations. Put another way, you expect laziness from a child who then conforms and confirms your initial expectations. Of course, it can work in a positive way, as a motivational tool where high expectations encourage positive behaviour and achievement follows.

In both cases the issue is essentially self-esteem, which at its positive and negative extremes can have potentially miraculous and/or crippling results. Low self-esteem results in low motivation, a lack of self-confidence and a lessening in the use of verbal and non-verbal communication. High self-esteem improves all of these, facilitating social interaction, persuasion, and increasing the quality and volume of communication.

ACTIVITY . . .

Self-esteem is a flexible 'substance', often extremely susceptible to fluctuation. What kinds of thing raise your self-esteem and make you feel good about yourself? What kinds of thing lower your self-esteem and make you feel bad about yourself?

It is likely that your lists were dominated by the influence of other people, those whose responses are likely to make a difference to you. These interested others act as a kind of validation of our behaviour, reflecting (if we're lucky) the kinds of versions of ourselves that we think we are projecting. This is what Cooley (1992) called 'looking-glass theory', the version of the self we find in others' responses. On a superficial level this is evident. When we get dressed up for a night out, we partly see ourselves in others people's reactions to us. The theory is similar to 'the self-fulfilling prophecy' in that expectation is created by response. We receive judgements and evaluations of our behaviour from others and then modify our behaviour accordingly. Cooley was interested in the ways we modify behaviour according to the differences between 'reflections'.

These variations depend very much upon our stability and consistency as *personalities* (for more of this see the next section), our capacity effectively to perceive and interpret feedback, the importance of the responses we are making to others. The depth of our engagement with a person or situation will usually influence the effectiveness of the mirror effect. The looking-glass effect is powerful but only at a fairly superficial level, due to its immediacy. Often this influence is seen in terms of the encouragement of conventional patterns of behaviour and attitudes rather than as infiltrating beliefs and values.

Attitudes, values and beliefs are terms used to describe our various responses to the world. To some extent they represent depth of response and breadth of influence.

KEY TERM

ATTITUDES Our tendency to react favourably or unfavourably to people, objects or situations. Attitudes are created and modified by rewards and punishments (real and implied).

BELIEFS Our views of existence; what we think is true. Belief includes knowledge and is often given to us by authority figures: we act on our beliefs.

VALUES The worth you place on things, events and people. Values are the bedrock of all behaviour. Society's values are found in the media.

Another factor that has bearing on 'looking-glass theory' is the degree to which we are able as individuals to read the often non-verbal feedback. In Gerbner's two-dimensional model, which we encountered in Part 3, perception is one of the dimensions. It is a key communication activity. Gerbner suggests that perception is subject to the qualifiers 'selection, context and availability' (what you choose to perceive; where you perceive from physically and psychologically; and how much of the perceived object is available to you). Selection is an interesting criterion as it suggests to some extent that we 'see' what we want to see.

KEY TERM

PERCEPTION A term used to refer to certain human processes and capacities. We gather sensory data from the world about us. We process that data and, in so doing, produce information about the world. We use that information to make sense of the world in the immediate sense and we also carry forward that perception as the capacity to make sense of things we will encounter in the future.

If the responses of others to us have importance, it is equally important to understand the role interpersonal perception plays in intrapersonal communication. We have already looked at the broad implications of low self-esteem. To these we can surely add 'uncertainty in perception'. If we feel badly about ourselves, we will see this reflected in others. Accurate perception is a precarious business to which all the various elements of the self mentioned earlier in this section contribute. Add to these the various environmental factors which might influence the process (largely what Gerbner calls 'availability' and 'context') and you see the difficulties. Dimbleby and Burton (1998) usefully sum up 'errors of perception' in the following way:

- **We miss out some piece of information** In other words, we interpret a person or behaviour without all of the relevant information, like when you later discover that the person who appears to have been 'giving you the eye' all night is in fact very short-sighted.

- **We make too much of something**. People often take one feature of a person and for no rational reason amplify this; this is the place that stereotyping and prejudice start.

- **We make false connections between one thing and another.** This is often the outcome of making too much of something; in gender terms, stereotypes make irrational connections between women and certain kinds of behaviour. For example, because women are weak, emotionally fragile and largely moral, you shouldn't swear in front of them.

- **We guess wrongly about the other person by making false association of traits and experience.** Given that perception is invariably partial, it is inevitable that part of the process [and processing] is estimation or guesswork. We take the exhibition of generosity as a character trait as the basis for a positive judgement or we read some other person's bad experience with the police as the basis of 'a dangerous personality'. This is classically the 'halo and horns' effect, privileging one piece of information, positively or negatively, over the rest.

With such potential problems of perception, the self-image has a key role as gatekeeper of the information about the self which is available both from without (the feedback of others) and from within ourselves. This is a balance between intrapersonal and interpersonal communication, between our own influence on the self and the influence of others: between looking-glass self and self-image. To some extent we control the information about ourselves that is made available both to ourselves and to others. What we choose to offer of the self to the world is termed 'self-disclosure', while our responses to what comes back constitutes 'feedback'.

This disclosure/feedback relationship is at the heart of the Johari Window, which is a useful model for setting self-image in the context of the self and other people. Luft and Ingham (1955), the creators of the Johari Window, drew axes that record self-image in terms of information available to the self and others. They then organised the resulting grid into four quadrants.

Diagram 5.3 **The Johari Window**

- **The open area** includes information that is available to all (your gender, race, name are examples).
- **The hidden area** is more intimate and private. Here are those items you choose not to reveal (perhaps the shameful acts we thought about earlier).
- **The blind area** is that which 'looking-glass' theory avoids, that which others can see but not you yourself (perhaps you are too self-critical).
- **The unknown area** is that part of us we cannot easily contact or understand; the subconscious, dreams and desires.

The Johari Window is a flexible model, with areas drawn according to the specific character or situation. Some people can't help but be self-disclosers, whereas others hold on to their private thoughts as if they were gold. You can use the Johari Window to plot these tendencies and to predict outcomes. Engaging in interpersonal communication is, according to this model, about further opening the 'open' frame and at the same time adjusting the 'hidden' and/or 'blind'. It is about self-disclosure as an effective response to feedback. This brings us neatly to the 'looking-glass self', because one thing that we manipulate in our response to others' feedback is information about ourselves that we were only partly aware of.

ACTIVITY . . .

If we encountered an individual whose hidden quadrant or frame is or was dominant, then that person would likely be secretive or inward-looking. This might be a feature of this person's personality or might be a response to a particular set of circumstances, such as a bereavement. What sort of situation or individual would you be encountering if the dominant (i.e. largest) frame was:

- open
- blind
- unknown?

Self-disclosure is not the only protective mechanism known to the self-concept and its attendant self-image. We may be theoretically vulnerable to the responses of others, which is why we have strategies through which to counter their effects. This is essentially a *dissonance theory*. The self is faced with two sets of oppositional data – positive information from the self-concept and negative information from the world. These 'informations' are cognitively dissonant (they do not 'rhyme' intellectually; they are difficult to reconcile). Dissonance theory suggests that the likely response to such a conflict of information is for us artificially to weaken one side of the argument. The classic example offered by Richard Gross (1996) is with smokers who believe, know and understand that smoking increases the risk of serious disease. Their response to this cognitive dissonance is often a sort of overreaction:

- They belittle the evidence.
- They associate with other smokers.

- They smoke low-tar cigarettes.
- They convince themselves that smoking is a highly pleasurable activity.
- They stress the dangers of smoking and make it a personality feature.

This is exactly what Gergen and Gergen (1981) were dealing with when they identified the various ways in which we protect our selves (ourselves) from negative feedback. These so-called 'self-maintenance strategies' are really a series of dissonant responses for keeping our idea of the self intact. What we do is one or more of the following:

- Mix with like people (how many of your closest friends like the same kind of music as you?)
- Mix with people of lower status or ability (we go around with our 'inferiors' in order that we look and feel good)
- Change our behaviour to conform to norms (one of the ways that the self protects itself is by changing its 'clothes' and adopting the 'uniform' of accepted ways of behaving in which it will be less likely to attract attention and challenge)
- Form low opinion of detractors (feedback is effective in proportion to the status of its source; if the source is stupid/unreliable/dishonest, then the feedback will be too)
- Disbelieve what others say (which is why we never believe our parents when they tell us our new boy/girlfriend will bring us nothing but trouble)
- Misunderstand negative feedback (if we don't fully understand criticism, it can't fully 'hurt' us)
- Consciously evoke response (we behave or dress in a way that will artificially provoke the feedback we want – like dressing smartly for an interview)
- Selectively evaluate self (a simple device which stresses some aspects of who we are instead of other less positive aspects)
- Self-handicapping (this is a favourite strategy with students of all ages; by not attending or trying or revising, we leave little room for real failure [and no room for success])

ACTIVITY . . .

Self-maintenance strategies are employed by us all to a lesser or greater degree: they are designed to keep us comfortable and sane. Spend some time observing your friends and colleagues, and try to collect evidence of Gergen and Gergen's strategies.

Gergen and Gergen offer a useful list of mechanisms which are a mixture of the internally defensive and externally offensive (the best form of defence being attack). We move to discuss the latter as part of self-presentation in section 5. Meanwhile the next section will try to explore further theories about the self and its internal operations, this self that we are so keen to develop and defend.

COMMUNICATION STUDIES: THE ESSENTIAL INTRODUCTION

▼ 4 INTRAPERSONAL COMMUNICATION: IDEAS ABOUT THE DEVELOPMENT OF THE SELF AND PERSONALITY

In this section we continue to examine intrapersonal communication and move to consider some ideas about the development of the self and personality.

- We look at the work of Harré, Freud, Laing, Jung, Cattell, Eysenck and Adorno.

Introverted & extroverted

The purpose of this section is to stimulate further discussion about the self as communicator and as communicated; in other words, about how the self is not only a primary sender of communication but also part of the message as well. What follows is intended to work in two ways: (a) to provide direct input into your understanding of intrapersonal communication and (b) to suggest methods of individual research into the self and personality. The section is largely concerned with other people's theories, many of whom have made important contributions to the study of psychology. In Freud's case he made vital contributions to the history of twentieth-century thought.

Given that we're going to devote this section to other people's ideas, let's begin by stating some principles of our own. Across the whole of this chapter our aims are:

- To define key concepts (such as role, perception, culture and context) *see pg 239*
- To identify forms and uses of communication at the level of the individual and the small group (in other words, to recognise what kinds of personal communication there are and what they do)
- To develop useful subject-specific terminology (which will make the communication of the above information more efficient)

If we lose sight of the key elements (the 'what', 'how' and 'why' of personal communication), no amount of theoretical knowledge will help. This section must enhance our understanding of the basic principles developed in the previous section and lay the foundations for the discussion of self as communicated text, which is important to the next section.

We left the self at the end of the last section battling to maintain itself in the face of the assault of the real world and other people. Psychologists identify a series of stages through which this desperate-to-be-maintained self must pass before it enjoys 'autonomy', the capacity to function independently. Piaget (1952), for example, argues that babies have no self-concept and see their own bodies in the same way as they see other objects in the world. There is no sense of self-ownership. As they adapt to their environment, so they find a sense of themselves. This is reinforced by self-recognition (the capacity to recognise your image or reflection) and in self-definition (the capacity to know the difference between 'I /me' and 'you').

SELF - RECOGNITION = Being able to recognize oneself

Developing alongside this is the child's emerging awareness of the inner self, invisible but clearly communicating and visually localised – even by young children – in the head. This is the beginning of what Mead (1930) called 'self-interaction', our unique capacity to have discourse with ourselves, through self-perception, through thinking about ourselves and through forms of intrapersonal communication (talking or writing to ourselves). This extended conversation is stimulated by the influence of objective categories like age and gender or by more subjective interpretations like role and personality. All of this is reinforced by the defining discourse (the authoritative voice) of language, through which personality and self are made and then communicated.

Harré has argued that language reflects our attitudes towards selfhood (Harré *et al.* 1985). This is essentially a standpoint which can be characterised as 'linguistic relativism'. This approach to language can be efficiently summed up in the philosopher Wittgenstein's (1953) famous saying: 'The limits of my language are the limits of my world'. In the case of understanding the self, Harré is saying that what we can say about the self is limited by the vocabulary that we and our culture and language possess. Harré suggests that even the existence and widespread use of the pronouns 'I' and 'me' give the (often false) impression that we are more coherent and unified than we actually are.

ACTIVITY . . .

Look up 'self' in a thesaurus and you'll be directed to two categories of related words:

- **'Identity'**, which includes 'selfness', 'selfsame', 'oneness', 'homogeneity', 'unity' and 'identification'

- **'Speciality'**, which includes 'I myself', 'ego', 'individuality', 'particularity', 'peculiarity', 'personality', 'singularity', 'special', 'specific', 'personal', 'original' and 'exact'

What do these associations tell you about our understanding of the self?

Partly Harré is engaged with Roland Barthes' (1973) concept of myth as a level of signification. You will remember that a myth is a sort of collective connotation, a story to explain some aspect of reality which groups of people can buy into. Harré is suggesting that language itself is a mythic structure in which values are enshrined. He is also suggesting that there are only a certain number of 'stories' which can be told about the self. Other cultures will, necessarily, have other stories in which the self is a more or less restricted idea. Moscovici (1985) goes even further to suggest the 'individual' is the greatest invention of modern times; in other words, it is a product of Western culture and language. In a comparative study of Western and non-Western culture, Smith and Bond (1993) found it useful to make a distinction between the independent self (favoured in the West) and the 'interdependent self', between the self as isolated and as part of a 'team'.

Make a list of traditional stories that are told to young European children (for example, 'The Three Little Pigs' or 'Jack and the Beanstalk'). How many of these are centred around what characters do *individually* and how many depend on collective effort (or *teamwork*)?

It is interesting to note that the English language has about 20,000 words which refer to aspects of the human personality, or personality traits as they are commonly called. This is arguably an aspect of the contemporary view in the West that personality is, as *The ABC of Communication Studies* has it, 'an individual's distinctive consistent and patterned methods of relating to the environment', or, more simply, 'individual differences and the typical ways people behave' (Gill and Adams 1998). Clearly, in both senses personality is of interest to the Communication Studies student in that 'distinctive, consistent and patterned methods' can be nothing other than communication. To some extent it could be argued that our personality defines the motivation for, and style and content of, all our conscious acts of communication.

We will certainly want to define and/or dissect the notion of personality if we are fully to understand what communication there is and particularly what it does.

Sigmund Freud had interesting things to say about human personality and communication. Basically Freud believed that the development of the self was forged in the conflict between what he called 'the pleasure principle' and 'the reality principle' (Freud 1984a). The pleasure principle describes the uncontrolled desire to be physically and immediately satisfied, which is the desire of a foetus in the womb. Growing up, for Freud, is simply the story of the ways in which this instinctive drive is checked by the influence of the real world and other people, which Freud labelled 'the reality principle'. The reality principle provides social roles and responsibility and notions of selfhood that go beyond immediate needs: to include such things as morality (conventions of behaviour) and self-image.

Communication (and language in particular) is implicitly central to Freud's analysis of personality, which in many ways is an impressive model of intrapersonal communication. Freud saw the 'reality–pleasure' contradiction as being contested through the forms of the conscious and unconscious mind. In this, communication in all its forms is a kind of context or even medium. To Freud lapses and slip-ups in spoken and written language are nothing more or less than the intrusion of the subconscious into the conscious (in other words, what we are thinking deep down comes to the surface and interferes with what we are saying). (Freud used the term 'parapraxis' to describe this phenomenon. This is commonly referred to as 'the Freudian slip'). In his book *The Interpretation of Dreams* (1999) he also proposed that a similar case can be made for dreams as an important symbolic intrapersonal code, another way in which one layer of the self communicates with another. 'Words', Freud claimed, 'are a half-way house to lost things'. In other words, they are properly, in a semiotic sense, symbols, though what is signified is for Freud very like the 'unknown' frame of the Johari Window, that which you barely know yourself.

Freud's analysis of personality dramatises it very effectively, modelling the debate within the self in a coherent and convincing way. For Freud the personality consists of three parts

– the id, the ego and the superego (Freud 1984) – and intrapersonal communication is the product of their various relationships. Let us take them in turn.

■ **The id** responds directly to the instinct. It is the mouthpiece of needs and desires. As Freud himself pointed out: 'It contains everything that is present at birth . . . above all the instincts.' The id operates according to the pleasure principle: 'I want it now'. Freud dramatises the id to make his point that it is primitive and primal: 'we call it a chaos, a cauldron full of seething excitations.'

■ **The ego** represents the conscious self responding to the physical needs of the id and the moral demands of the super-ego. It is the manager of the personality, continually making contingency plans to stave off the next crisis. The ego operates according to the reality principles, bringing the outside world to bear on the desires of the id. The ego is reason, whereas the id is passion. Freud estimated the ego gradually developed, starting at a few months old as the child turned his energies outwards.

■ **The super-ego** is the moral aspect of the personality and thus the last fully to develop. It is partly ego-ideal (a sort of ideal ego), which promises rewards for good behaviour, and partly conscience, which threatens punishment for transgressors. The super-ego is in constant conflict with the id, for one is moral and the other is amoral (the id has no sense of morality).

A crude way to demonstrate Freud's argument is to take a simple moral situation and dramatise the roles of id, ego and super-ego. If you were walking home and found a wallet containing some money lying on the ground:

■ The id would say 'take it, spend it, enjoy yourself, you won't be found out'.
■ The super-ego would say 'That would be stealing, and stealing is wrong. You will be caught and punished.'
■ The ego would have the job of working between these positions in order to make a practical decision. The ego would consider such factors as how much there is, how much you need it, who's around to see, and whose wallet it is.

ACTIVITY . . .

Try to apply Freud's theory in the same way to the following situation. You find yourself attracted to your best friend's girlfriend/boyfriend, and a string of coincidences has left you alone together at your place. There is no one else at home, and he/she seems 'keen'. What does your id say? What does your ego say? What does your super-ego say?

It is the ego's job to mediate (act as a go-between for) the demands of the id and super-ego. In other words, the ego is a representation of that 'voice' we all listened to in the previous section, when asked about shameful events from our past. The same would be true in a situation where we were asked to reveal something intimate or talk about a taboo subject such as masturbation. The super-ego represents that part of our internal communication which considers the accepted morality. The id represents that part of our internal communication which considers the instinctive reality. The ego acts as a go-between and forges a response. In Gergen and Gergen's (1981) terms, the ego is the self-maintainer. Freud's 'strategies' are unconscious and referred to as defence mechanisms, intrapersonal behaviours designed to (albeit temporarily) resolve the conflict between what we'd like to do and what we should do.

An understanding of defence mechanisms is invaluable for interpreting interpersonal behaviour because it offers a key to decoding a good deal of individual and group communication. A simple list of defence mechanisms would include:

- **Repression**: bottling up potentially painful experiences and feelings
- **Displacement**: transferring your feelings to a substitute object, for example being angry with your boss and coming home to pick a row with your partner
- **Denial**: refusing to accept reality, e.g. that your coursework is late, or that your relationship is over, or that your dog is dead
- **Rationalisation**: finding acceptable reasons for unacceptable things, like your failure in an examination because you didn't revise
- **Reaction formation**: consciously thinking the opposite of what you really feel – for example, being very nice to people you dislike
- **Sublimation**: working your unacceptable feelings out in a substitute activity, for example doing the washing up to avoid a vicious argument
- **Identification**: avoiding conflict by associating yourself with someone else's thoughts or experiences
- **Projection**: seeing your own faults or problems in other people
- **Regression**: exhibiting behaviour typical of an earlier stage of your development, for example crying or wetting the bed
- **Isolation**: compartmentalising problems, keeping different thoughts and feelings apart

ACTIVITY . . .

How far do you agree with Freud's descriptions of the ways in which we defend ourselves psychologically? Which of the above behaviours can you recognise in your own life and/or the lives of your closest friends and family?

Freud's model of a segmented self overseen by a dominant ego has a validity that can be easily supported by our everyday experiences. We do seem to have an inner voice which, among other things, settles both consciously and subconsciously disputes between what we'd 'like' to do and what we ought to do. In many ways the effectiveness and necessity of defence mechanisms is demonstrated by cases where all forms of defence fail.

R. D. Laing's work on schizophrenia (*The Divided Self*, 1962), for example, offers a model in which the patient's relationship with the world and the self has broken down. Here the patient's communication remains intelligible but only in terms of their own 'divided self' and its relationship with the world. Without the balance and control that Freud would see provided by the ego, schizophrenics, according to Laing, suffer from what he called 'ontological insecurity', an uncertainty which affects even their ability to know and understand anything. This comprises three experiences which Laing labelled:

- **Engulfment**: the fear of being swallowed up, suffocated by others' involvement. This makes love a particular threat
- **Implosion**: the fear that the world at any moment will come crashing in and obliterate their identity. Schizophrenics feel empty
- **Petrification/depersonalisation**: the fear of being turned to stone or becoming brainwashed

Laing's work was an assault on the treatment of schizophrenia as a disease. He came to feel that the way it was being treated made the condition worse, that schizophrenia was something the medical profession did to patients. Writing in the 1960s, which was a period of experimentation, it was not surprising that Laing also came to see schizophrenia as a gateway to a new perception. His 'psychedelic model' sees schizophrenia as an antidote to normality. 'Madness,' he claimed, 'need not be all breakdown . . . it may also be breakthrough.' At a time when access to the unknown self was valued highly, this was a persuasive manifesto.

Laing's theories are interesting now only as an aid; they properly belong to their time. Freud has made a more lasting contribution. Freud offers a challenging analysis of human personality, which we can take or leave but which, either way, stimulates thought about communication. Others have disagreed with Freud's theories of personality, condemning them as abstract and unscientific. However, as tools for analysing the various understandings of intention, they are invaluable.

A one-time colleague of Freud, Carl Jung broke away from Freud's teachings, seeing the personality as a combination of factors: heart, feelings, soul. 'Wholeness' for Jung was both vital and vitally missing from Freud. Jung (1963) identified three elements of the psyche:

- **Consciousness** (thinking, feeling, sensing, intuiting (knowing something without knowing how you know it)). This is the part of the psyche known directly to the individual. For Jung the conscious mind also has two attitudes: either introversion (looking inward) or extroversion (looking outward). The ego is the organisation of the conscious mind, the individual's sense of identity.
- **Personal unconscious** (depressed or forgotten experiences). This is the part of the psyche that is only indirectly available to us by means of therapy or traumatic experience. Sometimes feelings, thoughts and memories cluster together on the personal unconscious and become complexes, significant stand-alone influences within the psyche (these are our 'hang-ups').
- **Collective unconscious** (our genetic heritage, the fruit of evolution). This is the part of the psyche that we have inherited from our ancestors.

For Jung, the collective unconscious is a store of 'primordial images' (a sort of racial memory bank), both human and pre-human. Jung used this to explain various phobias such as the fear of spiders or the dark. These images are archetypes, 'original models' of aspects of human behaviour. There are four major archetypes in Jungian psychology:

- **Persona**: the outward face we present to the world
- **Anima/animus**: our feminine/masculine side
- **Shadow**: the dark, primitive source of creativity

- **Self**: the unifying force of the personality – selfhood is the aim of the Jungian model and achieved by only a few individuals

Jung's theories are attractive to students of communication in at least two ways. First, like Freud, Jung offers a provocative set of prompts which are useful as tools of analysis of personal acts of communication. Jung exposes the levels at which communication takes place in a way that is not unlike Barthes's explanation of levels of signification. In this way Jung's archetypes are not unlike Barthes's myths, though for Jung 'ideology' would probably be replaced by 'psychological programming'. Furthermore this allows us to examine the connections between the structure of the self and communication texts, especially in terms of such things as narrative theory. Much of the supportive evidence and informing basis of Jung's theories come from an examination of theories in world mythologies and a recognition of the similarities between these. The stories we tell, much like the dreams we have, may in fact be a 'royal road to the unconscious', a coded version of our intrapersonal structures. Stevens' diagram of the Jungian psyche (cited in Gross 1993) shows the levels at which communication might operate:

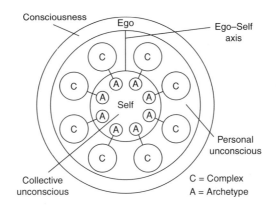

Diagram 5.4 Jung's psyche (after Stevens)

The controversy remains with the collective unconscious, the idea of cultural memory. Do we dream our culture at a superficial level because we are immersed in it on a day-to-day basis or as a profound retrieval of inborn and biological information? Certainly the case for archetypal themes in the stories we tell as cultures, in both traditional and contemporary contexts, seems very strong, as the success of the *Star Wars* movies indicates. In the case of George Lucas's nine-part epic story cycle, there is ample room to identify a cast of archetypal characters and themes working out their complexes on an intergallactic scale. After all, what is 'The Force' but Jung's 'shadow' – primal, troubling and creative? In Luke Skywalker and Princess Leia the animus and anima are acknowledged and reconciled, and when the persona of Vadar is eventually breached at least some reflected light is cast on the self.

Choose any mainstream Hollywood film or well-known novel or play and see if you can identify archetypal elements. Jung's list went well beyond the big four to include birth, rebirth, death, power, magic, the hero, the wise old man, the earth mother, the child, the demon. Remember these are symbolic forms, so, for example, the forty-something central character of a modern film may correspond to the archetype of 'the child'.

Both Jung and Freud offer guides or maps to the interpretation of behaviour. This certainty that all human behaviour can be explained (albeit from the point where the present interprets the past) has generated the criticism that these guides or maps are unscientific. Critics like H. J. Eysenck (1969), whose alternative theories of personality we will look at next, question the validity and usefulness of any theory that is unable either to predict behaviour or to measure it. Freud and Jung are strong on metaphor and symbol. Eysenck (1969) proposes a model through which the personality might be categorised and measured. This psychometric model of personality (in other words, one that hopes to 'measure' the psyche) suggests that there are central aspects of personality (or traits) which can be successfully cross-referenced with others to form clusters (or factors). By analysing these factors, or building blocks, of personality (assuming the tests can be validated) we will be able to build up a picture of the fundamentals of human personality and the range of differences across this idea.

At its crudest this simply identifies a range of character tendencies and asks individuals to plot their own characteristics or those of others on a continuum in order to create an impression of their personality. The problems of this approach are self-evident and have been implicitly addressed in the previous section, where the relationship between self-image, self-esteem and the ideal self were presented. However, systems like Cattell's (1965) do provide a useful starting and talking point. Where would you place yourself and your closest friend (use X and O) on the following model:

Reserved	⟷	Outgoing
Less intelligent	⟷	More intelligent
Affected by feelings	⟷	Unaffected by feelings
Submissive	⟷	Dominant
Serious	⟷	Happy-go-lucky
Expedient	⟷	Conscientious
Timid	⟷	Venturesome
Tough-minded	⟷	Sensitive
Trusting	⟷	Suspicious
Practical	⟷	Imaginative
Forthright	⟷	Shrewd
Self-assured	⟷	Apprehensive
Conservative	⟷	Experimenting
Group-dependent	⟷	Self-sufficient
Uncontrolled	⟷	Disciplined
Tense	⟷	Relaxed

Diagram 5.5 Psychometric model (after Cattell)

Using Cattell's list, plot the personalities, as far as you are able, of two of the following 'personalities':

- footballer Paul 'Gazza' Gascoigne
- a Spice Girl of your choice (old or new)
- the Prime Minister/Leader of the Opposition
- your parent/guardian
- a respected/feared/despised teacher
- Chris Tarrant or Anne Robinson

To 'discover' that Paul Gascoigne is, for example, very outgoing, extremely affected by feelings, always experimenting and too often uncontrolled may be of limited value. However, to have a set of proven tendencies of personality may help us to understand, for example, the different ways in which people are motivated. A drawback with Cattell's approach is that, for the perfectly defensible reason that it is undesirable to specialise any further, there are too many criteria to allow significant classification of individuals. That is to say, once you have made 16 statements about an individual, what you are left with is a convincing statement of their individuality rather than a feeling that they represent a type. Even to schematise Cattell's list into left–right–centre sections would permutate a massive 43 million combinations. (In other words, if we only allowed respondents to be reserved, outgoing or neither, the 16 category system would define more than 43 million personality types.)

Eysenck's approach is bolder for it proposes as a theory that there are a smaller number. He suggests four dimensions which deliver, in all, four distinct character types. Type theories attempt to classify all personalities into a limited number of groups. To some extent the theory of astrology is a type theory, given it assumes that roughly one-twelfth of the population have personalities that are broadly similar and governed by the stars. Eysenck's, in fact, is closer to the ancient Greek theory of the 'Humours'. This stated that human personality was determined by bodily 'chemical' balance; that our feelings and attitudes were aggravated by a predominance of one of the following 'bodily fluids':

too much yellow bile = choleric (angry, aggressive, restless)

too much blood = sanguine (warm, outgoing, lively)

too much black bile = melancholic (pessimistic, moody, quiet)

too much phlegm = phlegmatic (thoughtful, calm, reliable)

Galen, a doctor in second century AD Asia Minor, who contrived this theory, may have got the biology wrong but it is interesting that Eysenck incorporates these 'humours' into his own model of personality written some 1,800 years later. Eysenck proposed two axes of personality from which the four 'humours' might be derived. These axes, arrived at by analysing some 700 neurotic soldiers, are extroversion (and its opposite introversion) and neuroticism (and its opposite stability). Extroversion is simply the tendency to be outgoing, with introversion the tendency to direct ourselves inwardly. Neuroticism, or emotionality, describes the tendency to be excitable, changeable and unstable. According to Eysenck, the typical introvert is a quiet, retiring sort of person, introspective, fond of books rather than people, reserved and distant except to intimate friends. The typical extrovert is sociable, likes parties, has many friends, needs to have people to talk to and does not like reading or studying alone. He or she craves excitement.

ACTIVITY . . .

Which are you? The four designations are:

1   Stable – introvert

2   Stable – extrovert

3   Unstable – introvert

4   Unstable – extrovert

Find examples from public life or your own personal experience for each of the above.

If we look straightforwardly at Eysenck's model, it is easy to see its relevance to our study of communication. First, the qualities that define an individual's position on the axes are chiefly if not exclusively demonstrated in their communication. Second, this implies a conscious or unconscious communicative style for each designated grouping. Finally, if the model proves feasible, it simplifies the business of interpersonal perception and offers hope that we can improve skills of perception and, through this, our capacity to find the most appropriate communication.

Eysenck's dimensions offer us a basis for predicting behaviour, and he and others have pursued investigations into such matters as:

- Fatigue (extroverts tire more easily)
- Employment (extroverts change jobs more frequently)
- Relationships (extroverts divorce more readily)
- Pain (introverts have lower pain thresholds)
- Drugs (introverts are more difficult to sedate)
- Criminality (Eysenck claimed that criminals should classically be 'unstable' extroverts. Research has not confirmed this. Some studies have found criminals as a group to be slightly introverted. Hampson concluded that no verifiable link could be made between personality dimensions and criminality.)

Most useful for us is the work done by Eysenck and others on personality and conditionability, the relative ease or difficulty with which individuals can have the attitudes they hold changed. Eysenck (1947/1999) claimed that introverts were more easily conditioned than extroverts. However, the evidence is inconclusive and Eysenck has been criticised for assuming that any suggestion that introverts are easily conditioned by one kind of stimulus is proof of a general case about a broader range of stimuli.

The twentieth century was the century of Big Brother, so conditioning was always going to be a headline issue (George Orwell proposed in his 1948 novel *1984* a future in which we would be observed in our homes by representatives of the government; Big Brother was the novel's dictator). Partly theorists in the second half of the century were trying to understand and to come to terms with the large-scale political conditioning of the first half of the century, which had led to so many atrocities. Theodor Adorno (1950), who had himself fled Nazi persecution, first made the connection between personality and prejudice and between certain kinds of personality and certain kinds of 'collective ideologies' (such as Fascism). Adorno's research (which started in Nazi Germany and moved, as did he, to America) proposed the theory of the 'authoritarian personality'. According to Adorno, the authoritarian personality is:

- hostile to people with inferior status
- servile to those of higher status
- contemptuous of weakness
- rigid and inflexible
- intolerant of uncertainty
- unwilling to face feelings
- an upholder of traditional values and ways of life.

Adorno suggested that these individuals had often experienced a very strict upbringing, which gave them repressed feelings about authority which were re-channelled positively into 'political movements' and negativity into hatred for minorities.

Both Rokeach (1960) and Eysenck (1954) felt that the issue of prejudice (and its consequences) required a specialised scale. Rokeach proposed 'dogmatism' (the degree to which one's mind is open or closed) as a scale by which attitudes might be gauged. Eysenck called this the Toughmindedness and Tendermindedness factor. Both had a political attitudes axis (Eysenck's was radicalism–conservatism; Rokeach used Adorno's 'potentiality for fascism' scale). These allow us to plot a predictive position for various political varieties. The three theorists can be usefully combined in the diagram on p. 186.

While Eysenck largely confirmed a relationship between aspects of personality and authoritarianism (where toughmindedness was the significant trait), Rokeach stressed the greater importance of the compatibility of belief systems. Rokeach called this 'belief congruence theory', the idea that we are more positive in attitude towards people whose beliefs are congruent with ours (in other words which are similar in form and content). This will likely determine whom we communicate with, form relationships with, even work with. It was dealt with negatively in terms of cognitive dissonance theory in the previous section.

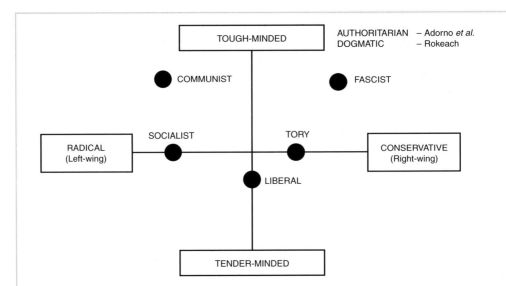

Diagram 5.6 *Example of a political attitudes axis (Gross 1993)*

▼ 5   # INTRAPERSONAL COMMUNICATION: SELF AND SELF-PRESENTATION

In this section we conclude our consideration of intrapersonal communication by looking at ideas about the self and self-presentation.

■   We consider the work of Argyle, Goffman and Berne.

Having given self-concept and personality a detailed examination, it is time to come to product and outcome. Intrapersonal communication is all very well in itself, but 'the audience of one' is a demanding one, particularly if you want to try out your range of communication skills. We can think a range of things from the philosophical to the erotic; we can whisper sweet nothings in our own ears (and, if we're desperate, answer in a different voice); we can write notes or a diary or even a poem or a song; but sooner or later we're going to want to communicate with others.

This section is about the influence of what's inside on what comes out. It's about the connections between intrapersonal and interpersonal communication. A common question asked in Communication Studies at all levels is 'What is the relationship between intrapersonal and interpersonal communication?' The first part of the answer is easy: a statement of the strength of this bond which is intimate, essential and significant. The boldest responses would claim that all communication is self-presentation, that the self is all we have to communicate. In this sense the self is both the source and the destination of communication; the motivation, the purpose, the content and the outcome.

Whichever model of motivation we adopt, the self is prominent, either providing us with the energy for pushing us into action or providing us with a set of higher-order needs, such as the need for self-esteem or self-respect, which must be fulfilled. Argyle's (1983) drives ('persistent tendencies to pursue goals') are of three varieties:

- **Social acceptance**: wanting to be a part of various groups
- **Bodily needs**: needing to be fed and watered
- **Specific task goals**: having to do specific things like getting to work on time or putting up a shelf

Once watered and fed, the self-concept is the driving force, pushing us into relationships, power struggles and good deeds, and all for its identity and self-esteem. The same is true of the most prominent 'needs' model. Maslow's (1984) hierarchy is dominated, literally, by *self*-esteem and *self*-actualisation.

ACTIVITY . . .

Think about all the things you have done so far today, every action and conversation. How far were these done (a) for some significant external reason, for someone else's sake, or (b) for yourself (for your *self*)? How many of those listed in (b) were really necessary?

The more we consider this matter, the more we realise that 'we' are at the mercy of the self, its needs and its desires. So all-controlling is it that it is almost impossible to think of a genuinely selfless act, one that has no reference to our own intrapersonal needs. Even when giving generously to others of time and money, we are often consciously increasing our self-esteem and thinking of our perceived mirror self. Some psychologists identify three forms of motivation for people doing things: egotism, altruism and psychological altruism. To be motivated by egotism is to act in your own interests. To be motivated by altruism is to act in the interests of other people. To be motivated by psychological altruism is to act apparently to meet other people's needs whilst actually fulfilling your own needs – that is your need to meet others' needs.

The uncontrollable elements are of course our own personal skills, abilities and understandings. Servicing the self is all very well in theory, but in practice it is fraught with complications: in our ability to understand or know the self (the 'Unknown frame' of the Johari Window); in our capacity successfully to interact with others; in the special problems that reality always brings as a context. To some extent we always talk a better game than we play.

Key to understanding the relationship between the self-concept and the self as communicator is the idea of self-presentation, which Argyle (1983) has defined as 'behaviours designed to create an impression for others'. Self-presentation implies that our interactions with the world are largely conscious attempts to influence other people. In his important book *The Presentation of the Self in Everyday Life* (1990), Erving Goffman offers what is described as a dramaturgical model of self-presentation, in other words one that sees self-presentation as a sort of extended dramatic performance for which we prepare and at which we constantly work. As Goffman himself claims, 'life itself is a dramatically enacted thing'. His extensive work takes its cues from this understanding and from his assertion that 'we all act better than we know'. Goffman sees self-presentation in six aspects or key elements, all of which are related in some way to the idea of life as drama:

- Persona
- Performance
- Staging
- Teams
- Role
- Personal style

PERSONA

The first aspect, similar to one of Jung's key archetypes, is persona, the various personality 'masks' we might wear when undertaking roles. While these personae are to some extent selected or encouraged by their respective roles or contexts, they are not bound to them (persona is the singular form and personae is the plural form). The idea is that we have a number of viable selves, or variations on the self, and that we select the version that best fits the situation or role. In extremes it is easy to see this as a viable argument. The persona adopted for a Sunday afternoon picnic with your family may be very different from the one you need for your job as a prison warder or for your journey through the early morning rush hour or even your attendance with friends at a heavy metal concert. In between these there is a grey area in which such aspects as your mood, the setting or your simple lack of engagement or interest work against any coherent 'character' persona. Persona in fact works best as an explanation of formal situations, where conscious performance is an issue – at work, in an interview, even in an examination. Here the way you play is a matter of choice; it is about strategy. Elsewhere it is often not a real issue.

ACTIVITY . . .

How far is Goffman's theory realistic? If it works, we should notice a difference in the way we communicate in different situations. Try to identify some of your personae and suggest some of the differences in the ways they communicate.

To some extent we see persona most at work in the world of the media, where presentation is a matter of marketing. The Spice Girls are a classic case of created personae, with each 'girl' representing a subset of attitudes and characteristics. When the presentation of the persona is professional, as in film acting, some people are better at it than others. Some actors present a range of personae across a range of roles, while others cannot (or do not).

Performance

If personae are masks, performance describes the different ways in which they can be worn. These ways range crudely from 'for real' to 'ironically/for laughs/ for reward'. This partly describes the degree to which the self is honestly and wholeheartedly engaged in the act of self-presentation. At the 'sincere' end of the scale, the persona is a device that allows us to be ourselves, or as close to this as is possible. It is worth reminding ourselves why this is not an attainable goal. We have dealt with too much evidence that suggests that the self is ultimately unknowable. Hopefully, most of the time we are working on the 'sincere' end of the scale, trying as we might to present ourselves as we really are. This, after all, is the key even in formal (and fake) situations like interviews and examinations.

However, on occasion, we also need to 'play the game', to put on a show merely to fulfil the demands of a situation. This is what Goffman calls 'cynical' performance, where the persona you employ is disconnected from the self and simply 'exhibited'. The 'cynical' self in performance represents us rather than presents us, for it is largely dealing with the audience's rather than our own needs. (We are literally giving them what they want.) This is very like a theatrical performance.

ACTIVITY . . .

Suggest how you would be likely to perform on the sincere–cynical axis in the following situations:

Sincere Cynical

1 On a first date

2 In your Communication Studies examination

3 At your wedding/on the day you move in with your partner

4 In an Internet chatroom

5 Visiting a sick relative

6 Listening to your best friend's problems

Clearly, there cannot be a definitive answer, but in most of the above there will probably be pressures from both ends of the line.

STAGING

Obviously performances need a context, and Goffman suggests that for our self-presentations these are carefully constructed and controlled. 'Staging' is the term he uses for all of the ways our self-presentation is 'set' – the physical locations, the props, the costume. Here he makes a distinction between that which he refers to as front, which is the routine combinations of location and costume we come to expect, and those stagings which are more spontaneous or infrequent. Front then might cover those aspects of a male teacher's self-presentation that you see on a day-to-day basis – his classroom, his limited wardrobe of style-less clothes, his supermarket carrier bags full of student work. The staging might be very different if the same teacher were called in to staff a school or college disco or gig. The physical setting is a dimly lit hall, the costume an unfortunate attempt at trendy gear, and the significant 'prop' an overbearing smell of an ancient aftershave.

The best examples of active staging are probably to be found in what the research rather archaically calls 'courting rituals', the sometimes ridiculous lengths we go to in order to attract prospective partners. Men and women in pubs and clubs on the lookout for men and women often use extravagantly artificial stagings, presenting themselves in strategic locations and in supposedly appropriate postures. In a more modest way staging is also important when we meet and greet someone. Rising from your chair and moving towards someone you are greeting is clearly about staging, fixing the physical relationship between you and your audience. Taking this kind of initiative is a particularly good way of beginning to dismantle the barriers that are often put up in formal communication contexts like interviews by their own staging.

ACTIVITY . . .

A common assessment activity in Communication Studies is the formal or semi-formal oral presentation, in which you are asked to deliver an illustrated talk to a small group audience you invite. You are invariably asked for your own staging. In other words, you are allowed to arrange the room and your audience as you wish. Assuming your own presence, the need to use visual aids, and an audience of five friends, suggest two contrasting stagings for this talk. Evaluate the strengths and weaknesses of each, e.g.

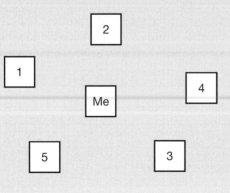

COMMUNICATION STUDIES: THE ESSENTIAL INTRODUCTION

Strengths:

- self is central
- element of surprise

Weaknesses:

- intimidating for all
- limits use of visual aids
- difficult to address members equally

How might 'costume' affect the success or failure of your two 'models'? What would it be best to wear in each case? Do different stagings suit different costumes? (If you have them sitting on the floor on beanbags, will informal clothing be a necessity?)

TEAMS

What is also implied by the oral presentation scenario is what Goffman described as teams, in other words the company we keep – our friends and fellow actors. These teams may be part of what we have identified as front, 'that part of the individual's performance which regularly functions in a general and fixed fashion to define the situation for those who observe the performance'. Staging is often shared or enhanced by by the participation of others who form the groups (Goffman's 'teams'), which will be the focus of the next three sections. The teams that Goffman refers to range from the structured and specialised sets of people (who, for example, allow television presenters to do their job) to the small (as small as one other person) friendship groups which form a context for much of our communication.

If you're selling burgers at a major fast food chain the notion of teamwork will not be unfamiliar. Those people who are part of your team support your self-presentation as a competent employee or undermine it by making you wait too long for chicken nuggets. Goffman argues that the situation is the same even if the context is very much more informal. First, teams are part of your front, they are part of the furniture of your staging, reflecting aspects of your personal front (your age, your fashion sense, your attitudes). This can turn out to be a considerable psychological barrier in terms of the in-group/out-group dynamics (where people are mildly put off by the presence of other people who already know one another). Add to this the characteristic costume of a youth subcultural group (nose ring, make-up, Marilyn Manson T-shirt) and a team becomes a gang and the cause of a minor moral panic.

ACTIVITY . . .

Gender is assumed to play a significant part in explaining the differences between kinds of team. What team behaviour is expected from the following teams? (What sort of context will they create for an individual's self-presentation?)

- a boy band
- a girl band

- five girls/women 'out on the town'
- five boys/men 'out on the town'?

Your team may be only one other person. This does not detract from a theory that sees observed relationships as a significant context. The very ease we have with our closest friends makes the notion of team performance very persuasive. In this sense, getting to know someone is to become part of their team, to communicate with them and alongside them. If you think of the smallest group (of two), it is useful to think theatrically in terms of 'double acts' and then of your own 'work' with your closest friend.

If we consider high-profile comedy pairings (for example Morecombe and Wise, the Two Ronnies, Smith and Jones, French and Saunders, Newman and Baddiel), we are immediately aware of the front that is being established. We are being 'sold' physical differences as an index (a connection is being made) of character differences. These are used consciously to create a context for comedy, a staging for humour. The teamwork is often slick and professional but the principles are the same as for our own two-person performances. We play off other people, and that play begins with appearance and goes from there.

ACTIVITY . . .

Choose three friends whom you might see individually. Briefly describe the 'teamplay' in each of the three pairs you form when you're with them individually. How does it differ and what difference, if any, does it make to you as a presented self?

ROLE

Given that Goffman uses a theatrical metaphor, it seems surprising that it should have taken us so long to come to role. Role refers to the parts we play and is, in essence, the focus of Goffman's model. Though Goffman admits that 'All the world is not, of course, a stage', he also points out that 'the crucial ways in which it is not are not easy to specify'. When we considered the business of defining who we are, when we first looked at intrapersonal communication, we identified 'social role' as a significant theme of the responses. The research, by Kuhn and McPartland (1954), also indicated that 'definition by role' becomes more prominent as we mature (undergraduates referred to the idea of role twice as often as 7-year-olds did).

ACTIVITY . . .

What is the role we play when we are alone? For example, 7.36 am: Woke up. Thought about the day ahead. This is what Mead (1930) called 'self-interaction'. Is this the meta-role, the role of roles? Is this the maskless self? Is it, in fact, the 'casting' role: who will I be today?

COMMUNICATION STUDIES: THE ESSENTIAL INTRODUCTION

Goffman sees the parts we play as an organising principle of our self-presentation. He would see most of us moving from role to role across the day. We may wake up as a wife or husband, walk downstairs into the role of father or mother, before playing the commuter in the early morning rush hour. We may arrive at work to the unexpected role of friend or confidante before we assume the role of employee or employer. The workplace is alive with role differentiation, and potentially role conflict, where the role of 'mother of a sick child' conflicts with the role of 'full-time worker'. Work is often obsessed with rank and status. This makes offices and staffrooms settings for conflicting and overlapping roles. The evening may produce a new set of roles; you may be the guest at a party, a diner at an expensive restaurant, or a part-time worker in a pub (though these may not be the roles of an average student).

ACTIVITY . . .

Keep a fanatically accurate record of one day's interaction with other people (take a notebook with you). For each of the listed interactions, try to define the role you were playing (either consciously or subconsciously).

PERSONAL STYLE

That leaves only personal style. How can this be last on the list? It almost seems an afterthought, as if Goffman isn't entirely convinced it exists. More than this, personal style is marginalised simply because Goffman's extensive model has left very little space in which this style can operate. Surely we'd like to believe our individuality counts for more than that? Surely, to extend the metaphor, we are more like actor-managers than actors. After all, we provide the script and allow the show to be put on.

We may provide the script but that does not mean that in any significant way that we 'write' it. Script is the unspoken element in all of this. Goffman would see it as intimately connected to each of the other aspects. Personae bring language or at least register and tone; performance gives clues as to how language might be used; staging sets the idiom more precisely in the way that foreign words in a phrase book might be clustered around 'the tobacconist' or 'the swimming baths'; teams sensitise or desensitise language to audience needs and expectation; roles often have their own dialects, or at least registers (technical, specialist and restricted). The more fragmented the analysis becomes, the harder it is to see a place for the personal voice, the authorial voice, even personal style.

This is perhaps the function, even the justification, of creative or aesthetic communication. When we write something personal or imaginative – a story, a poem, even a memoir – we are in fact writing ourselves, and for ourselves. The same is true of our drawing, painting, performing, sculpting, singing and some of our speaking. We are imposing our personal experiences and personal style and in doing so are emphasising the unity rather than fragmentation of the self. Poetically this could be described as a healing process, a mending. This idea is central to Jungian psychology and a potential role for Goffman's notion of personal style as a sort of 'synoptic' element (one that unites the others).

Personal style is therefore that which gives coherence to self-presentation, that which lends it its voice. Without personal style (or if this element is underdeveloped or stilted), performance has no fluidity, no coherence; we are merely 'rude mechanicals', bad actors. With a mature personal style we can be artists, authors of our own 'stories', *auteurs* (the French term used to signify those film directors who stamp their own identity on their work).

ACTIVITY . . .

Choose an artist or musician or writer or film-maker whose work has an individual or personal style. Try to define this 'style' as a bullet-point list. Now do the same for someone you know very well (close friend or family member), looking at the key characteristics of their personal communication.

The strengths of Goffman lie in the detailed way he has worked through the elements of self-presentation and the coherence with which he has brought them together. Goffman offers a set of prompts which act as a useful starting point for examining interpersonal behaviour. It is not an approach that dwells too long on the self as such, but rather as it is demonstrated in performance, as it appears 'dressed' in the world. An alternative approach, which pays greater attention to the state of the self and which offers an alternative metaphor for the relationships between individuals and the world of others, is Transactional Analysis.

The writer most frequently associated with Transactional Analysis (or TA as it is known) is Eric Berne (1968). At the heart of Berne's theories is the notion that communication is transactional, that it consists of innumerable 'transactions' (or interpersonal deals). A transaction is an exchange of communication. It might be an acknowledged smile of greeting or part of an involved and sophisticated negotiation. Berne argues that when we communicate with others we are involved in negotiations and in game-playing with the intention of either reaching a compromise or outplaying our opponent in order to overcome them. This is an interesting view, if not a startling one, but Berne goes further to relate these transactions and these games to what he called ego-states, conditions of the self.

KEY TERM

TRANSACTIONAL ANALYSIS An approach to understanding and ultimately improving interpersonal communication introduced by Eric Berne in his book *Games People Play* (1968). Berne proposes three 'ego states': child, parent and adult.

The essence of Eric Berne's theories of personality is that each of us is really three people. These are identified as 'the child', 'the parent' and 'the adult'. These are not stages of maturity, they are options within all of us. They have their own patterns of behaviour and particular uses of speech and body language. In the course of normal communication each will become dominant in its own contexts. The idea is that when we are communicating we choose from which ego-state to speak and our receiver does the same. When we get recognition for our communication, in the form perhaps of a smile or a nod, we receive what Berne called a 'stroke'. A stroke is a form of positive reinforcement, a boost to our self-esteem and for Berne it is the most important reason we communicate. We transact to receive strokes. With small children strokes are literally physical, whereas with adults strokes tend to take a verbal form. Berne claimed that without strokes 'the spinal cord will shrivel up'. Clearly, negative recognition produces negative strokes and everything deteriorates.

According to Berne, there are three ego-states:

■ **The child**: the child state is emotional and poorly controlled but also creative and affectionate. The child is prey to its emotions; it is sulky, physical and inconsistent. When drunk or hyped up on emotion of any kind, we often retreat to the child state.

■ **The parent**: Claude Steiner describes the parent ego-state as 'like a tape-recorder . . . it is a collection of pre-recorded, prejudged and prejudiced codes for living'. When we are in our parent state we become our parents or the people who raised us. Berne distinguishes between the 'Critical Parent' and the 'Nurturing Parent'. For Steiner, 'The parent uses old tapes to solve problems and is therefore at least 25 years behind'. We probably have all known teachers who are stuck fast in their 'Critical Parent' state.

■ **The adult**: the adult uses reason and logic to solve problems. It thinks and feels in relation to experience. In Steiner's words, 'The adult is a human computer'. The adult has its emotions under control.

Berne's work is useful as a tool for analysing interpersonal exchanges and the role of the self in these. It is widely used in counselling as a therapeutic tool. In his book *Games People Play* (1968), Berne motivated discussion on TA by offering compelling and often amusing examples of the way the ego-states interact and literally of the 'games people play'. Steiner identifies, for example, five ways in which people can get strokes.

■ **Rituals**: 'a pre-set exchange of recognition strokes'. For example, you might pass a friend in the corridor early in the morning and take part in this kind of exchange:

> 'Alright, Chloe?'
> 'How are you?'
> 'Great.'
> 'See you later, then.'

This would be described as a 'four-stroke ritual'.

■ **Pastimes**: 'a pre-set conversation around a certain subject'. These might include the weather, old friends, school/college/work, television, music.

■ **Games**: 'a repetitive, devious series of transactions'. Games are a risk. They can be won; they can also be lost. We are not always aware we are playing.

■ **Intimacy**: 'a direct and powerful exchange of strokes'. This is about touching and being close. It may involve sex, but sex may also feature in all the other categories.

- **Work**: 'an activity which has a product as its result'. Along with intimacy, this is the most satisfying way of getting strokes. Without meaningful work, people resort to rituals, pastimes and games.

Berne's work gives a satisfying new angle on behaviour and potentially a fresh way to look at communication problems. Berne would put down many of the disruptions in communication we experience on a day-to-day basis to a mismatching of ego-states. Berne conceived of two significant sorts of transaction:

- **The complementary**: where the ego-states of the participants are matched.
- **The crossed**: where the ego-states are mismatched. This is where problems start.

Consider, for example, a teacher–student relationship in two versions:

> TEACHER: 'What do you think the issue is here?' (Adult–Adult)
> STUDENT: 'Depends where you're looking from.' (Adult–Adult)

This is a complementary transaction. Compare this to the following:

> TEACHER: 'What do you think the issue is here?' (Adult–Adult)
> STUDENT: 'Just get off my back, will you?' (Child–Parent)

> This is a crossed transaction, and communication has already deteriorated.

Although the language of TA is simple, and deliberately so, its insights are certainly not superficial. Berne developed the approach as a practical way to make a difference. He was interested in empowering people, in allowing them to see that they have choices, in promoting thinking and self-respect. TA is about understanding the factors that got us to where we are and then using this understanding to inform a better future. On one level it is about de-parenting, for the Parent is the significantly poorest ego-state and Berne himself has suggested that most parents take princes and princesses and turn them into frogs. TA is also a model for understanding the smallest groups, the dyad or group of two. Group communication is what we'll consider next.

▼ 6   GROUP COMMUNICATION: WHAT GROUPS ARE AND WHAT THEY DO

We now move to consider group communication.

- We begin by looking at a range of definitions of what constitutes a group.

The most common approach to the study of group communication is to begin by attempting some kind of definition of what a group is, or to line up a number of competing definitions.

Before we load 'group' with all manner of theoretical baggage, it is important that we see it for what it is, an important label for the place where we experience a large amount of communication on a day-to-day level. This section will locate the practice of group communication within the practice of day-to-day communication of which it forms a significant proportion and then use that experience to attempt to reconcile various academic definitions of 'group'.

ACTIVITY . . .

Imagine the communication that usually happens across your average student or work day. List the people you usually talk to or with whom you interact.

The list you have made is a crude list of the groups to which you belong. These are collections of people you habitually communicate with, often in limited and specific contexts. Hartley identified three types of these, all of which may be included in your list:

- Family groups
- Friendship groups
- Work groups

If we consider these three types of group, we can begin to describe the dimensions of our experience of significant others. We may, for example, conclude that there are certain general differences across these three designations. Work groups tend to be rather more formal than the other types. Some groups are 'ascribed' (like our families) and others 'achieved' (like the membership of teams). Some groups are large and others are small. Moreover, within friendship groups there is considerable variation of intensity and commitment which may result partly from how well established these groups are.

ACTIVITY . . .

Answer the following questions in the order they are given:

1   Who were your FIVE best friends at the end of junior school?

2   Which of these people went on as friends to secondary school?

3   Who were your FIVE friends in Year Nine (at age 14)?

4   Which of these remained by the end of secondary school?

5   How many of these went on with you to college?

6   How many of these (in question 4) do you still keep as friends?

7   Who are your FIVE best friends now?

8   Are any of these those you listed in answer to question 1?

Clearly, a dimension of groups is their longevity, whether they are short term or long term. Another dimension is their significance to us and the resulting frequency of interaction that entails. Those groups that you spend most time with are referred to as primary groups, with secondary groups as those with which you have intermittent contact. In terms of friendship, this is directly related to the level at which you have bonded with the other person or people. Button suggests four levels of companionship:

- Close friend
- Other friend
- Associate
- Acquaintance

If these are the starting point for the designation of 'kinds of friendship groups', it is clear that any definition of a group must range in size from the dyadic one-to-one, which is the staple unit of interpersonal communication, to the reasonably large social groupings which are a natural spin-off of work groups and sports groups. Stanton has suggested that in all cases there is an optimum number. This is dependent on such variables as context, task and personality, and stands somewhere between the need for participation and the need for a breadth of knowledge and experience. An example might be discussions about the optimum size of teaching groups in a school or college. Too many students means some will be unable fully to participate in the work of the group; too few students will limit the range of opinions and responses available.

ACTIVITY . . .

Compare two groups of which you are a member. They could be family, friendship or work groups. Consider the extent to which size is a factor in their success or lack of it.

Douglas (1979) includes number in his extensive list of criteria by which groups may be assessed, with size as its classification. It would be useful to carry the two groups you have just considered through this substantial list of classifications:

Criterion		Classification
1	Nature	natural/artificial
2	Origin	spontaneous/created
3	Leader	directive/non-directive
4	Location	environmental influences
5	Members	selection criteria
6	Outcome	group purpose
7	Number	size
8	Throughput	open/closed
9	Orientation	approach
10	Programme	choice of activity
11	Duration	time factor

COMMUNICATION STUDIES: THE ESSENTIAL INTRODUCTION

A one-year Communication AS group would in this way be described as artificial, created, directive, based in the room ET30, largely self-selecting, determined to pass AS Communication Studies, of a specific size, closed, enthusiastic, studying Communication Studies, and lasting one year. Each of these is a useful prompt, not only for understanding this or any specific group, but also for uncovering the paradigms of 'group' as an idea. In identifying a specific group as artificial, we are being prompted to consider what a natural group would be like.

ACTIVITY . . .

Find examples of groups which can be classified in the following ways according to Douglas's criteria.

A) Natural   (nature)

B) Spontaneous   (origin)

C) Non-directive   (leader)

D) Open   (throughput)

E) Short term   (duration)

We began with a deliberate non-definition of what group was – a vague term that describes all of the habitual communication we have with significant others. By merely pricking the surface of our experience, we have exposed the immense variety in these contexts, what could be termed units of communication practice. We are now ready, in the light of this experience, to construct and test out definitions of 'group'.

Clearly, group is a descriptive term that can be applied to a wide variety of communication practices. In terms of personal communication, it is fair to say that we are mostly engaged in group communication, communication with or within groups. There is a significant amount of redundancy or predictability in personal communication in groups – established routines, patterns, even networks of communication that we occupy. What this entails can be clarified if we bring together a number of academic explanations:

What is a group? In order for a group to exist, the following must apply:

- **Individual members must exist in some kind of relationship.** According to Burton and Dimbleby (1995), 'If there is no interaction between the individuals, then a group cannot be formed'. Hartley talks of a regular pattern or structure of interaction. Judy Gahagan (1975) asserts 'A group should be conceived of as a system whose parts interrelate'.

- **Groups share common interests, goals and purposes.** In *Between Ourselves*, Burton and Dimbleby define a group as 'a collection of individuals who interact in some way and share some common goals or interests'.

- **Groups share common values and norms.** O'Sullivan *et al.* (1994) define norms as 'Those sets of social rules, standards and expectations that both generate and regulate social interaction and communication.' In most groups these norms are unwritten and unspoken.

- **Groups develop set roles of behaviour which members accept.** O'Sullivan *et al.* (1994) define roles as 'socially defined positions and patterns of behaviour which are characterised by specific sets of rules, norms and expectation'. To some extent these developed roles are the manifestations of the values and norms of the group; in other words the theory is put into practice.

- **Group members have an identity.** Hartley (1997) talks about the existence of a group depending on the perception that it exists, logically both inside and outside the group. Turner (1991) categorised this effectively when he claimed, 'A group exists when two or more people define themselves as members of it and when its existence is recognised by at least one other.'

A handy summary of these descriptions of group is provided by Douglas (1979), who declared that a group was 'the largest set of two or more individuals who are jointly characterised by a network of relevant communications, a shared sense of collective identity and one or more of shared goal dispositions with associated normative strengths'. Or as Gahagan (1975) more succinctly puts it, 'a group of people is significantly more than the sum of its parts'. In mathematical terms it is not about addition but about integration.

So far we have established what kind of groups we are in and what kind of things they are. In doing so we have recognised a distinction between those groups that we are 'assigned' to (those which are ascribed to us) and those which we join of our own free will. In terms of the latter we might reasonably ask why we join these groups. Douglas lists seven reasons beyond 'the individual is born into the group':

- They choose to do it
- It is part of doing something else (e.g. a job)
- They are compelled to do so
- They are compelled to do so by specific changes in circumstances (e.g. an accident)
- They drift into it over a period of time
- They are invited to do so
- They are proud to do so (this is the 'achieved' idea, for example gaining entry to a prestigious sports team)

Douglas adopts a pragmatic approach to the business of joining groups; others have adopted a more psychological one. Abraham Maslow (1954), for example, offered social needs as one level of his hierarchy, suggesting that companionship in whatever configuration was a basic human necessity. Dimbleby and Burton (1998), similarly, define the reasons people join groups in terms of two simple socio-emotional and task-orientated criteria. In other words, in terms of intrinsic social and emotional needs, and extrinsic instrumental needs; the need to support and protect the self, and the need to get things done. Their twin criteria were:

- To achieve a shared goal or resist a common threat
- To have a sense of belonging and security

COMMUNICATION STUDIES: THE ESSENTIAL INTRODUCTION

These have a primal feel, as if all groups were essential and extreme. It may be difficult to square the interactions within your work social group with 'shared goal' and 'common threat' or even 'belonging' and 'security'. Many viable groups are more mundanely constructed. A more tentative list was compiled by Nicholson (1977) who set out to establish the factors that had bearing on the formation of friendships. His list is less striking but perhaps more realistic:

- The need for stimulation
- The need for reassurance
- The attraction of similarity (mixing with People Like Us)
- The recognition that friendships are expendable (we are prompted into relationships by the knowledge that some, and potentially all, will fail)
- The fact of proximity (we join with people we constantly see)
- Physical attractiveness

Nicholson suggests that relationships and the joining of groups are primarily about finding something to do and less to do with those factors that influence other personal relationships like love. Clearly, though, there are the same intrinsic and extrinsic motivations: the desire to be whole and strong; to have a sense of group identity; and a desire to do things, to complete tasks and achieve goals. Stanton (1996) has related these primary functions of groups to roles members play within them. Stanton describes these as Task Roles (functions required in carrying out a group task) and Group Building and Maintenance Roles (functions required in strengthening group life and activities).

▼ 7 GROUP COMMUNICATION: INSIDE GROUPS

In this section we look at how groups form and function.

- We will consider how groups communicate internally.

- We will examine the roles group members perform when in groups.

- We will look at Moreno's work on sociometrics and at Douglas's work on group processes.

The previous section ended by suggesting some of the reasons why people join groups either formally or informally. This section will take that process a step further by exploring how groups form, how they function, and how they are structured. As with all of this work, it is useful to test the theories offered against your own experience in groups.

Choose two groups to which you consider you belong, one informal group (a friendship or family group perhaps) and one formal group (a work or school/college group). For each group respond to the following prompts:

- Status of group: family/friendship/work/other?
- Who?
- When?
- Where?
- Why did this group form?
- How did this group form?

Any explanation of how groups form and how they work needs to ring true with your experience of groups.

Tuckman (1965) and others have suggested that there are four stages in the life and work of groups. Argyle described them as 'formation', 'rebellion', 'norming' and 'co-operation'. In Tuckman they are more dramatically and memorably termed forming, storming, norming and performing:

- **Forming**: the initial stage of basic interaction in which a number of people come together and communicate regularly
- **Storming**: the crucial stage of disorder and sometimes conflict through which relationships are forged; the testing stage, which determines whether a group will develop
- **Norming**: the explicit result of storming, the establishment of group 'rules', ways of working, thinking, communicating and self-presentation
- **Performing**: the stage at which a functioning group emerges as a significant communicator, complete with its own 'personality' and patterns of behaviour

In practice groups do not conform neatly to this evolutionary plan and it is more useful to see these stages as fluid, dynamic aspects of the life of groups rather than successive phases of development. It is likely that this pattern will be repeated often across the life of a group as the group develops. As a general guide, however, these are accurate descriptions of the life of most groups.

Within these general descriptors of the stages through which groups are continually working or ceasing to work, two factors are constantly at play – the roles of individual members and the patterns and processes of intra-group communication.

KEY TERM

INTRA-GROUP COMMUNICATION Communication going on inside a group, between its members.

Burton and Dimbleby (1995) have described the roles we undertake in relation to the three kinds of group we have considered as interdependent. The model they offer suggests that the role we play in one sort of group influences the roles we play in other groups.

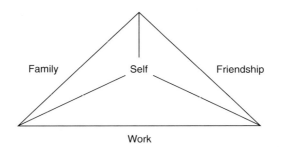

Diagram 5.7 Burton and Dimbleby's group communication model

What Dimbleby and Burton are suggesting is that role is an organising concept of our behaviour in groups: that if our roles within our family are relatively passive, then that fact will make our likely roles within our work groups more or less passive. We may conform to our given or chosen role stereotype or react against it. Either way there is a significant influence. When considering role as a concept, it is important to distinguish between roles that are 'ascribed' or 'assigned' (like membership of a family) and those that are 'achieved' or 'assumed' through being earned (like membership of a team).

'Assigned' carries with it connotations of the group being 'directive'; 'assumed' might imply initiative or the lack of it. All four descriptors are useful for indicating the complexity and subtlety of role as an idea and clarifying some of the differences between one situation and another. For example, is the role of 'father' 'ascribed' or 'achieved'? All we can really say is that this is a good question, and good questions are what education is about.

ACTIVITY . . .

List the roles you perceive yourself to have, from son/daughter to college member or sportsperson. Describe each role using one or more of the following descriptions:

- Achieved
- Ascribed
- Assigned
- Assumed

The 'perceive yourself' part of the last activity introduces another variable or, to put it another way, complication. Shaw (1981) has argued that it is vital to distinguish between three versions of any role:

- Perceived role
- Enacted role
- Expected role

In other words, Shaw makes an interesting distinction between the role we think we're filling, the role we fill, and the role others expect us to fill. Much in-group conflict might be seen to derive from these discrepancies. The 'storming' process, which we discussed earlier, is partly about ironing out critical differences between these three ideally harmonious 'states'.

ACTIVITY . . .

Choose a group you feel happy and confident in, ideally your Communication Studies group, and write down:

- What you think your role in the group is.

- What are the roles of three others in that group?

Ask others in the group to do the same and compare results.

At the end of the previous section we briefly considered Stanton's (1996) description of two types of role in groups: Task roles, and Group Building and Maintenance roles. Stanton relates these to types of behaviour and communication skills, suggesting that being a group member is about having a portfolio of skills. 'Task roles' includes such things as initiating activity, seeking information and co-ordinating, whilst 'Group Building and Maintenance roles' includes encouraging, gatekeeping and standard setting. Kurt Albrecht, on the other hand, is much more rigid in his designations of the specific role needs of groups. He describes five kinds of group member:

- **Energisers**: those who provide group motivation
- **Ideas people**: those who think what to do
- **Action people**: those who get things done
- **Organisers**: those who make sure things are done efficiently
- **Uncommitted**: those who make no real contribution

These can easily and more flexibly be seen as four group functions and one group dysfunction. At a general level they probably do offer recognisable character generalisations but they also constitute those elements that every group needs.

ACTIVITY . . . .

For the two groups you identified in the first activity in this section, complete the following:

COMMUNICATION STUDIES: THE ESSENTIAL INTRODUCTION

Who are the:

- Energisers
- Ideas people
- Action people
- Organisers
- Uncommitted?

It is likely that in most groups these functions will vary according to such variables as task (what the group are doing), personnel (who the group are) and environment (where the group are). Knowing this, it may be more satisfactory to see intra-group communication in terms of skills or processes rather than in terms of roles, in terms of in-group activities rather than personal specialism.

Dimbleby and Burton (1998) identify a number of interpersonal communication skills, which are valuable to group members. The implication is that these might and will be developed and will be present in group members to varying degrees. Being in healthy groups will presumably help these develop, just as possessing these skills will help groups be healthy. The Dimbleby and Burton list of group skills runs as follows:

- To be able to offer praise for ideas and actions
- To be able to show agreement with group ideas
- To be able to offer information and ideas
- To be able to evaluate ideas and information
- To be able to invite opinions and involvement
- To be able to bring together ideas and opinions
- To be able to suggest actions involving the groups

ACTIVITY . . .

In your opinion rank these group skills according to their significance to groups. In your own contexts, which of these skills can you identify and which do your fellow group members lack?

Albrecht and Dimbleby and Burton essentially offer differently focused accounts of what goes on in groups. Albrecht is concerned primarily with individual members and their specific functions; Dimbleby and Burton with individual behaviour and performance. A third approach focuses on the group itself and the processes within it. Bales's Inter-action Process Analysis (1950) is an attempt systematically to describe what goes on in groups.

Bales identifies socio-emotional and task-orientated needs as the basis of group motivation and then proceeds to clarify the specific ways in which these are made evident in group behaviour. He labels these 'ways' as 'interaction processes', a series of specific responses individuals make in groups:

Socio-Emotional Area: Positive — A
- 1 Shows solidarity
- 2 Shows tension release
- 3 Shows agreement

B
- 4 Gives suggestions
- 5 Gives opinion
- 6 Gives information

Task Area: Neutral

a b c d e f

C
- 7 Asks for information
- 8 Asks for opinion
- 9 Asks for suggestions

Socio-Emotional Area: Negative — D
- 10 Disagrees
- 11 Shows tension
- 12 Shows antagonism

Key:

A	Positive reactions	a	Problems of communication
B	Attempted answers	b	Problems of evaluation
C	Questions	c	Problems of control
D	Negative reactions	d	Problems of decision
		e	Problems of tension reduction
		f	Problems of reintegration.

Diagram 5.8 Bales's Interaction Process Analysis (IPA) model

Bales offers a sophisticated model of the implications of certain kinds of group behaviour, both positive and negative. He identifies six significant levels at which problems might occur, in other words six points at which barriers might impede communication. Like Albrecht he identifies negative factors in the interaction of group members, replacing 'uncommitted' with 'socio-emotional behaviour: negative'. Bales has clipped them down to 'disagrees', 'shows tension' and 'shows antagonism' and in all cases connected them to the dynamic of the group. Bales sees these negative elements as essential to the active processes through which groups work. The problems are all subtly couched in positive terms: 'reintegration', 'tension reduction' and 'decision'.

Stanton (1996) is less convinced about the value of dissident elements in groups. He sees certain member characteristics as potentially harmful to the functioning and long-term future of some groups. He talks of the 'hidden agendas' of some group members, whereby what these members want and need is often at odds with what the rest of the group wants and needs. His examples of 'hidden agenda' behaviour include trying to impress; defending vested interests; responding negatively to other group members; and using the group for amusement.

Stanton lists types of non-functional behaviour as:

1 Being aggressive
2 Blocking
3 Self-confessing
4 Competing
5 Seeking sympathy
6 Special pleading
7 Horsing around
8 Seeking recognition
9 Withdrawal

You may already recognise some of these behaviours in yourself or in others. One of the things to which they relate is the degree to which members commit themselves to groups. The problems of interaction which Bales elegantly identifies are often less elegant and less identifiable in practice. The very essence of 'hidden agendas' is the fact that they are hidden. If we are to understand how group members interact, we will need to back up this theory with some practice.

ACTIVITY . . .

Arrange to observe a group in action, perhaps one of your own, and simply tally the number of times each member of the group makes a contribution to what the group is saying or doing. Observe over a significant period (for example 30 minutes) and on more than one occasion. Look at the results and see how far they match your expectation and experience. Could you have predicted the most frequent contributor and the least frequent?

If you take your tally evidence and relate it to relative group positions, you may arrive at something like:

In a group such as a teaching group, there may be something to be learned from the relationship between positioning in relation to the teacher and group interaction. Some positions may in fact be inherently stronger than others and may as a result be occupied by those who have the greatest influence. Similarly, those who are not so keen to interact may occupy weak positions. The arrangement of a group around a single desk may or may not tell us much about their interaction but it does offer likely variables.

X = teacher
O = powerful position
△ = weaker position

Diagram 5.9 Teacher–group model

In these kinds of 'directive' groups, member positioning is rarely uninformative. Members might on occasion find weak positions by default (by arriving late for example) but across a significant period of 'storming', weaker positions will usually go to the uncommitted or communicatively reluctant. In the example above, it would be unsurprising that in an interaction tally A, B and C will enjoy a significant share. This is a statement of power not structure. To understand what goes on beyond these simple axes we need a more sophisticated tool, a measurement of the way individuals react to and with others.

Moreno's work on sociometrics, literally the measurement of social relationships, offers a handy next step. If we are trying to discover how a group is patterned, structured or aligned, Moreno would argue that we must look at more than the behavioural evidence of their frequency of interaction and their physical interaction. We need to consider the alignments they are playing out with other people in the group (in other words who in the group likes/respects/admires who else). Sociometrics asks how socially inclined we are towards others, how keen we are to interact with them. For example, members of a small group might be asked to express their preference for working with any two other group

COMMUNICATION STUDIES: THE ESSENTIAL INTRODUCTION

members. To be effective the question would stress the context, whether it be work or social. Their decisions would then be plotted in this way:

Diagram 5.10 *Network of group interactions I*

This simple mechanism offers a significant confirmation or challenge to practical observation. To a limited extent it goes beneath the surface to explore the underlying relationships within any group. What the diagram above reveals is a significant network of interactions which can be quickly 'read'. There are clear bonds between members 1 and 3, 1 and 2, 2 and 4, and a basic solidity about most of the group. Members 1 through 5 conform to what Moreno called a 'cluster', a series of significantly interacting individuals, who clearly constitute a subgroup. On the other hand, member 6 shows signs of being an 'isolate', an individual not significantly bonded with the rest of the group. The suspicion that member 6 is an isolate could be followed up through observation or, with sensitivity, by couching a negative question: 'Which group member would you be least likely to work with?' It is always interesting to relate these social 'maps' to the physical ways in which groups behave. The individuals plotted above sat in this configuration:

Diagram 5.11 *Network of group interactions II*

The focus of this small group is easy to see and it would not be difficult to predict the results of an analysis of the frequency of interaction. One of the crudest group norms relates to members' 'territory' within the group 'lands', whether it be a seat in a classroom or a place in the car park. In most established groups, changing this pattern is likely to prompt a significant response. This is partly to do with habit and an innate conservatism (wanting things to stay the same) but Moreno would argue that it is also to do with the fact that changing your position may in effect be changing your whole social outlook. If in any of the group situations you are habitually in you have a set place to stand or sit, try a change of position. You will be surprised how radically different the group looks from your new perspective. What you are in fact doing is disrupting patterns of social behaviour, those norms that time and experience have generated and reinforced.

ACTIVITY . . .

Conduct a sociometric survey on a group you know, confidentially asking a simple question about preferences for small group or paired work. Predict the shape of this group and then anonymously plot your results. Ask members of the group to comment on your sociometric plan.

The question might read something like:

'You have been invited to select from this group the *three* other people with whom you would choose to work. Please rank these below:

1 ....

2 ....

3 ....

The shape of groups tells us a lot about them, and sociometry is one of the ways in which we might get a picture of how groups are intrinsically organised. In this respect all groups are subtly different. One aspect of any group's sociometric layout which is worth considering is the extent to which the revealed structure is centred around either an internal or external influence. To put it another way: does the group have leaders? Teaching groups, for example, are good examples of centralised groups whilst friendship groups are more often decentralised.

The importance of group structure is emphasised by Douglas's model of group processes which usefully pulls together many of the ideas contained in this section. Douglas (1979) identifies four kinds of processes, or categories, which also mark four stages in group development:

Category	1 Basic	Interaction
	2 Structural	Group development
		Social structure
		Subgroup formation
	3 Locomotive	Decision-making
		Purpose and goal formation
	4 Motor	Formation of norms, standards, values
		Development of cohesion
		Development of group influence
		Development of 'climate' (this refers to a group's specific 'atmosphere' or 'character')

Having arrived at structure and subgroup formation and predicted the progress from here, we will leave the final section to deal with 'locomotive' and 'motor' processes.

▼ 8   **GROUP COMMUNICATION: HOW GROUPS WORK AND WHEN THEY DON'T: LEADERSHIP AND LETHARGY**

In this last section we will bring our consideration of group communication and of personal communication to a close by looking at how groups work, what motivates them to work, and what happens when they don't work.

■   We will look at the notion of conformity within groups, and the positive and negative outcomes this may lead to.

■   We will examine ideas about leadership.

This section will look at fully operational groups as they move into action and how they are directed. As groups develop, so the benefits and obligations of individual members develop, too. We enjoy being part of the group but also feel responsible to it. Hartley has expressed this two-sided experience in terms of 'liberation' and 'conformity', suggesting that membership of functioning groups both sets you free and in a strange way confines you:

> On the one hand a group can develop norms which restrict its members' behaviour and communication; on the other hand a group can provide support and under-standing for its members and allow them to express themselves in ways that they otherwise would not have done.
>
> (Hartley 1997)

We can all think of groups that especially restrict or support us, but most do both to different degrees at different times. Moreover, we are ourselves differently committed to different groups, and so our 'conformity' is itself subject to variation.

CONFORMITY This might usefully be defined as the tendency of individuals to adhere to or follow the conventions or norms of a particular group or situation. It refers to the way we fit in with the expectations of a particular group or situation.

Conformity in fact operates at a number of levels or depths. In some groups our 'fitting in' is only skin deep; it is put on to keep face or to avoid conflict. This level of conformity is described as 'compliance'; there may be many occasions with our families where we conform at this level because it's easier.

Conformity at a more significant level might see the recognition that certain situations or groups provoke certain kinds of response. In other words, we begin to associate certain kinds of attitudes and behaviour with certain situations. This is 'identification'; the willingness to use the group concerned as a cue for certain types of behaviour, attitude and communication. This is still some way from a sincere performance but it does offer a coherent set of responses tied to a particular context. In more significant cases a third, and potentially disturbing and/or enriching, stage is reached whereby the group's norms sincerely become those of the individual members. The goal of all advertisers,

ACTIVITY . . .

Try to identify situations where you have 'conformed' at the three levels suggested:

- Compliance
- Identification
- Internalisation

What are the benefits and problems of conformity at each of these stages?

propagandists and cults is 'internalisation', the stage at which the values, attitudes and beliefs of others become part of the self.

Conformity as an idea is a sort of inverse measurement of group influence on individuals; the lower the level, the less 'pull' the group has. In all cases it has significant positive and negative elements.

Allen (1965) suggests that conformity is a complex idea which is subject to a series of pressures and that these, both individually and collectively, dictate the level of conformity. Allen's factors are:

- Level of commitment to group
- Level of attractiveness of the group
- Status of the group
- Degree of interdependence within the group
- Composition of the group
- Size and unanimity of the group
- The extent to which group norms are extreme
- Whether the group is task-competent
- Level of task confidence
- Difficulty and importance of task

Much of Allen's work focuses on the coherence and quality of the group to whose norms the individual is conforming. It is tempting simply to break down groups into 'good' and 'bad' ones or, more academically, into functional and dysfunctional ones. Kell and Costs (1980) have refined this in their identifications of group maturity. The following is a checklist against which you can measure your own groups. A mature group:

- Offers the facility for individual growth
- Offers an atmosphere of trust
- Offers equality of membership
- Adapts to points of disagreement
- Encourages participation
- Encourages sacrifice for group benefit
- Has a good time

What Kell and Costs are essentially suggesting is that a mature group functions like a rich soil; it allows individual members to grow. Immature groups thus function like the proverbial 'stony ground', offering little in terms of support and harming rather than helping individual members.

We began this section by addressing the balance between what groups allow and what they restrict. Restriction in the extreme case can have harmful implications whereby a group becomes an unhealthy context for individual work. Marilyn Brewer and Norman Miller begin their book *Intergroup Relations* (1996) with this description of where unhealthy, immature groups can lead ultimately:

> On November 18 1978, more than 900 men, women and children committed suicide at Jonestown in Guyana. Told that their group was under siege, members of the

Reverend Jim Jones's People's Temple lined up to receive glasses of red Kool Aid laced with cyanide. All drank the liquid as they were told, and almost all died within 30 minutes.

This is a shocking description of a real-life group. It is shocking, too, that, on the limited evidence offered, the Jim Jones's People's Temple seems to demonstrate some signs of group maturity – the atmosphere of trust, the encouragement of participation, the sacrifices for the group's benefit. However, it is difficult to see how mass suicide offers genuine evidence of a facility for individual growth.

The extract gives much clearer evidence for what Irving Janis in 1972 labelled 'GroupThink', a sort of psychological disease associated with some groups. GroupThink was identified by Janis as the psychological degenerative condition which afflicts group members, undermining their facility for individual response.

KEY TERM

GROUP THINK This is described by Janis (1972) as 'a deterioration of mental efficiency, reality testing and moral judgement which results from in-group pressure'.

These three areas of deterioration – mental efficiency, reality testing and moral judgement – all seem particularly pertinent to the Jim Jones tragedy. Janis published a list of symptoms of GroupThink which might function as an early-warning list:

- Illusion of invulnerability (thinking you can't be harmed)
- Collective rationalisation (explaining things away as a group)
- Belief in inherent morality of group (irrespective of others)
- Stereotypes of out-groups
- Direct pressure on dissenters (taking action against those who disagree)
- Self-censorship (removing the bits they don't like)
- Illusion of unanimity (imagining the whole group thinks the same)
- Self-appointed mind-guard (someone to keep reality out)

Much of what GroupThink consists of amounts to what Zimbardo (1988) has called 'de-individuation', the undermining of individuality for the good of the group. Most of us will have experienced this first hand or observed it in our political leaders or celebrities. The behaviour of the members of successful pop groups read like a casebook on GroupThink – the illusion of invulnerability, the direct pressure on dissenters, the illusion of unanimity. Perhaps in the context of international super stardom, mental efficiency, moral judgement and especially reality testing are always going to take a battering.

More disturbing examples are found in the context of criminality, where groups can provide a sometimes murderous reinforcement of deviant behaviour. Certain criminal acts would appear to result from the way in which groups generate a 'collective rationalisation' which finds reasons for the unreasonable.

GroupThink, as a dysfunction of group, is a complex combination of factors – membership, context, task. Stanton (1996) has defined group effectiveness in terms of two sets of variables – those that cannot be controlled and those that can. In the 'uncontrollable' set he lists three sets – group variables, environmental variables and task variables (all of which might be seen to contribute also to the ineffectiveness which GroupThink essentially is).

These variables in fact correspond to the questions 'who', 'where' and 'what'. By implication Stanton is saying that the effectiveness of your Communication Studies group is dependent on:

■ Who's in it
■ Where it is – physically and structurally
■ What it's doing

These are uncontrollable in the sense that they are largely given.

ACTIVITY . . .

If these factors are 'uncontrollable', what sort of elements can we influence in groups? Try to construct a list of controllable variables.

What is always available as an influence is member activity and motivation. The size and shape of a group might be largely set whereas the behaviour is open to amendment. Motivation may vary from task to task and members may be more or less able to participate. Often this motivating role becomes a function of the group or the motivator becomes something like a group leader. Stanton in fact lists 'leadership style' as his first controllable variable, underlining its importance. The problem is that across a range of different groups leadership does not appear to be a consistent feature. It is relatively easy to define in a formal context like a work or educational situation but rather more difficult in personal and social contexts.

ACTIVITY . . .

What differences are there between the 'leadership' of these kinds of group:

■ Family

■ Friendship

■ Work?

Think of groups to which you belong: who are the leaders?

Leadership is something that is communicated through the form and style of messages. It works on individuals and motivates them to the achievement of certain goals. How it operates and what forms it takes has been addressed by Myers and Myers (1992), who suggested four 'approaches' to the understanding of leadership.

LEADERSHIP Tedeschi and Lindskold (1976) have defined leadership with reference to three factors – social influence, behaviour and authority. They suggest that leadership, when we experience it, consists of an impact on the way people interact, a set of actions and a sense of power. Tannenbaum has more formally defined leadership as 'interpersonal influence exercised in a situation and directed through the communication process toward the attainment of a specialised goal or goals'.

The first approach identified by Myers and Myers is the 'trait' approach. This great person theory approaches leadership through personality. Leaders are those with special character 'traits' or excess of quality. Leaders are born, not made.

This approach is supported by Stogdill (1981), who proposed a substantial list of those qualities that leaders might possess in greater abundance than the rest of us. It might be useful to think how far you can find leaders to match each of these categories or how far your own teachers excel or excelled in any of these:

- Intelligence
- Scholarship
- Dependability
- Activity
- Social status
- Initiative
- Persistence
- Self-confidence
- Insight
- Popularity
- Adaptability
- Verbal facility

Stodgill proposes that leaders are those who are more intelligent, more dependable, more persistent and so on.

The second approach identified by Myers and Myers (1992) is the 'situational' approach. Contexts make leaders. Leadership is simply a particular response to a particular situation.

It might be argued that each situation has its own character. This character arises out of the sometimes opposed factors of the need for quality and the need for acceptance or content. Leadership styles are responses to this relationship between quality and acceptance. A range of leadership styles could be mapped as follows:

- If quality is more important than acceptance: preferred decision style = COMMAND (leadership style is 'autocratic')

- If acceptance is more important than quality: preferred decision style = CONSENSUS (leadership style is 'collective')

- If quality and acceptance are both important: preferred decision style
  = CONSULTATION (leadership style is 'democratic')

- If neither quality nor acceptance is important: preferred decision style
  = CONVENIENCE (leadership style is *laissez-faire*)

LEADERSHIP STYLES Four styles are often identified:

- **Autocratic (authoritarian):** leadership by command; the leader is sole source of decisions.

- **Democratic:** leadership by consultation; decisions are made by group or its elected representatives.

- *Laissez-faire*: leadership by instinct; decisions are made by whoever can make them.

- **Collective:** leadership by consensus; decisions are made by whole group together.

ACTIVITY ....

Which leadership or decision-making style might be appropriate in the following situations?

- *Family Fortunes*
- Electing a member of parliament
- Electing a student council representative
- Selecting a venue for a special celebration
- Choosing where to go next Friday night
- Choosing your A Level subjects
- Appointing the captain of a sports team
- Awarding a promotion to a member of staff
- Choosing a friend to share a 'Holiday of a Lifetime' prize
- Choosing an audience for an oral presentation

This is a flexible enough approach to allow a range of answers, though research often attempts to discover which works best. When Lewin, Lippett and White (1939) set children to make soap models under various kinds of supervision, they found that the 'autocratic' approach produced most models while the 'democratic' created best group morale; *laissez-faire* simply let things go, and little was achieved. In a modern welfare state the 'collective' of some models is replaced by 'bureaucratic'; leadership by faceless administration and written justification.

The third approach identified by Myers and Myers (1992) is the 'functional' approach. Leadership is a collection of jobs a group needs doing. These jobs might be done collectively. Myers and Myers identify three sorts of job:

- **Procedural**: running the group
- **Substantive**: giving input .
- **Maintenance**: keeping the group going

There is no reason why different members of the group might not offer these very different kinds of function. The key to successful leadership might in fact be appropriate skills rather than talented individuals, for example openness, information and persuasion.

The fourth approach identified by Myers and Myers is the 'contingency' approach. Leadership is a mixture of the other approaches. Argyle (1983) offers a good example of contingency in his checklist of the sources of leadership:

- Personality
- Composition of group
- Context
- Group structure
- Character of task
- Ability to motivate

Leadership is a factor of all groups from the group of two to the largest organisations. It may be explicit or implicit, formal or informal. It affects us all either as leader or as led; it shapes the character of our experience of much communication. We see it in action in our political leaders, our work and social environments, even in our family situations. What kind of leaders we make depends largely on the groups we are in and the attitudes we have.

A study of political leaders by the American Psychological Association, presented to their 2000 conference, suggested that leaders fall crudely into eight types. These might also function as an alternative list of leadership styles. They were derived from a large-scale critical analysis of the first 41 American presidents but might easily be applied to leaders in a range of situations from managers to opinion leaders.

Eight types of leader (Rubenzer 2000):

- Dominators
- Introverts
- Good guys
- Innocents
- Actors
- Philosophers
- Maintainers
- Extroverts

Identify leaders, either public or personal, who might fit each of these types.

PAST QUESTIONS ON UNIT 3.

FURTHER WORK

1 Verbal/non-verbal communication:

a Non-verbal communicative behaviour appears to be governed by unwritten 'rules' which regulate such behaviour in a particular culture. List ten such unwritten rules which appear to regulate public behaviour in Britain today.

b How might the regulation of social encounters be influenced by body movement and the use of body adornment?

c Conventions such as punctuation, spelling and grammar serve to regulate written communication. To what extent are conventions used to regulate face-to-face oral communication?

d Outline the uses and limitations of language as a means of communication.

e Assess the importance of non-verbal communication in social interaction.

f 'Women are better communicators than men.' Discuss.

g 'Language most shows a man. Speak that I may see thee.' How far is this true?

h To what extent can you rely upon non-verbal communication alone?

i 'Actions speak louder than words.' Discuss.

j 'The limits of my language are the limits of my world'. Discuss.

k Evaluate the ways in which purpose, role and context affect body language.

l How do people use verbal and non-verbal communication to regulate their interpersonal exchanges?

m Language is man-made. Discuss.

2 Intrapersonal communication:

a Analyse the importance of self-image and self-esteem in interpersonal communication.

b How useful and accurate is Maslow's 'Hierarchy of Needs' in analysing the motivation of communicative behaviour?

c Evaluate the factors that affect the playing of roles.

d How does intrapersonal communication influence interpersonal communication?

e To what extent does our own self-image influence the way we communicate with other people?

3 Group communication:

a Choose any contrasting groups or organisations with which you are familiar. How do they use communication to (i) achieve goals, (ii) reinforce norms, and (iii) display identity?

b How important is leadership to the successful functioning of a group? Answer with reference to two groups of which you are a member.

c To what extent is a knowledge of role useful in understanding group communication?

d Analyse the ways in which groups communicate either externally and internally.

e Evaluate the reasons people join groups.

f How might a knowledge of group dynamics help someone to lead a meeting?

All of the above questions are taken from past papers of the pioneering AEB (now AQA) Communication Studies A Level (1976–2001).

FURTHER READING

Burton, G. and Dimbleby, R. (1988) *Between Ourselves*, London: Arnold.

Hartley, P. (1997) *Group Communication*, London: Routledge.

Hartley, P. (1999) *Interpersonal Communication*, 2nd edn, London: Routledge.

FURTHER VIEWING

Morris, D. (1994) *The Human Animal*, London: BBC Worldwide.

PART 6: USING YOUR COMMUNICATION SKILLS TO PASS EXAMINATIONS

In this part we will look at how your communication skills can be used to help you prepare for and to sit examinations.

- We will explore approaches to revision.

- We will look at how you can be more personally effective when preparing for, and sitting, examinations.

- We will offer you useful techniques to assist you when taking examinations.

The purpose of this part is to offer both general and specific advice on how to improve your chances of gaining high marks in the examinations you may sit in Communication Studies (and elsewhere). Its rather clumsy title is a deliberate attempt to develop this process from the start. Communication Studies is a discipline which encourages effective communication and a personal critical response to all manner of contexts and texts. Examinations, and particularly examination advice, cannot be immune to the need to be both rigorously criticised and effectively communicated.

The skills we need in examinations will of course include reading and writing, speaking and listening, drafting and dealing with questions. It is equally important to practise critical skills to deal with the examination as yet another text, and to plan in both a general and specific sense. There will also be a need for common sense. This is not a skill but all too sadly and too often it isn't demonstrated in the examination room.

It is easily said but examinations should not be feared. It is likely that you will have worked hard all year on your Communication Studies course. In truth it would be very frustrating if the knowledge you acquired there was never tested or called upon. Exams are merely the rather artificial opportunity you get to demonstrate what you know and to receive some, hopefully much, credit for it. They are a time- and money-saving alternative to having a visiting examiner come to your house to quiz you in depth on your knowledge of the subject. Positively, examinations usually ask you about what you know rather than what you don't know: after all, to 'examine' means 'to look at in detail', not 'to catch out'.

EXAMINATIONS

There are lots of places to go for advice on examination preparation and technique: study skills guides, websites, your teachers/fellow students, Radio One's annual series of radio and television revision programmes. What common sense tells you is that there can be no single definitive answer any more than there can be a single effective general model of communication. At the centre of the examination process is the examinee, just as at the centre of the revision process is the reviser – in other words, you! What helps is whatever helps you to be relaxed, to be confident, to be clear-headed and clear-sighted. If, for you, this means eating garlic harvested at a full moon with a platinum sickle, then so be it!

What follows is a debate between received wisdom and an individual approach; not a contest, but a conversation. It partly rehearses the advice which everybody knows to give to prospective students; it is largely the advice which you would give to yourself if you were writing this part of this book. It also challenges that advice to suggest that there are a large number of potential 'negotiated' readings, or even 'oppositional' readings, of this advice. This is partly meant to function as a viable alternative to the all-too-common position of knowing what you should do both to revise and to prepare for your examinations and equally knowing that you will never actually do this. Too many students buy into the self-fulfilling 'prophecy' which begins with despair, moves to an unrealistically extensive revision plan, and ends with no revision (and despair).

Some of the advice that follows is deliberately provocative because its very purpose is to make you all as individual learners think about how you learn best and how you might best prepare for examinations which judge your quality as learners. Nothing here is advocated, save the need for individual students to make rational and personal decisions about their own revision and preparation. All too often the most important lesson of education is that 'you shouldn't let other people get your kicks for you'.

Communication Studies is not a subject that lends itself to 'right answers'. You are mostly asked for analysis and evaluation in contexts where the choice of evidence and treatment is yours. Much of what has been covered in this textbook remains a matter for debate, and it is your job to join these debates rather than attempt to bring them to a satisfactory conclusion. What is often being marked is your ability to fashion a convincing argument and support it with relevant evidence: it is the quality of your argument not the character of your argument that is important here.

Advice on examination practice, or rather examinations in practice, falls into three phases:

1 **Revision:** which looks at the various ways in which the knowledge gained from a course of study can be recalled, marshalled and reorganised so as to be useful in the examination
2 **Preparation:** which covers the period from the arrival in the examination room to the first time your pen is used
3 **Technique:** which deals with how different forms of question might be approached – from design to realisation

Let's look at these three phases in more detail.

REVISION

Literally 'the act of seeing again', revision is a taboo word for many students, describing a process they only vaguely understand and one that, even when done thoroughly, offers questionable results. Revision has a dubious reputation; stereotypically it involves sitting still for long periods of time and suffering. There is a profound moral dimension to this. In fact it is treated by society at large and by the educational community specifically as a kind of moral performance indicator. Good students do revision in the same way that they don't do sex or drugs. Bad students on the other hand spend their time doing the last two and thus have no time for the former. For, above all things, revision takes time.

Every institution, whether it be school, college or self-help guide, has its own timescale: 'start at Easter', 'at least three months' or 'Christmas is a good time to start'. Courses are cut short, curtailed to allow for the 'revision period', the part of the course where the dynamic that is learning is brought to a standstill. At some point the revision timetable must be drawn up – provided by your school or college, or constructed with a sharp pencil and 30cm ruler. This is a statement of intent, an attempt formally to engage in a self-fulfilling prophecy.

A good example is found in our sister volume *Media Studies: The Essential Introduction* (Rayner *et al.* 2001).

Drawing up a revision plan

A revision plan is the essential first step towards preparing yourself for your Media Studies exam. You may find the following steps a useful way to guide you in drawing up such a plan:

1   Make sure you know what you need to revise. Either check with the specification or syllabus yourself, or ask your teacher what you need to do. In some cases you may find that there is a choice of topic areas and you may have to decide how many of these you are going to prepare for the exam.
2   Make a list of the topics you have decided you need to cover. Check where you can best find the information you need on these topics. Start with your own notes and then look at how textbooks, such as this one, may be able to help you.
3   Draw up a revision timetable devoting a suitable amount of time to each topic. Be realistic about how many hours you can devote to this. There will almost certainly be other subjects making demands on your time, as well as all of those diversions you will have to succumb to.
4   Put together a list of up-to-date examples that you can draw upon to illustrate your answers. If you have made good notes throughout your course, you should have a good range of texts such as films, television and radio programmes, newspaper and magazine articles you can call upon. It is also worth thinking in advance about how you may be able to use these in the exam. Remember, too, to keep an eye on such sources as the *Media Guardian* for up-to-date information on key media issues and debates.
5   Remember that revision you do at the very last minute may be of little use. Revising is like preparing yourself for a sporting event. A sustained programme of preparation will always be more effective than a last-minute panic.

This is sensible advice but it is not the only approach to revision. One problem with revising in this semi-formal way is that you run the risk of putting unwanted pressure on knowledge that has been organically and contextually acquired. You also simply put pressure on yourself over a significant period of time and stress the skills of recalling information instead of the skills of analysis and evaluation.

An alternative approach is to see revision as both a more general and more focused activity. First, this would see revision as a course-long activity and would see the regular activity pattern of this book as a reasonable representation of most teaching within the area. In applying knowledge in practical and semi-practical situations, we are in fact revising our understanding of the key concepts of topics and particularly of our singular central topic, communication itself. This process may regularly lead to topic summary sheets on which you record the key ideas of some topic, but these are merely the regular reminders of how the course is to be assessed.

ACTIVITY . . .

Do you know how the course you are currently doing is assessed?

- How many examinations?
- How long are they?
- What is the mark breakdown across papers/units?
- What does the mark scheme for each paper reward?

Too often the course is seen as something to remember when in fact it is something to experience. The principle of 'study leave' is well established in this country but not well founded on any significant evidence. Letting students leave school or college to revise reinforces the separation between the course and the examination and restresses the importance of memory over analysis. Examinations need not be viewed like this. They are a small but significant part of the course and one of the 'audiences' that any course must have. Most often the courses we do are defined by the qualifications we seek, in other words by the examinations we sit.

This fact can be approached sincerely or cynically. Partly we must dismiss the need for specific revision altogether, for if we have engaged with intrapersonal communication what question can we fear? More practically we might think early about the amount of knowledge necessary to 'fill' an answer planned and written within as little as 30 minutes. We may in fact 'knock up' our own revision plan which will serve as a gloss to the previous one or perhaps define a continuum within which we all can work.

A substantial engagement with the course, its form and its content, is the essential first step towards preparing yourself for your Communication Studies examination. Revision is all very well but 'vision' is actually much more important. Make sure you 'see' it clearly first time around so you won't struggle to recall it. The following steps may form a useful guide.

AN ALTERNATIVE REVISION PLAN

1 Make sure you know how you are to be assessed. Get hold of past questions and mark schemes. Check the range of topics to be assessed and the number of questions to be attempted. Calculate the minimum number of topics to be prepared for the examination and the frequency with which they occur. Give yourself an amount of security according to your temperament (if you are by temperament cautious, revise extra topics).

(NB: The new specifications at AS and A Level are by their design easier to predict because they specify not only what you must know but also that this knowledge must be tested.)

2 Consider each topic you cover in terms of (a) its most important content and (b) the amount of information you could reasonably use, if known, in between 30 and 45 minutes. Compile the essential information, together with quotations and/or notes, on no more than one side of A4 paper for each topic. This is an indication of the amount of knowledge you can need or use in an examination. Given that no examination is longer than two hours, and that three questions is the maximum request, revision cannot consist of more than six sheets of paper or six sides of A4 paper.

(Psychologically and symbolically the information and content knowledge that you need for any formal examination should be able to be comfortably located on your table/desk. You should end up sitting with no more than six separated and organised A4 sides, perhaps fewer. In this way 'what is to be known' is put in its place and you are in a position to think about what you are being asked and how your response will be structured.)

3 If you have clarified the significant content for each topic and reduced it to a single side of A4, the fixing of content detail is in fact best done close to the examination. If there are things you feel you need to remember, two days is a much more sensible timescale than two months. Try as far as you can to think about one examination at a time and to concentrate your knowledge-fixing on the two days before the examination. This may seem like a heresy but remember we are not here talking about things you don't know but rather about things you do. Obviously other examinations in other subjects will interfere, but ideally you should deal with one examination at a time and not begin to revise the second paper until the first is over.

What this approach advocates is that knowledge of assessment – of what examinations are and what they do – is as important as knowledge of subject. Study at Advanced Level must involve more than the regurgitation of knowledge, and the more that is crammed in, the more likely it is to emerge in an unprocessed fashion. In Communication Studies in particular there is an established equality between theory as such and the evidence of communication in practice. The latter can be rehearsed across the course but there must ideally be room for 'live' performance, the act of coming to an examination question in an examination room and drawing freshly upon your experience as a communicator. This is the first lure of the subject: we are all experienced and mainly skilful communicators.

This subject asks us to draw on that experience and skill. The more that we try to learn this 'experience', the less like experience it becomes.

Knowledge of assessment begins with the classification of your exams which you attempted earlier. Different kinds of examination require different kinds of preparation as well as different kinds of skills. However, there are simple statements to be made which cover general features of the examination experience.

PREPARATION

However much good advice you're given and take, the problems of the examination room come down to a simple problem: you need to be calm, relaxed and clear-headed – and you're not! However cool you are in the face of a formal examination, by the time you've stood around for 10 minutes outside the exam room with 25 to 50 fellow students who are bombarding you with trivial questions about the coming examination, you are likely to be a little wound up. The way you behave in the first 5 minutes of the examination is therefore vital.

Unfortunately it is not uncommon to find candidates filling this vital opening 5 minutes with frantic writing. No sooner has the invigilator's 'The time is 9.30, you may now begin' died in the air than the first task response is finding an introduction. This is simply an impossibility if you are interested in maximising your achievement. Clearly, the first 5 minutes are for reading, for getting to know the paper, and for discovering across a couple of readings at least the opportunities that the paper offers. Better not to open the paper at all for the first 5 minutes than attempt an immediate answer to the first question.

You are partly allowing yourself time to acclimatise to the examination environment, making yourself familiar with the overall picture before the real work begins. This may give you ideas, albeit crude ones, about which questions are most demanding and about which questions should be tackled first. Often in this initial assessment questions are clarified and what appeared easy and attractive at first sight now seems problematic and confusing. This is not the only safeguard against poor question selection but it is the first of a number of filters.

You are also moving into 'examination time', the medium of examinations. Being asked to perform to time is the essence of the examination experience and thus nothing is more important than keeping to time. Do not be fooled by the theory that two good answers are better than three mediocre ones; siphoning time from one question to another rarely allows a significantly greater performance. Unfinished papers simply and literally wipe marks and thus grades off a candidate's achievement. Your performance in the questions you attempt can never compensate for the question you have missed. In fact the latter dilutes the former. Hear this loud and clear: you must attempt the number of questions you're asked to. This is the ugly reality of examinations: if you attempt a three-question AS paper but in fact only manage two questions, the level of performance required in these two answers, just to reach a basic pass mark of, say, 40 per cent, is in fact 60 per cent (this may be the difference between a B grade an an E grade).

The great myth of examination time is the suggestion that, to arrive at your time allocation for each question, you divide the number of questions to answer into the time allowed.

This in fact overlooks all the other advice that we are giving about the psychology of doing examinations. What you are asked to do is write *in* 3 hours (or two examinations of 1½ hours) not write *for* 3 hours. In the new 1½ hour AS examination you must allow at least 10 to 15 minutes for examination management time – reading the paper in a considered way; moving from one topic area to the next; and checking that all words have been successfully transferred from your head via your pen to the page (and that most of them are spelled correctly). This leaves 25 minutes to plan and execute your answer, not 30. This seems a minor point but if you don't time realistically and 10 minutes are spent reading followed by lots of 30 minutes, then the final question may be squeezed down to next to nothing.

SCORING AND EXPLODING: PAPER VANDALISM APPROVED

The other thing you must do, and this can start pretty much with the first reading, is to make the examination paper your own. You do this in a primitive way by defacing it, leaving your own marks on it. These marks are the evidence that you have ruthlessly explored the questions' potential and have identified any potential problems with them. If you do not do this, you have not justified your entry. If your paper can be handed back and reused, or even effectively photocopied, you really haven't made the examination your own – it still belongs to the examiner and the examining body.

The longer you stay in the examination system the more likely you are to have a tragic examination story – about the friend of yours who read 'First World War' when it said 'Second World War' or answered eight questions when the instructions said 'choose ONE'. These stories are told up and down the country in the lead-up to examinations, and much fun is had at the expense of these buffoons who could not be us. Yet the catalogue is added to every year without fail. Candidates answer on books they haven't read, attempt six hours' work in three hours or even sit the wrong examination. If defacing the paper does nothing else, it reduces this risk. Educationists and psychologists frequently assert that the most effective learning is active – and not passive – learning. Taking your pen to the examination paper is a sound extension of this principle. You claim and maintain your status as an active examination candidate; you will not settle for being a passive examination candidate for whom examinations are something that happens to them.

Underachievement in public examinations is in fact rarely the result of a hideous lack of ability, skill or knowledge but more often a result of a hideous lack of relevance. Most examiners report that most papers they mark are hampered by the fact that the candidate, even if the paper is complete, has not responded to questions in their entirety and thus has made it impossible for the paper to access the upper range of marks available. To get full marks is unlikely, but to put yourself in the game and get a mark out of the full allocation must be a primary goal. In some scripts (this is examiner-speak for a candidate's examination answer book) the answers are so negligent of the questions that the final mark is low because only a third or even less of the question's scope has been addressed. Let's say this again: physically marking the paper makes this broader response to specific questions significantly more likely.

Looking for key words is part of your starting point, but even so it is vital to be aware that there are two sets of key words:

- Words that instruct, direct or govern (e.g. 'analyse', 'describe', 'state', 'evaluate', 'consider', 'compare')
- Subject-specific words (e.g. 'self-concept', 'feedback', 'semiotic').

If you can discover what it is you have to do and what is the precise focus of subject content of your examination, you are well on the way to success. Be careful you don't make the identification of key words your only goal; the next stage is necessary, too. Successfully identifying the key words of a question should always clarify the question but it may lead you to conclude that this is a question you should avoid.

Once the key words have been 'scored' they then should be 'exploded' into the margins of your question paper for note-form explanation. If the question addresses 'feedback', it is important that you should be able to write in your own words what 'feedback' is. Similarly, if the question asks you to consider the effectiveness of a text for its intended audience of '8-year-olds', it is important that you are able to understand not only that '8-year-olds' is an important part of the question but also what that phrase might mean. In this case your exploded notes might include words and phrases like 'restricted code', 'highly visual', 'energetic'.

ACTIVITY . . .

Consider (a) the key words and (b) their implications in the following sample examination questions (NB do *not* answer the questions themselves):

1 Explain how and why individuals often reject evidence that appears to contradict their self-image.

2 Using material from EITHER or BOTH of the documents, prepare a revision sheet for your fellow A Level students on 'what signs are and what form they take'. The revision sheet should contain no more than 250 words of text. (*You will be rewarded for your organisation of the revision sheet, for your clarification of key semiotic ideas and for your choice of accurate and appropriate examples.*)

Once you've dealt with the paper in this way, you're ready to offer your responses. Here the advice we offer must take account of the different kinds of examination that Communication Studies favours.

UNSEEN PAPERS

Most examining bodies set a paper that requires you to write about a communication text that you will see for the first time in the examination itself. This is often called the unseen paper. Typically the examination will consist of a print-based text, such as a magazine article, which you will be asked to consider in the examination room. Usually you are asked to respond to the text in around 1½ to 2 hours. The type of text – video, sound, print – may vary, as will the precise instructions telling you what to do. The principles for approaching this type of exercise, however, remain very similar. In fact it is likely you will have had a go at some practice papers in class to help you get the hang of it. Moreover this examination task is also probably very close to the sorts of activities you'll have experienced in Communication Studies classes, when your teacher has brought in a communication text and has asked everyone to discuss and analyse it.

A good way of practising for the unseen paper is to look at texts you have chosen yourself. Magazine covers, advertisements, extracts from television programmes, cinema trailers and CD covers are all good examples. Then try to get down some notes as quickly as you can on what specific aspects of the text you would want to point out if you were writing an analysis. In this way you will help prepare yourself mentally for the task of unseen analysis in the examination itself.

The current trend in unseen papers is to provide fairly detailed information advising you what you should look for in your commentary on the text. This guidance provides a useful checklist of points to cover. It is important to bear in mind that it may not be a good idea to work mechanically through the list trying to get something down under each heading. Each text that you will be asked to consider is unique. As such it needs an individual response. Your potential to identify the unique qualities of the text and base your commentary on these is the real test of your performance in such a paper. The checklist is, however, a useful mechanism for ensuring that you have not ignored a key element of the analysis which is important.

Organising your response is an important aspect of this question. A brilliantly perceptive textual analysis is of little use if it is confused and difficult to follow. The guidance or checklist may come in useful here as a way of suggesting to you headings under which to organise your response. However you decide to organise what you have to say, make sure that it is both logical and user-friendly for the examiner. The easier it is for someone to digest what you have to say, the more likely you are to be rewarded for it.

It is important that you also spend some time thinking before you start to write your response. This is true for all examinations, but it is especially important for an unseen paper. This is probably the first time you will have seen the text you are to deal with. You need, therefore, to spend time getting familiar with it and preparing yourself to develop your idea on the text. If the examination rubric permits, by all means start scribbling down some notes to help remind you of the important points; but, whatever you do, do not try to start writing your analysis straightaway. Give yourself time to see the text as a whole before you look at the individual parts.

KEY TERM

RUBRIC   These are the instructions that appear on the cover of the examination paper and at the head of each section of the examination paper. Typical rubrics are: 'Answer two questions' or 'Answer one question from each section'.

Analysing texts is a test of your skill in applying key Communication Studies concepts. It follows that if you can use the technical terminology of the discipline with accuracy and authority you will produce a convincing analysis. Understanding key terms such as connotation, anchorage, paradigm or ideology is important. Using them appropriately to describe how the text functions is even more important.

The mistake that many students make in this sort of paper is that they focus too much on simply describing the text itself. You can safely assume that the examiner has already seen the text. Your job is to analyse. This means you should be able to explain how the text works by exposing some of the underlying thinking that has gone into its construction. It is the complexities of the text that you should attempt to reveal; simply describing what is in front of you goes little way to achieving this.

ESSAY PAPERS

The other type of paper you are most likely to encounter is the essay paper. In this you are expected to write a number of essays in a given period of time. It is always a good idea to make yourself familiar with the type of paper you are sitting in advance of the examination. It is common for a paper to be split into sections, each reflecting an area of the specification you have studied. For example, there may be a section on verbal and non-verbal communication, another on intrapersonal communication and a third on group communication. If you are sitting such a paper, two things are important. One is to make sure just what questions you are supposed to attempt. Look out for an instruction on the paper telling you what to do. For example, it may say: 'Attempt one question from any two sections'. Clearly, you will not do well in the examination if you disregard such an instruction. The second important issue is about preparing yourself for an examination of this sort. If you know that you are to answer two questions on two different topics from a choice of four, how are you going to prepare? Some students will only prepare for the questions in two sections, while others may prepare three or even four topics to give themselves the widest choice on the day.

There are arguments for and against both approaches, and your teacher may be the best person to advise you on a strategy. However, do be absolutely certain that you follow the instructions on the paper and answer the specified number of questions.

Much of the advice that we can offer about dealing with essay papers is relevant to most other subjects. However, the problem of repeating advice you may already have been given is much outweighed by the advantages you will get in the examination by hearing it a second time.

Once you have decided what the question is asking you to do, it is important that you then try to answer this question. Clearly, essays at this level must be planned and planned realistically with reference to the reasonable expectations of what might be achieved within as little as 25 minutes and never more than 40. What follows is an approach to these limitations, which also includes a final 'poor question selection' filter.

A PRACTICAL APPROACH TO ESSAY PAPERS

An A/AS essay is a five-paragraph essay. The paragraphs will normally function as follows:

1 **Introduction**: address key words; set the essay's agenda
2 First main point and evidence
3 Second main point and evidence
4 Third main point and evidence
5 **Conclusion**: air other points; leave the reader with something to think about

No essay can be attempted without three main points (at least). If you can't find three, choose again.

Do not decide that the question is close to an answer you have already prepared and write that down without regard for what the question is actually demanding. Be aware of the scale of the response required; be modest and realistic.

Once you have decided which questions you are going to attempt, you need to consider the order in which you are going to tackle them. Experience of marking examination papers suggests that the last answer that candidates attempt is often their weakest.

One strategy you might like to consider is to spend time planning all the questions you are to answer as soon as you have chosen them. This means mapping out your response to each in note form before you actually start writing the first one. This will mean that you can then use your notes as the basis for each response and allocate the remaining time equally between the questions. It also means that if other points occur to you as you are working on another question, it is simple to note it down ready for use later on.

Rough notes are an invaluable help in producing a good essay response. One approach that many students find effective is to use a sheet of paper and write down in note form all the relevant points that come into their head. Once this has been done, it is a good idea to put together points that have an obvious link between them. You can use the five-paragraph plan to impose a structure on what you are going to write. It is surprising how often you will find that there will be five or six points that you want to make. If you number these in order of importance, this can form a useful route through your essay.

ACTIVITY . . .

Using one of the questions at the end of Part 5, try noting down and numbering the points you would want to make as your response.

Your style of writing is an important element of how well your essay is received. Rambling, unstructured or disorganised responses full of waffle do not get good marks in examinations. Examiners are not easy people to fool. The best approach is a simple and straightforward style of writing. Try to avoid seeming pretentious, for example by trying to use words that you do not properly understand but which you think sound impressive.

A good essay answer will also start in an interesting way. Do not think that the first paragraph has to be a mere rehash of the question. If you can think of a bright attractive introduction, perhaps a quotation or even something controversial, then do not be afraid to use it. Similarly, try to end on a high note. Do not just let your essay trail off at the end but try to find a positive ending that will help sum up what has gone before.

A particularly important point to bear in mind is to support your arguments. This can be done specifically in two ways. The first is by drawing on published authorities to give weight to the point you are making.

Similarly, you should refer to practical examples of communication or communication texts that you have considered to support your point of view. For example, you may allude to a particular communication context with which you are familiar to support an answer on the importance of paralanguage to interpersonal communication. The best examples are generally those you have found for yourself, rather than texts that the whole class has studied and which all students are likely to refer to in the same examination.

Finally, it is to be hoped that you will have had a lot of enthusiasm for your Communication Studies course. Do not be afraid to let this shine through in the examination. Examiners do enjoy reading scripts that demonstrate genuine engagement and commitment on the part of students and always try to reward this.

FURTHER WORK: TEXTS AND MEANINGS

In January 2001, Communication Studies students and teachers were offered a concrete example of the new AS examination. Copies of this paper are available from the examination board, so it will be useful to look at the questions in some detail. The key here is both to understand the prompts offered by the tasks and to connect the tasks to the content of this chapter, which has provided you with significant analytical tools.

The first 'Texts and Meanings in Communication' paper presented two documents for analysis:

- DOCUMENT ONE: 'The BBC's Promises to you 2000–2001': a full-colour, glossy, illustrated leaflet, stating the BBC's promises: it is slightly bigger than A4 and folded three times to present 4 sides inside [coloured green, blue, orange and purple respectively] and 4 outside [largely green with a full-colour cover side]: the inside sides are bordered on the bottom third of their faces with full-colour illustrations from BBC programmes [*Gormenghast*, *Today*, *The Royle Family*, *Robotwars*, *Tweenies*] and services [Radio 1 website, BBC Knowledge, BBC Information].

- DOCUMENT TWO: 'This week's RADIO': Full-page programme projections for the following week's radio from *Radio Times* (the BBC's listings magazine): black and white reproduction: largely text with one major (a photomontage of different kinds of home) and two minor (actress Patricia Hodge and three opera singers in head-and-shoulder shots) illustrations.

Clearly, there is a contrast here, at least in terms of format and finish, which comes as no surprise. The difference between the documents clearly suggests the range of print-based texts. Task 1 leads us straight into a critical analysis of the first document and a set of 'hand-holds' to encourage uncertain candidates. It is important that you, as candidates, are able to identify the key words:

Task 1

DOCUMENT ONE lists the BBC's promises to its <u>viewers and listeners</u> [*television and radio*]. <u>In addition</u> [*don't talk about lists!*] the leaflet attempts to communicate a <u>positive impression of the BBC</u> [*this is the content/theme*]. Using <u>techniques of textual analysis</u> [*in other words, what I've learnt: semiotic and process approaches*] <u>explain how</u> [*detail the ways in which this is done*] the leaflet communicates this positive impression.

Your analysis should include reference to <u>some or all</u> [*all is safer!*] of the following:

- Choice of illustrations
- Use of colour
- Typography
- Layout
- Specific use of language

From this you should be able to construct an agenda for the question. In this case the key ideas are 'positive impression' and 'techniques of textual analysis': a 'what' and 'how' of the task. You can now begin to examine the text in detail, using the given prompts and the ever-necessary fields, 'first impressions' and 'overall feelings'. These should direct your note-making on a full A4 side of your answer book (always the left-hand side since notes from which to write need to be seen). You are only going to get 45 minutes to write, so A4 is just enough. You have been asked to use the tools of analysis that you have acquired from your course, so this should be reflected in the notes you make.

From here on the task is largely about organising your notes and writing them up efficiently. Clearly, the subheadings could be retained in the final written piece but this often makes for a dislocated response. The question asks 'how' the leaflet communicates 'a positive impression': it is asking for the means, the ways, the themes of this communication. The best way is to identify these themes and then draw on all parts of the leaflet for your evidence. In this particular case, for example, 'variety' might be identified as a theme. Variety is delivered in the leaflet through illustrations, typography, use of colour and layout. The five-paragraph essay model works well here:

- **Introduction**: clarify task and confirm it (comment on the fact that the BBC does indeed communicate on a number of levels); record first impressions (that this high-quality, glossy, colourful and attractive artefact is an index of the BBC as a high-quality, glossy . . . organisation); indicate a number of methods are used.

- **Main point 1**: method one: backs up verbal communication. The leaflet evidences the claims, e.g. 'offer children a wider range of UK made programmes' alongside illustrations of *The Tweenies* and 'BBC Knowledge'; 'experiment with new ideas especially in drama and entertainment' above a still from *The Royle Family* (which interestingly offers an alternative domestic group to the *Tweenies* image: the images are fairly similar, the effects very different [this is a case of two choices from the same paradigm producing very different results])

■ **Main Point 2**: method two: communicates the range and variety of the BBC.

1   The leaflet opens out to reveal the extent of the BBC's activities
2   The symbolic 'spectrum' of coloured sides
3   Text lists indicate abundance (and organisation)
4   Images range in content, form and style
5   The 'cover' tries and fails to contain the amount of material
6   Illustrations 'sprout' on the frontispiece; where the 'anchor' is 'We promise . . . ' and the images connote class and scope

■ **Main point 3**: 'aesthetic': it communicates by being a very slick, smart, sharp leaflet via:

1   The construction, which leads us to 'enter' through plain green doors and reveal the inner spectacle
2   Sophisticated range of styles; iconic but also symbolic
3   Myth of the BBC supported: classy, educational, responsible
4   Pictures are engaging and invite us to tell a story
5   Language is elegant and economic

■ **Final thoughts**: overall impression: express any doubts about whether it really works. Is it too skilful? Does it try too hard?

It is not a matter of getting these particular points, but rather of the need to approach the given text as a confident reader. This is also the case in Task 2, where Document Two turns out to be a much less accessible text. This task builds on the work you have done in the first task.

Task 2

DOCUMENT TWO on page *two* is a page from the Radio Times [*the BBC's 'house' TV magazine*], the BBC's all-channel listings magazine. It includes a selection of radio programmes for the following week. In DOCUMENT ONE the BBC promises to 'do more to reflect and serve [*what images of these people are offered and how are they helped and/or encouraged?*] the different people and cultures in the UK' [*implies minorities of various kinds: the notion of society as a vibrant mixture of cultures*].

In the light of this promise compare the representations [*representations may be words and pictures: 'compare' asks us to look at the documents together*] of 'different people and cultures' in DOCUMENT ONE and DOCUMENT TWO.

[*You may wish to refer to representations and stereotypes of ethnicity, gender, social class, ability and age.*]

Here the annotation (note-making) has already been done for you and the 'different people and cultures' has been initially addressed. This is a question about 'representation', a key concept in the study of what texts do. The first step again is to employ some prompts and make some notes. Clearly, the function of the hand-hold (the bracketed and italicised advice section) is to encourage you to focus your response on one or more of the sets of 'different people' listed there. This done, it is largely a matter of 'content analysis', for which job Gerbner's formula is always useful. Gerbner said we might look at four aspects of any representation:

- **Existence**: What is actually there?
- **Priorities**: What 'bit/aspect' of it are we being offered?
- **Values**: What is 'good' about it?
- **Relationships**: How does it connect to other things?

Applied to significant representations, this formula can aid analysis. The leaflet cover, for example, includes a colour photograph of a black pianist, which might be considered this way:

- **Existence**: a black man sits at the piano; smart, casual wear
- **Priorities**: the piano and by implication his musicianship
- **Values**: the BBC champions 'serious' music (rather than Black Music, which is something different)
- **Relationships**: it fits into a cultural pattern, whereby the BBC is seen as a guardian of British culture

The idea is to find representations in both documents and then compare them. Document two is rather inaccessible but it does offer a useful contrast, being fairly traditional in its content and layout. It is there to show the BBC in practice alongside their manifesto of promises. It is, however, worth remembering that 'This Week's RADIO' is but a small part of the BBC's output and it is across this range that the BBC fulfils promises, not on a programme-to-programme, station-to-station basis.

THEMES IN PERSONAL COMMUNICATION

One of the key tests for any course, and any book that claims it is suitable for that course, is the degree to which the work you have done before the inevitable examination prepares you for it when it comes. We have said a lot about Personal Communication in Part 5, but it is worthless if you are not able to use it to pursue a qualification in the subject. This is not to suggest that the examination is more important than the course, but rather to point out that as a simple test of knowledge and understanding of the subject the examination should be a natural end point and 'no big deal'. Given that public examinations are rigorously evaluated, assessed and scrutinised, it is likely that if you cannot recognise the exam as something you can do (or could have done if you'd done more work), then something has gone wrong with your course (or your course text).

AS Communication Studies Unit 3 is such an examination: a straightforward test of knowledge and understanding of what they and we have called 'Themes in Personal

Communication'. It was first sat in January 2001 and offered the following 'menu' in three courses entitled:

- Verbal and Non-verbal Communication
- Intrapersonal Communication
- Group Communication

The fact that one choice was to be made from each 'course' and that the whole thing should be executed in one and a half hours reinforced the emphasis on knowledge rather than response. In such a limited amount of time there is hardly room for anything more than a demonstration of knowledge of key concepts and the application of these to real-life communication. The first choice was as follows:

SECTION A

Answer **one** question from this section.

Verbal and Non-verbal Communication

1   It has been claimed that language is the most sophisticated form of communication ever developed but that only human beings have the capacity to learn and use language. What are the arguments for and against this point of view?

2   Explain the role which paralanguage can play in a conversation between two people.

Keywords are our first priority. Question 1 offers 'claimed' (denoting a point of view), 'language . . . most sophisticated form of communication' (which begs the question, 'Is it?'), 'only human beings' (which rules out other animals) and 'learn and use' (which may be separate issues). It goes on to ask for 'arguments' (series of linked reasoned statements) 'for and against' (though not necessarily balanced). If we adopt the five-paragraph essay plan suggested earlier in this chapter, it might pan out like:

1   Introduction: which generally addresses the details of the claim by defining/commenting on terms of reference: language, sophisticated, humans/non-humans
2   Arguments for
3   Arguments against
4   Your own view in the light of these
5   Final thoughts: comment on unresolved elements

Question 2 is much more practical, applying knowledge to practical situations. The keywords are 'Explain' (suggests detail and analysis), 'role' (the part played/function discharged), 'paralanguage' (the non-verbal aspect of speech) and 'conversation' (the classic model of dyadic communication). A plan might look like this:

COMMUNICATION STUDIES: THE ESSENTIAL INTRODUCTION

1   Introduction: define paralanguage and outline its vital role
2   Main point 1: 'it expresses attitudes and emotions' with 2–3 good examples
3   Main point 2: 'it regulates communication': pitch and intonation punctuate communication and assign functions to language (e.g. questioning by rising intonation)
4   Main point 3: 'it emphasises/supports verbal communication': volume and speed do this especially
5   Final thoughts: on the importance of paralanguage

Having negotiated the first section, it is time to tackle 'intra'. The January questions were as follows:

SECTION B

Answer **one** question from this section.

Intrapersonal Communication

3   How helpful is Transactional Analysis in explaining the relationship between ego-states and acts of communication?

4   Explain how and why individuals often reject evidence which appears to contradict their self-image.

'How helpful' is a question which, daft as it sounds, does require you to come to some sort of decision on the scale 'totally helpful', 'very helpful', 'quite helpful', 'not very helpful' or 'totally unhelpful'. This is a classic theory question in that it deals with the most important criterion: how useful (in this case 'helpful') the theory is when applied to practical situations. Given the range of possible responses, the structure, too, will be variable. You might structure your three central points/paragraphs around TA's ego states (parent, child and adult) or conversely around evidence of TA's advantages and deficiencies.

Question 4 is more directed, although the explanations themselves are up for grabs. The 'trick' is in 'how *and* why', which demands two lists; the 'how' list led by the preposition 'by' (e.g. by discrediting the source); the 'why' list led by the phrase 'in order to' (e.g. in order to undermine the criticism they are making). 'Self-image' is clearly a key term that will need defining in the introduction, a paragraph that should also site the question where it belongs, in the discussion of 'self-maintenance strategies' and/or 'defence mechanisms'. Gergen and Gergen, as well as Freud, will be useful here as a theoretical foundation which then can be tested against experience.

Group comes last in sequence but do remember you can attempt these sections in any order you wish. Altering the printed order is once again a way of showing your control over the exam time and experience. In this case the group questions were perhaps the most straightforward, whatever order the questions were attempted in.

SECTION C

Answer **one** question from this section

Group Communication

5   Why do groups develop in different ways?

6   Some groups are more successful than others in achieving their goals. Discuss the key factors which contribute to the success of these groups.

The first group question is deceptively simple and as such makes particular demands on the candidate. Common sense must be your guide here; for, while the question appears simply to ask for your opinion, in the context of the exam, what it is really asking for is a response that surveys critically the opinions of others. This is not to prescribe your response: good answers might focus on any or all of group variables, group motivation, group functions, group dynamics and intra- and intergroup communication.

The above list of content is also a starting point for uncovering potential factors in response to question 6. A very useful piece of theory here might be Kell and Corts (1980) on 'group maturity', which offers a checklist of criteria for defining 'mature' groups (for 'mature' read 'successful'). This list of factors would likely form the basis of a very competent answer.

COMMUNICATION STUDIES: THE ESSENTIAL INTRODUCTION

▼ GLOSSARY

actor synonym for communicator

anchorage the process by which the meaning of a text is fixed, usually by means of a caption or voice-over to visual images

archetype an ideal or model after which others are patterned

attitudes tendencies to react favourably or unfavourably to things

audience the receiver(s) of a message

autonomy the ability to act independently

barrier anything that interferes with the communication process

beliefs things you know but which can't be proved

broadcast to communicate to a mass audience

channel a communication route or connection

closed text a message that is capable of being read in a limited number of ways, sometimes only the one way

codes systems of communication using agreed rules and meaning shared by the participants

cognitive dissonance a state of conflict between a person's belief system and the way in which they may choose to act

communicate to share experiences

communication barrier see *barrier*

communication text anything that has the potential to communicate (see also *text*)

competence the capacity to perform an act, e.g. speaking a language

complexes ideas or impulses that compel habitual or obsessive behaviour (psychological barriers to communication)

conformity the tendency to go along with the majority view

connotation the meanings in a text that are revealed through the receiver's own cultural experience

conscience our moral self

consciousness the state of being conscious

consumer the receiver of a message

content analysis a quantitative methodology that involves counting and the analysis of large amounts of data contained within communication texts

convention the accepted, or commonly used, method for producing a text

critical thinking the process of arriving at an objective and reasoned assessment or evaluation, e.g. of your own work

cue a prompt

culture shared beliefs, knowledge and experiences which form and reinforce communities

data raw, unprocessed facts; once data have been processed, information results

decode to convert an encoded message into a form that can be understood

deconstruction the process of taking apart a text in order to analyse its parts

defence mechanisms anything that seeks to protect the self from harm

denotation the specific, direct or obvious meaning of a sign rather than its associated meanings

determinant something that exerts influence in communication, for example, social class, economics, technology

dialect a type of speech specific to a particular area within a country

disclosure the act of opening oneself up

discourse a particular type of language associated with communication between groups with common interests, e.g. the discourse of the law

discourse analysis a branch of linguistics that concerns itself with conversations between two or more people

displacement the capacity of language to refer to things removed in place and time

dissonance theory the idea that, when faced with conflicting information about ourselves, we subconsciously handicap those parts of the argument that are most unacceptable to us.

ego the conscious self (Freud)

elaborated code communication that allows the expression of individuality, identified particularly through the use of a wide vocabulary

elite a privileged group of people

empathy the capacity to experience imaginatively someone else's feelings and emotions

encode   to convert a message into a form capable of being transmitted, e.g. words

entropy   a measure of the uncertainty or randomness contained within a message

extrovert   an outward-looking person

feedback   the response received by the sender to a message

foil   overhead projector transparency (see *overhead transparency*)

front   what is offered by a first impression

gatekeeping   the process that controls the flow of information

genre   a means of classifying texts into groups that share common characteristics, e.g. documentaries

grammar   the conventions governing our use of language

group   a collection of individuals

groupthink   a disease of groups whereby individual performance is inhibited by the priorities of the group as a whole

halo effect   the tendency to overpraise

Harvard referencing system   a method of acknowledging quotation or reference from other published sources

horns effect   the tendency to demonise or to overcriticise

icon   a sign that works by its similarity to the thing it represents

id   the unconscious, animal urge (Freud)

ideal self   the kind of person we would like to be

index   a sign that works by reminding us of the existence of something else; for example, smoke is an index of fire

information   data that has been subjected to specific enquiry

intention   purpose

intergroup communication   communication between different groups of people

interpersonal communication   communication between people at an individual level

intertextuality   reference within one text to another text, often across different media or genres (e.g. a television advertisement may parody a scene from a famous film)

intragroup communication   communication within a group

intrapersonal communication   communication within the self (e.g. thinking)

introvert   an inward-looking person

jargon   vocabulary specific to a particular group

Johari Window a formula for analysing intrapersonal communication

kinesics the study of the ways meanings are communicated by bodily movement.

language an abstract system of communication using words and sentences to convey meaning

langue the shared system which all speakers of a language use

leakage see *non-verbal leakage*

linguistic relativism the process by which language can influence or control one's view of the world

linguistics the scientific study of language

looking-glass theory the idea that we develop ourselves in response to how others see us

medium the method we use to communicate (e.g. speech)

mirror self the tendency to see oneself through a reflection of how others see one

moral panic a scare, often ill-founded, spread by the media which shocks people into calling for action

mode of address the means by which a text speaks to its audience

motivation In addition to the everyday meaning of 'a force that drives us', motivation is a term used in semiotics to refer to the relationship between a sign and what it represents: the higher the motivation of the sign (be it word, symbol, drawing or photograph), the closer the resemblance to whatever it is representing.

narrative the way in which a text reveals information to the audience in order to create a 'story'

narrowcast texts that are intended for transmission to a limited (as opposed to mass) audience

negotiation a relationship between sender and receiver that shapes meaning

netiquette the conventions for using e-mail, derived from a contraction of the two words 'network' and 'etiquette'

noise source the origin of any barrier to communication

non-verbal communication (NVC) messages, such as body movements and facial expression, which do not use language to communicate

non-verbal leakage the tendency of non-verbal codes to contradict or undermine intentional and verbal communication, e.g. lack of eye contact may betray the telling of a lie

open text a text that is capable of a wide range of different interpretations

overhead projector (OHP) equipment designed to show an image or text to a roomful of people

overhead transparency (OHT) a clear plastic sheet used with an OHP on which information for projection is displayed

paradigm a set of signs from which choices can be made

paralanguage communication that is in the form of utterances other than the words themselves, e.g. the volume of one's voice

parole the everyday use of language as opposed to the system of language and the conventions that govern it

patriarchy social organisation in which men occupy the key positions of power

perception the process of making sense of sensory data

performance communicative behaviour

persona an adopted form of the self/identity

personality what we are like

phatic communication aspects of language that serve to reinforce social relationships rather than communicate information, e.g. saying 'Have a nice day' when meeting someone

phonetics the study of the sounds used in speaking a language

phonology the study of sounds and their role in language

pitch the intonation of speech which determines the way in which our voice may rise and fall

polysemy the capacity of a text to have more than one meaning or to be open to a range of different readings

postural congruence the tendency to mirror another person's body language by adopting similar postures

PowerPoint computer software for creating visual aids, such as OHTs

preferred reading the reading of a message that the producer guides the receiver towards, the reading they would like the reader to make

process school a school of thought in which communication is conceived as a process whereby information is transmitted

producer the sender of a message

prompt a cue

proxemics the study of how we handle the space around us, especially in relation to other people

psyche the soul, the inner being

psychometry a scheme for measuring psychological behaviour

Pygmalion effect a byproduct of selective perception

Q&A (question and answer technique)   the phase in a presentation in which the audience are able to ask questions

reading   can be categorised as being of three different types:

   (a) dominant-hegemonic: the 'intended' message contained within a text that the majority of readers are likely to accept

   (b) negotiated: an interpretation of a text that identifies the dominant reading but seeks to question its validity

   (c) oppositional: an interpretation of a text that rejects the 'intended' message and makes a different or contrary interpretation

received pronunciation (RP)   'standard English' or the generally accepted means of speaking without regional accent

receiver   someone who gets a message

register   adopting a specific use of language appropriate to the situation in which communication is taking place and the audience being addressed

regulator   a controller

report   a formal account of something that has taken place, either written or verbal

representation   the act of presenting the world again

restricted code   communication that reinforces the shared values of a group, characterised by a limited vocabulary

role   a part we play

rubric   written instructions usually found on an examination paper

school of thought   where groups of academics come together because they feel the same way about particular issues

self   what we are

self-concept   the idea we have of ourselves

self-definition   the capacity to know the difference between 'I/me' and 'you'

self-disclosure   the act of revealing ourselves, consciously or otherwise

self-esteem   what we think of ourselves

self-fulfilling prophecy   the concept that the way in which we treat people (because of our expectations of them) may influence their behaviour in such a way that they fulfil these expectations

self-image   how we see ourselves

self-maintenance strategies   the ways in which we keep ourselves going

self-presentation   the conscious process through which self becomes text

self-recognition the capacity to recognise an image or reflection of oneself

self-reflexivity the act of consciously thinking about oneself or one's behaviour

semantics the study of the relationship between signs and meanings

semiotics (semiology) the study of signs and how they communicate

sender the originator of a message

sign that which stands for or represents an object, idea or mental concept

signification the process of signifying (see *signify*)

signifier/signified the two components of a sign: the physical aspect such as a sound or word and the mental concept.

signify to use a sign in order to represent an object, idea or concept

skill a capacity that can be learned, practised and refined

slide see *overhead transparency*

sociometrics the study of personal interrelationships within a social group

stereotype to represent a person by attributing to them simple characteristics supposedly shared by a larger group

superego the controlling part of the self (Freud)

symbol an arbitrary sign that works by the agreement among people as to what it represents

syntagm an ordered sequence of signs

syntax the conventions governing the use of language

text any form of communication that can be read/interpreted (e.g. advertisement, film, book)

Transactional Analysis (TA) theory in which interpersonal communication can be studied in relation to different ego states adopted by people

typography the use of different types and styles of lettering in printed texts

values fundamental responses to reality

▼ RESOURCES

COMMUNICATION, CULTURAL AND MEDIA STUDIES INFOBASE

www.cultsock.ndirect.co.uk/MUHome/cshtml/
A really useful resource for the student of Communication Studies. A helpful index provides access to key terms and concepts which are considered in an accessible manner. Provides useful links to further reading and information.

THE MEDIA AND COMMUNICATION STUDIES SITE

www.aber.ac.uk/media/index.html

Another useful site that breaks the disciplines down into useful topic areas. Provides links to articles, some of which students will find more accessible than others.

CRITICAL THEORY AND CULTURAL STUDIES

http://eserver.org/theory/
Generally quite a high-powered site, although with a searchable database.

www.theory.org.uk
A lively and challenging site with an interesting focus on popular culture.

www.popcultures.com/
A searchable site with useful links to articles by and about key theorists.

VOICE OF THE SHUTTLE

http://vos.ucsb.edu/shuttle/media.html
Generally a site focused on Media Studies but containing material on broader cultural issues.

▼ BIBLIOGRAPHY

Adorno, T. (1950) *The Authoritarian Personality*, New York: Harper & Row.

Allen, R. E. (1990) *Oxford Writers' Dictionary*, Oxford: Oxford University Press.

Allen, V. L. (1965) 'Situational factors in conformity', in L. Berkowitz (ed.) *Advances in Experimental Social Psychology*, Vol. 2, New York and London: Academic Press.

Argyle, M. (1983) *The Psychology of Interpersonal Behaviour*, 4th edn, Harmondsworth: Penguin.

Bales, R. F. (1950) *Interaction Process Analysis*, New York: Addison-Wesley.

Barrass, R. (1984) *Study! A Guide to Effective Study, Revision and Examination Techniques*, London: Chapman & Hall.

Barthes, R. (1967) *Elements of Semiology*, London: Cape.

Barthes, R. (1973) *Mythologies*, selected and translated by A. Lavers, New York: Hill & Wang.

Berne, E. (1968) *Games People Play: The Psychology of Human Relationships*, Harmondsworth: Penguin.

Bernstein, B. (1971) *Class, Codes and Control*, London: Routledge & Kegan Paul.

Birtwhistell, R. (1970) *Kinesics and Context: Essays in Body Movement Communication*, Philadelphia, PA: University of Pennsylvania Press.

Brewer, M. and Miller, N. (1996) *Intergroup Relations*, Milton Keynes: Open University Press.

Burton, G. and Dimbleby, R. (1995) *Between Ourselves: An Introduction to Interpersonal Communication*, 2nd edn, London: Edward Arnold.

Carey, G. V. (1971) *Mind the Stop*, Harmondsworth: Penguin.

Cattell, R. B. (1965) *The Scientific Analysis of Personality*, Harmondsworth: Penguin.

Chambers, E. and Northedge, A. (1997) *The Arts Good Study Guide*, Milton Keynes: Open University Press.

Cherry, C. (1978) *On Human Communication: A Review, a Survey and a Criticism*, 3rd edn, Cambridge, Mass./London: MIT Press.

Chomsky, N. (1968) *Language and Mind*, New York: Harcourt Brace & World.

Cobley, P. (ed.) (1996) *The Communication Theory Reader*, London: Routledge.

Cohen, S. (1980) *Folk Devils and Moral Panics*, Oxford: Blackwell.

Cooley, C. H. (1992) *Human Nature and the Social Order*, New York: Transaction Publishers.

Coopersmith, S. (1967) *The Antecedents of Self-Esteem*, San Francisco: Freeman.

de Saussure, F. (1983) *Course in General Linguistics*, trans. R. Harris, ed. C. Bally and A. Sechehaye, London: Duckworth.

Dimbleby, R. and Burton, G. (1998) *More than Words: An Introduction to Communication*, 3rd edn, London: Routledge.

Douglas, W. D. (1979) *Groups: Understanding People Gathered Together*, London: Tavistock.

Drew, S. and Bingham, R. (1997) *The Student Skills Guide*, Aldershot: Gower.

Eco, U. (1973) 'Social life as a sign system', in D. Robey (ed.) *Structuralism: An Introduction*, Oxford: Clarendon Press.

Eco, U. (1979) *The Role of the Reader: Explorations in the Semiotics of Texts*, Bloomington, Ind.: Indiana University Press.

Eysenck, H. J. (1947/1999) *Dimensions of Personality*, London: Routledge.

Eysenck, H. J. (1954) *The Psychology of Politics*, London: Routledge & Kegan Paul.

Eysenck, H. J. and Eysenck, S.B.G. (1969) *Personality Structure and Measurement*, London: Routledge.

Fiske, J. (1990) *Introduction to Communication Studies*, 2nd edn, London: Routledge.

Fiske, J. and Hartley, J. (1978) *Reading Television*, London: Methuen.

Fowler, H. W. (1983) *A Dictionary of Modern English Usage*, Oxford: Oxford University Press.

Freud, S. (1984) *On Metaphysics: the Theory of Psychoanalysis. 'Beyond the pleasure principle', 'The ego and the id' and Other Works*, ed. J. Strachey and A. Richards, The Pelican Freud Library Vol. 11, Harmondsworth: Penguin.

Freud, S. (1999) *The Interpretation of Dreams*, trans. J. Crick, Oxford: Oxford University Press.

Fry, R. (1997) *How to Study*, London: Kogan Page.

Gahagan, J. (1975) *Interpersonal and Group Behaviour*, London: Methuen.

Gerbner, G. (1970) 'Cultural Indicators: the case of violence in television drama', *Annals of the American Association of Political and Social Science*, 338.

Gergen, K. J. and Gergen, M. M. (1981) *Social Psychology*, New York: Harcourt Brace Jovanovich.

Gill, D. and Adams, B. (1998) *The ABC of Communication Studies*, Walton-on-Thames: Nelson.

Goffman, E. (1963) *Behaviour in Public Places*, New York: Free Press.

Goffman, E. (1990) *The Presentation of the Self in Everyday Life*, Harmondsworth: Penguin.

Gowers, E. (1987) *The Complete Plain Words*, 3rd edn, Harmondsworth: Penguin.

Gramsci, A. (1971) *Selections from the Prison Notebooks*, ed. and trans. Q. Hoare and G. Nowell Smith, London: Lawrence & Wishart.

Gross, R. (1996) *Psychology: The Science of Mind and Behaviour*, London: Hodder & Stoughton.

Guiraud, P. (1975) *Semiology*, trans. G. Gross, London: Routledge & Kegan Paul.

Hall, E. T. (1959) *The Silent Language*, New York: Doubleday.

Hall, S. (ed.) (1980) *Culture, Media, Language*, London: Hutchinson.

Halliday, M. A. K. (1978) *Language as Social Semiotic*, London: Edward Arnold.

Harré, R., Clarke, D. and de Carlo, N. (1985) *Motives and Mechanisms*, London: Methuen.

Hartley, P. (1997) *Group Communication*, London: Routledge.

Hartley, P. (1999) *Interpersonal Communication*, 2nd edn, London: Routledge.

Hawkes, T. (1977) *Structuralism and Semiotics*, London: Routledge.

Jakobson, R. (1962) *Selected Writings*, The Hague: Mouton.

Janis, I. L. (1982) *Groupthink: Psychological Studies of Policy Decisions and Fiascoes*, 2nd edn, Boston: Houghton Mifflin.

Jung, C. G. (1963) *Memories, Dreams, Reflections*, ed. A. Jaffé, trans. R. and C. Winston, London: Collins/Routledge.

Kell, C. L. and Corts, P. R. (1980) *Fundamentals of Effective Group Communication*, New York: Macmillan.

Kuhn, H. H. and McPartland, T. S. (1954) 'An empirical investigation of self-attitudes', *American Sociological Review*, 47.

Laing, R. D. (1962) *The Divided Self*, London: Routledge.

Lasswell, H. (1948) 'The structure and function of communication in society', in L. Bryson (ed.) *The Communication of Ideas*, New York.

Lewin, K., Lippett, R. and White, R. (1939) 'Patterns of aggressive behaviour in experimentally created social climates', in *Journal of Social Psychology*, 10.

Luft, J. (1969) *Of Human Interaction*, Palo Alto, Calif.: National Press Books.

Luft, J. and Ingham, H. (1955) 'The Johari Window: a graphic model for interpersonal relations', University of California Western Training Lab.

MacDougall, J. (2000) 'Finding the "ism" of the real', in *itp Film Reader 2*, ed. Stafford.

McEwan, I. (1987) *The Child in Time*, London: Cape.

McLuhan, M. (1964) *Understanding Media*, London: Routledge.

Maslow, A. (1954) *Motivation and Personality*, New York: Harper & Row.

Mead, M. (1930) *Growing up in New Guinea: A Comparative Study of Primitive Education*, London: G. Routledge & Sons.

Mepham, J. (1974) 'The theory of ideology in capital', *W.P.C.S.* no. 6, University of Birmingham.

Moreno, J. L. (1951) *Sociometry, Experimental Method and the Science Society*, Beacon House.

Morris, D. (1994) *The Human Animal*, London: BBC Books.

Moscovici, S. (1985) 'Social influence and conformity', in D.T. Gilbert, S.T. Fiske and G. Lindzey (eds) *The Handbook of Social Psychology*, Westminster, Md.: Random House.

Murphy, G. (1947) *Personality*, New York: Harper & Row.

Myers, G. and Myers, M. (1992) *The Dynamics of Human Communication*, 6th edn, New York: McGraw-Hill.

Nicholson, J. (1977) *Habits*, London: Macmillan.

Orwell, G. (1948) *1984*, London: Penguin.

Orwell, G. (2001) 'Politics and the English language', in *Inside the Whale and Other Essays*, Harmondsworth: Penguin.

O'Sullivan, T., Hartley, J., Saunders, D., Montgomery, M. and Fiske, J. (1994) *Key Concepts in Communication and Cultural Studies*, London/New York: Routledge.

Partridge, E. (1999) *Usage and Abusage*, Harmondsworth: Penguin.

Piaget, J. (1952) *The Child's Conception of Numbers*, London: Routledge.

Peirce, C. S. (1966) *Collected Papers of Charles Sanders Peirce*, Cambridge, Mass.: Belknap Press of Harvard University Press.

Potter, D. (1996) '*Karaoke*' and '*Cold Lazarus*', London: Faber.

Pound, E. (1961) *ABC of Reading*, London: Faber.

Roget's Thesaurus of English Words and Phrases (2000) ed. B. Kirkpatrick, Harmondsworth: Penguin.

Rayner, P., Wall, P. and Kruger, S. (2001) *Media Studies: The Essential Introduction*, London and New York: Routledge.

Rogers, C. R. (1961) *On Becoming a Person*, Boston: Houghton Mifflin.

Rokeach, M. (1960) *The Open and Closed Mind*, New York: Basic Books.

Rubenzer, S. (2000) paper given to the American Psychological Association, reported in *The Independent*.

Sapir, E. (1956) *Language, Culture and Personality*, ed. E. G. Mandelbaum, Berkeley, Calif.: University of California Press.

Shannon, C. and Weaver, W. (1949) *The Mathematical Theory of Communication*, Champaign, IL: University of Illinois Press.

Shaw, M. (1981) *Group Dynamics*, 3rd edn, New York: McGraw-Hill.

Smith, P. B. and Bond, M. H. (1993) *Social Psychology across Cultures*, Brighton: Harvester Wheatsheaf.

Spender, D. (1998) *Man Made Language*, 4th edn, London: Pandora.

Stanton, N. (1996) *Mastering Communication*, 3rd edn, Basingstoke: Macmillan.

Stogdill, R. M. (1981) *Stogdill's Handbook of Leadership*, 2nd edn, New York: Free Press and London: Collier Macmillan.

Strinati, D. (2000) *An Introduction to Studying Popular Culture*, London and New York: Routledge.

Tedeschi, J. T. and Lindskold, S. (1976) *Social Psychology: Interdependence, Interaction and Influence*, New York: Wiley.

Tuckman, B. W. (1965) 'Developmental sequence in small groups', *Psychological Bulletin*, 63.

Turner, J. C. (1991) *Social Influence*, Oxford: Oxford University Press.

Whorf, B. L. (1956) *Language, Thought and Reality*, ed. J. B. Carroll, Cambridge, Mass.: MIT Press.

Williams, R. (1962) *Communications*, Harmondsworth: Penguin.

Wittgenstein, L. (1953) *Philosophical Investigations*, Oxford: Blackwell.

Zimbardo, P. G. (1988) *Psychology and Life*, 12th edn, Glenview, Ill.: Scott, Foresman.

▼ INDEX

accent, 147, 148, 162
Acquired Immune Deficiency Syndrome,
  69
Adams, B.: *ABC of Communication Studies*,
  177
Adorno, Theodor, 185
adult ego state, 195
advertisements, 28, 61–3, 67, 80–1, 90–2,
  96–7, 98, 102, 113, 117, 121, 163
aesthetic function, 102
agenda, 42–3
AIDS, *see* Acquired Immune Deficiency
  Syndrome
Alas, Smith and Jones, 192
Albrecht, Kurt, 204, 205, 207
Alexander, Frederick, 160
Allen, V. L.: 'Situational factors in
  conformity', 213
American Psychological Association, 218
anchorage, 82–3, 85, 88, 90
anima/animus, 180
animal communication, 21, 148–9
annotation, 106
architecture, 58
Argyle, Michael: *Psychology of Interpersonal
  Behaviour*, 153, 187, 188, 202, 218
Art Alive!, 92
attitudes, 171
audience-building, 97
audio tapes, 10, 128, 129, 132
authoritarianism, 216
autocracy, 217

babies, 88, 175
Bales, R. F.: *Interaction Process Analysis*,
  205–7
Barber Institute of Fine Arts, 92

Barthes, Roland: *Elements of Semiology*, 82,
  83; *Mythologies*, 176, 181
Bayeux tapestry, 95–6
BBC, *see* British Broadcasting Corporation
beliefs, 171
Bell telephones, 23
Benetton, 99
Berne, Eric: *Games People Play*, 194–6
Bernstein, Basil: *Class, Codes and Control*,
  144, 145
Big Breakfast, The, 88
Birtwhistell, R.: *Kinesics and Context*, 134
Blair, Tony, 121
Blair Witch Project, The (film), 99–100, 121
Blanchett, Cate, 83–5
blushing, 151
body: adornment, 159; image, 167–8;
  language, 154, 155; needs, 187
Bond, M. H.: *Social Psychology across
  Cultures*, 176
books, 44; referencing, 17, 19; selecting, 15
Brewer, Marilyn: *Intergroup Relations*, 213
British Broadcasting Corporation, 147, 232,
  234, 235
British Psychological Society, 128
broadcast/narrowcast: defined, 88
Budweiser, 96
buildings, 54–6
bureaucratic leadership, 216–17
Burton, G.: *Between Ourselves*, 199, 200,
  205, 293; *More than Words*, 168, 171–2

Caine, Michael, 73, 74, 147
California Institute of Technology, 6–7
Cambridge Youth Project, 80–1
Carrey, Jim, 71–4
cartoons, 114–16

COMMUNICATION STUDIES: THE ESSENTIAL INTRODUCTION

Cattell, R. B.: *Scientific Analysis of Personality*, 182–3
CCTV, *see* surveillance cameras
CDs, *see* compact discs
Channel Four, 69, 88
channel/medium, 72
Charles, Prince, 114
Chaucer, Geoffrey: *Canterbury Tales*, 142
Cherry, Colin: *On Human Communication*, 21, 23
Chicken Run (film), 121
child ego state, 195
Chinese, 140, 142
Chomsky, Noam: *Language and Mind*, 146–7, 148
cinema, *see* film
Clarke, D.: *Motives and Mechanisms*, 176
cliché, 30
closed/open text, 66
clothing, *see* dress
codes, 22–3, 70–9; defined, 74; elaborated, 144–8; presentational, 75, 79; representational, 74–5, 79; restricted, 144–8
Cohen, S.: *Folk Devils and Moral Panics*, 69
collective ideology, 185
collective leadership, 216–17
collective unconscious, 180, 181
comic book, 114–16
commercial design, 58
common sense, 133
communication, 21–5; barrier, 55, 134; text, 55
compact discs, 75–9, 121
complementary transaction, 196
computers, 2, 44–5; back-up copies, 14, 46; CD-ROM, 108, 111; creating documents, 47; diary, 8; e-mail, 44, 48–51, 122, 148; Flesch Reading Ease Score, 47; formats, 47; Information Technology, 2, 148; Internet, 14, 15, 17–18, 19, 34, 44, 99, 122, 148; letters, 47; netiquette, 50; notes, 13; Outlook Express, 48; PowerPoint, 39, 40, 44; search engines, 18; security, 51; storing information, 10, 13, 18, 45; templates, 47; typography, 45, 47; using, 45–7; websites, 99–100, 120–1; word processing, 45–7
conative function, 101–2
conformity, 212–13
connotation, 85

consciousness, 180
content analysis, 63
convention, 65, 88, 90
Cooley, C. H.: *Human Nature and the Social Order*, 170
Coopersmith, S: *Antecedents of Self-Esteem*, 168
Corts, P. R.: *Fundamentals of Effective Group Communication*, 213, 238
courting rituals, 190
critical thinking, 20–1
crossed transaction, 196
cues, 164
cultural memory, *see* collective unconscious
cultural studies, 2
cynicism, 189

Daily Star, The, 57
data/information, 150
de Carlo, N.: *Motives and Mechanisms*, 176
decoding, 70–9, 106–112
deconstruction, 74
democracy, 217
denial, 179
denotation, 84
depersonalisation, 180
dialect, 147, 148, 162
Diana, Princess of Wales, 96
DiCaprio, Leonardo, 100
digital technology, 2, 44
Digital Video Disc, 7
Dimbleby, R.: *Between Ourselves*, 199, 200, 205, 293p; *More than Words*, 168, 171–2
discourse analysis, 144
displacement, 148, 179
dissonance theory, 173
dominant discourse, 65, 67, 73
dominant-hegemonic reading, 67, 69, 70
Douglas, W. D.: *Groups*, 198–9, 200, 210
dress, 58, 59, 157–9; uniform, 157–8
DVD, *see* Digital Video Disc
dyadic communication, 134, 198

Eco, Umberto: 'Social life as a sign system', 59, 65–6
Egg Card, 113
ego, 178; *see also* transactional analysis
Eliot, T. S., 30
Elizabeth (film), 83–5
Elizabeth, the Queen Mother, 116

Elizabeth II, 114
e-mail, *see* computers *and* television
emotional self, 167
emotive function, 101–2
empathy, 27–9, 35, 50, 135, 137
emphasis, 134
encoding/decoding, 56
engulfment, 180
entropy, 67, 88, 145, 164
ethnicity, 79
Eve, 102, 103
evidence: statistical/critical, 129
examinations: communication skills and,
   221–38; defacing the paper, 227–8;
   essay, 37, 123, 133–5, 230–2; evaluation,
   20; oral presentation, 37; preparation
   for, 226–7; revision for, 223–6; sample
   paper, 232–8; sample project, 123–37;
   sample question, 110; unseen papers,
   228–30
eye contact, 13, 39, 153–4, 164
Eyes Wide Shut (film), 97
Eysenck, H. J.: *Dimensions of Personality*,
   184–5; *Personality Structure and
   Measurement*, 182, 183–4; *Psychology of
   Politics*, 185

facial expression, 36, 37, 70, 150, 154–6,
   164
Falklands War, 57
familiarity, 137
family life, 126–7
fascism, 185
Fawlty Towers, 134–5, 136–7
fax, 33
feedback, 29, 35, 36, 37, 39, 98–9, 169,
   171, 172, 173, 174
feminism, 149
F.H.M., 121
film, 14, 87, 181–2, 194
FilmFour, 83–5
Finney, Albert, 147
first impressions, 76, 104–6, 135
Fiske, John: *Introduction to Communication
   Studies*, 23, 74; *Key Concepts in
   Communication and Cultural Studies*, 61,
   85, 144, 164, 200; *Reading Television*, 85
Flesch Reading Ease Score, 47
football, 54–6, 57
French and Saunders, 192

Freud, Sigmund, 175, 177–9, 180, 181,
   182, 237; *Interpretation of Dreams*, 177;
   On Metaphysics, 177
friendship, 59
frowning, 154

Gahagan, Judy: *Interpersonal and Group
   Behaviour*, 199, 200
games, 195
Gascoigne, Paul, 183
gatekeeping, 96, 165–6, 171
gazing, 70, 153
gender, 79, 122, 149, 153, 191–2
genre, 63, 87
Gerbner, George: 'Cultural Indicators' 62, 63,
   67, 93–5, 97, 100, 171
Gergen, K. J. and M. M.: *Social Psychology*,
   174, 179, 237
gesture, 156
Gibbons, Dave, 115
Gill, D.: *ABC of Communication Studies*,
   177
goals, 8, 187
Goffman, Erving: *Behaviour in Public Places*,
   153; *Presentation of the Self*, 126, 137,
   188–94
Google, 18
Gormenghast, 232
Gramsci, Antonio, 67, 69
greetings cards, 118–19, 121
Gross, Richard: *Psychology*, 173–4
group communication, 196–201, 201–11,
   211–19
group jargon, 22
GroupThink, 214
Guevara, Che, 121
Gulf War, 57

hairstyle, 58
Hall, E. T.: *Silent Language*, 134, 151
Hall, Stuart: *Culture, Media, Language*, 67
Halliday, M. A. K.: *Language as Social
   Semiotic*, 100
handshakes, 155
Harré, R.: *Motives and Mechanisms*, 176
Hartley, J.: *Key Concepts in Communication
   and Cultural Studies*, 61, 85, 144, 164,
   200; *Reading Television*, 85
Hartley, Peter: *Interpersonal Communication*,
   12, 13, 85, 197, 200, 212

COMMUNICATION STUDIES: THE ESSENTIAL INTRODUCTION

Harvard System, 19
hegemony, 69
hesitation, 37, 162–3
Hodge, Patricia, 232
home life, 126–7
Hughes, Ted, 104–8
humours, 183–4
hypothesis, 127, 142

icon, 90, 116, 140
id, 178
identification, 168–9, 179
ideograms, 140
ideology, 85
implosion, 180
Independent on Sunday, The, 116
indexes, 90–1, 92, 116
industrial design, 58
information: data and, 150; obtaining and
    retaining, 6–7; organising, 29; sources,
    15–16, 35–6
information rich/poor, 44
information technology, *see* computers
Ingham, H.: 'Johari Window', 172–3, 177,
    187
inner monologue, 165
intellectual self, 167
intention, 80–93; outcome and, 97
interactive technology, 2
interior design, 58
Internet, *see* computers
intertextuality, 108
intimacy, 195
intonation, 37, 39, 134, 150, 161
intra-group communication, 202
intrapersonal communication, 165–74,
    175–86, 186–96
isolation, 179
Italian Job, The (film), 73

Jakobson, Roman: *Selected Writings*, 101–2
Janis, Irving: *Groupthink*, 214
jargon, 22, 31, 32
Jewel, 104–8
Johar Window, 172–3, 177, 187
Jones, Rev. Jim, 214
Jung, Carl Gustav, 188, 193; *Memories,*
    Dreams, Reflections, 180–1, 182

Keeping Up Appearances, 145

Kell, C. L.: *Fundamentals of Effective Group*
    Communication, 213, 238
kissing, 152
Kitchiner, Lord, 57
Kubrick, Stanley: *Eyes Wide Shut*, 97
Kuhn, H. H.: 'Empirical investigation of self-
    attitudes', 167, 192

Laing, R. D.: *Divided Self*, 179–80
laissez-faire, 217
Lancaster University, 117
language, 139–49
Lasswell, Harold: 'Structure and function of
    communication', 25, 72, 73, 85, 93, 104
laughing, 13
leadership, 215–16; styles, 216–17, 218
leakage, non-verbal, 59, 134, 154; defined,
    60
Lennon, John, 94, 96
letters, 33–4, 51; computers, 47
linguistics, *see* language
literacy, 30
Logan's Run (film), 121
looking-glass theory, 170–1, 173
Lucas, George, 181
Luft, J.: 'Johari Window', 172–3, 177, 187
Lycos, 18

MacDougall, J.: 'Finding the "ism" of the
    real', 65
McEwan, Ian: *Child in Time*, 97
McLuhan, Marshall: *Understanding Media*,
    126
McPartland, T. S.: 'Empirical investigation of
    self-attitudes', 167, 192
magazines, 61–6, 67, 102, 121
male dominance, 149
management psychology, 170
Marilyn Manson, 191
Marxism, 85
Maslow, Abraham: *Motivation and*
    Personality, 187, 200
mass media, 126
Mathematical Theory of Communication,
    87
Mead, M.: *Growing Up in New Guinea*, 176,
    192
meanings, *see* text
medium/channel, 72
meetings, 42–4; agenda, 42–3; minutes, 43–4

INDEX

Mepham, J.: 'Theory of ideology in capital', 60

metalingual function, 101, 103

metaphor, 30

Miller, Norman: *Intergroup Relations*, 213

minidisc, 128, 129, 132

minutes, 43–4

Mission Impossible 2 (film), 96

Mr Bean, 128

mobile telephone, *see* telephone

montage, 119–20

Montgomery, M.: *Key Concepts in Communication and Cultural Studies*, 61, 85, 144, 164, 200

Moore, Alan, 115

moral panic, 69

Morecambe and Wise, 192

Moreno, J. L.: *Sociometry*, 209

Morris, Desmond: *Human Animal*, 55, 154–5

Moscovici, S.: 'Social influence and conformity', 176

motivation, 89, 90, 135

Munch, Edvard: *Scream*, 67–9

Murphy, G.: *Personality*, 166

Myers, G. and M.: *Dynamics of Human Communication*, 215, 216, 218

myth, 176, 181

narrative, 106

narrowcast/broadcast, 88

National Union of Students, 98

Nazism, 185

negotiated reading, 67, 70

negotiation, 74

netiquette, 50

New Fowler's Modern English Usage, The, 30

Newman and Baddiel, 192

News at Ten, 148

News of the World, 69

Newsnight, 148

newspapers, 33, 44, 56–7, 121

Nicholson, J.: *Habits*, 201

Nietzsche, F. W., 133

nodding/shaking the head, 13, 36, 150

noise, 24; source, 85–7

non-verbal communication, 150–64; blushing, 151; body adornment, 159; body language, 154, 155; dress, 157–9; emphasis, 134; eye contact, 13, 39, 153–4, 164; facial expression, 36, 37, 70, 150, 154–6, 164; frowning, 154; gazing, 70, 153; gender and, 153; gesture, 156; handshakes, 155; hesitation, 37, 162–3; intonation, 37, 39, 134, 150, 161; kissing, 152; leakage, 60; nodding/shaking the head, 13, 36, 150; orientation, 134, 152–3; paralanguage, 37, 134, 161–3; posture, 39, 70, 150, 159–61; proxemics, 151–2; silence, 37; smell, 151; smiling and laughing, 13, 154, 155; verbal and, 163–4; volume, 37, 134

notes: annotating text, 106; making, 38–9, 110–11; taking, 13, 16, 36

Oasis: *Standing on the Shoulder of Giants*, 96

observation sheets, 129–33, 137

observation, 128–33, 137

Old Trafford, 54–6, 57

Once Were Warriors (film), 58

onomatopeia, 140

open/closed text, 66

oppositional reading, 67, 69

oral presentations, 20, 37, 123, 124, 135–6, 137; notes for, 38–9; visual aids, 39–42

organisation, 29, 37

orientation, 134, 152–3

Orwell, George: *Nineteen Eighty-Four*, 185; 'Politics and the English Language', 30, 31, 47

O'Sullivan, T.: *Key Concepts in Communication and Cultural Studies*, 61, 85, 144, 164, 200

outcome/intention, 97

overhead projection, 37, 38, 39, 40, 114, 136

packaging, 121

paedophiles, 69

Panorama, 148

paradigm, 59, 78, 79, 106

paragraphs, 33

paralanguage, 37, 150, 161–2

Paramount Studios, 72

parapraxis, 177

parent ego state, 195

Parkinson, Norman, 86

Parklife, 121

pastimes, 195

patriarchy, 149, 153

PC Format, 61–6

Peirce, Charles, 1–2, 24, 79, 90–2, 116

People's Friend, The, 121

perception, 171
performance, 126, 137
persona, 180, 188–9
personal space, 134, 151–2
personal style, 193–6
personal unconscious, 180
personality, 167, 170, 175–85
petrification, 180
Peugeot, 59
phatic communication, 97, 101, 103, 137
philosophy, 2
phone-ins, 98
phonetics, 144
phonology, 143
photocopying, 16
physical self, 168
physiological self, 168
Piaget, J.: *Child's Conception of Numbers*, 175
Pitman shorthand, 144
plagiarism, 17, 19, 46
Plain English Campaign, 31
Planet Happy, 118
pleasure principle, 178
poetic function, 101–2
political attitudes axis, 185–6
polysemy/polysemic, 66, 70, 82, 87
posters, 40, 121
Postman, Neil, 22
posture, 39, 70, 150, 159–61
Potter, Dennis: *Karaoke*, 119–20, 121
Pound, Ezra: *ABC of Reading*, 140
preferred reading, 69, 73
presentations, *see* oral presentations
process, 23–4, 71, 87, 93–103
projection, 135, 179
proxemics, 151–2
psychology, 2
public self, 168
punk rock, 69
Pygmalion effect, 170

Q, 104–8
question, 127
quotations, 16

race, 142
Radio Times, 232, 234
rationalisation, 179
reaction formation, 179

reading effectively, 16–17
reality principle, 177
received pronunciation, 147–8, 162
redundancy, 16, 88, 164; entropy and, 87
referencing sources, 17, 19
referendums, 98
referential function, 101–2
reflexivity, 101
register, 32, 100, 134, 137
regression, 179
regulator, 163
representation, 61
repression, 179
review, 123, 136–7
rituals, 190, 195
road signs, 22–3, 24
Robinson, Anne, 183
Robot Wars, 232
Rockwell, Norman, 89
Rogers, C. R.: *On Becoming a Person*, 168–9
Rokeach, M.: *Open and Closed Mind*, 185
role, 192–3
role model, 168
Rowling, J. K.: *Harry Potter and the Goblet of Fire*, 96, 121
Royle Family, The, 145, 232
Rubenzer, S., 218
rubric, 229

Saturday Evening Post, The, 89
Saunders, D.: *Key Concepts in Communication and Cultural Studies*, 61, 85, 144, 164, 200
Saussure, Ferdinand de, 1–2, 24, 78, 83, 90, 145
saying/seeing, 93
school of thought, 23
S Club 7: *Bring It All Back*, 75–9
Scrank, 116
screenplay, 119–20
seeing/saying, 93
self, 168, 181; development of, 175–85; ideal, 168
self-concept, 135, 165–74, 187
self-definition, 175
self-disclosure, 172
self-esteem, 169–74, 187
self-image, 166–8
self-interaction, 176, 192
self-maintenance strategies, 174
self-presentation, 126, 186–96

self-recognition, 175
self-reflexivity, 20
semantics, 65, 142–3
semiotics, 23, 24–5, 71, 79–93
sex, 79, 142
shadow, 180
shaking/nodding the head, 13, 36, 150
Shankley, Bill, 56
Shannon, Claude E.: *Mathematical Theory of Communication*, 2, 23, 85–7, 93
Shaw, Bernard: *Pygmalion*, 170
Shaw, M.: *Group Dynamics*, 203–4
shorthand, 144
sign, 24
sign language, 147
signifier/signified, 83, 88–9
silence, 37
simile, 30
Simpsons, The, 96, 111
Sims, The, 108–12
sincerity, 189
situation comedy, 88
smell, 151
smiling, 13, 154, 155
Smith, P. B.: *Social Psychology across Cultures*, 176
soap opera, 40, 63, 148
social acceptance, 187
social life, 126–7
social role, 167
social self, 168
sociology, 2
sources, 15–16; referencing, 17, 19
Spair, Edward, 142
Spender, Dale: *Man Made Language*, 149
Spice Girls, 121, 183, 188–9
sport, 54–7; psychology, 170
SQ3R model for study, 11
staging, 190–1
Stanton, N.: *Mastering Communication*, 198, 201, 204, 207, 214, 215
Star Wars (film), 78, 181
statistical/critical evidence, 129
Steiner, 195
stereotype, 62
Stevens, 181
storyboard, 120, 121
strangers, 59
strokes, 195
structure, 32–3

studying, 5–21; achievements, 9; climate for, 9; critical thinking, 20–1; effective reading, 16–17; evaluation, 20; goals and rewards, 8–9; gratification, 8–9; information retrieval, 14; Internet, 17–18; listening, 12–13; location, 9–10; motivation, 7–8; notes, 13, 16; organisation, 14; previewing, 10; questioning, 11; reviewing, 10; sources, 15–16; SQ3R model, 11
style, personal, 193–6
sublimation, 179
summary sheets, 110–11
Sun, The, 96
super-ego, 178
surveillance cameras, 126
swear words, 142
symbol, 90, 92, 116
syntagm, 59, 78, 79, 106
syntax, 143

Tannenbaum, 216
Tarrant, Chris, 183
tattoo, 58
teams, 191–2
Tedeschi, J. T. and Lindskold, S.: *Social Psychology*, 216
tele-conferencing, 44
telephone, 29, 33, 34, 36–7, 44, 87; answering system, 36; caller ID, 37; mobile, 2, 33, 44, 118, 141; Ringback, 37; text messages, 33
television, 7, 40; breakfast, 88; digital, 44; e-mail, 44, 51; interactive, 44–5; situation comedy, 88; soap opera, 40, 63, 148
territory, *see* personal space
text, 53–60; closed/open, 66; first impressions, 104–6; human figure as, 57–60; mass media, 56–7; meanings, 60–70; world as, 54–6
time management, 8, 14
Titanic (film), 100, 126
title, 127
Today, 232
Toy Box, The, 91–2
Trainspotting (film), 74, 75
transactional analysis, 194–6, 237
Truman Show, The (film), 71–4
Truth Machine, 163
Tuckman, B. W.: 'Developmental sequence in small groups', 202

Turner, J. C.: *Social Influence*, 200
Tushingham, Rita, 147
Two Ronnies, The, 192
typography, 32, 40, 45, 47, 88, 119–20

uniform, 157–8

values, 171
verbal communication, 34–5, 139–49;
    meetings, 42–4; non-verbal and, 163–4;
    presentations, 37–42; seeking information,
    35–6; telephone, 36–7
video, 7, 40–1, 100, 111–12, 128, 129, 132;
    home, 126
visual aids, 37, 38, 135–6, 137
vocabulary: variations in, 147
volume, 37, 134

Watchmen, The, 115
Weaver, W.: *Mathematical Theory of
    Communication*, 2, 23, 85–7, 93

websites, *see* computers
Weir, Peter, 71, 72
Westlife, 121
White, 165
Whorf, Benjamin Lee: *Language, Thought and
    Reality*, 142
Williams, Raymond: *Communications*, 53–4
Winslet, Kate, 100
Wittgenstein, Ludwig: *Philosophical
    Investigations*, 176
women, 62, 63, 65, 85, 149; *see also* gender
Woolf Virginia, 122
word processing, *see* computers
working life, 126–7, 195
written communication, 29–32; letters, 33–4,
    51; response, 110–12; structure, 32–3

Yahoo, 18

Zimbardo, P. G.: *Psychology and Life*, 214
Zulu (film), 147

AB
657
H38899
£18-00

AAT

and Treasury Management

Level 4
ssional Diploma in Accounting

Course Book

For assessments from September 2017

Second edition 2017

ISBN 9781 5097 1215 1
ISBN (for internal use only) 9781 5097 1234 2

British Library Cataloguing-in-Publication Data
A catalogue record for this book is available from the British Library

Published by

BPP Learning Media Ltd
BPP House, Aldine Place
142-144 Uxbridge Road
London W12 8AA

www.bpp.com/learningmedia

Printed in the United Kingdom

Your learning materials, published by BPP Learning Media Ltd, are printed on paper obtained from traceable sustainable sources.

BPP
LEARNING MEDIA

AB
657
438899
£18-00

AAT

n and Treasury
Management
Level 4
ssional Diploma in
Accounting
Course Book
For assessments from
September 2017

Second edition 2017

ISBN 9781 5097 1215 1
ISBN (for internal use only) 9781 5097 1234 2

British Library Cataloguing-in-Publication Data
A catalogue record for this book is available from the British Library

Published by

BPP Learning Media Ltd
BPP House, Aldine Place
142-144 Uxbridge Road
London W12 8AA

www.bpp.com/learningmedia

Printed in the United Kingdom

Your learning materials, published by BPP Learning Media Ltd, are printed on paper obtained from traceable sustainable sources.

BPP
LEARNING MEDIA